More advance praise for
JOURNEYS TO WAR & PEACE
and Stephen J. Solarz

"This fascinating book shares with the reader what many of us who worked along-side him already knew — that he was a savvy and effective public servant, dedicated to promoting U.S. interests and advancing the causes of democracy and human rights worldwide. *Journeys to War and Peace* is more than an engaging illumination of Congressman Solarz's international activities, it is a testament to what one individual can accomplish when armed with determination, creativity, and an irrepressible desire to help others."

SENATOR CHRIS DODD

"Steve Solarz was both a statesman and a member of Congress, a rare combination. No American did more to help restore democracy to the Philippines, and few members of Congress had as much impact globally in steering U.S. foreign policy towards peace-making and democracy-building. *Journeys to War and Peace* helps us understand what a wise Congressman has done and what Congress can do to further U.S. interests abroad."

JIMMY CARTER

"The literature on Congress and foreign policy suggests that its role has either been destructive or marginal. Steve Solarz's career and memoir provide compelling evidence that Congress can be constructive and central in steering the President toward infusing American foreign policy with its values and reinforcing the President to make necessary and unpopular decisions to advance U.S. interests abroad. Also, unlike most books on Congress, Solarz's is insightful, readable, and entertaining. I would recommend this for every student and course on Congress and on U.S. foreign policy."

ROBERT A. PASTOR
Professor of International Relations, American University

"Steven Solarz's *Journeys to War and Peace: A Congressional Memoir* is a succinct and sharp introduction to the most significant international conflicts of the last two decades. Written from the perspective of an influential American Congressman of his time, Solarz examines the core issues of the Middle East Peace Process, Apartheid, the birth of Zimbabwe, the tragedies of Zaire, Cambodia, the fall of Marcos, the India and Pakistan conflict, the Gulf War, Turkey, Kosovo, Korea, Taiwan, and other conflicts.

It is an absorbing, fascinating and well-written account and will certainly be included in libraries and collections.

"This book will be most useful for students of politics, diplomats, negotiators and decision-makers because they will gain valuable insight into why elected politicians take the actions they do, how they work the political process to achieve policy objectives, and why they are successful. His last chapter, 'Lessons Learned,' is an important legacy to pass on to others. In the case of Steven Solarz, he became one of the U.S. Congressmen who can reasonably claim to have had an impact on American foreign policy. It was his immense persistence and fighting spirit."

LEE KUAN YEW
Minister Mentor, Singapore

"Steve Solarz's *Journeys to War and Peace* is one of the most illuminating commentaries on the role of Congress in foreign policy in many years. By dramatically showing how an individual congressman can make a difference on a broad range of foreign policy issues he demonstrates that foreign policy is not the exclusive prerogative of the presidency. A must and enjoyable read for anyone who wants to understand the ways in which Congress can influence American foreign policy."

ROBERT DALLEK
presidential historian and author of biographies
about John F. Kennedy and Lyndon Johnson

"Steve Solarz's book is both a touching personal memoir and a quiet demonstration of how a dedicated, determined, and intensely knowledgeable congressman could exert real influence on American foreign policy over two decades. His contributions to democracy in the Philippines and South Korea modestly recounted here are a lasting testament of a Solarz foreign policy."

MORT ABRAMOWITZ
former U.S. Ambassador to Turkey and Thailand

"More than an eyewitness to history, Congressman Steven Solarz bent history — towards greater human freedom and democracy. He tells this compelling tale in scenes that stick with the reader long afterwards. His book is as superb as was his decency and dedication in public life."

KENNETH ADELMAN
former Deputy U.S. Ambassador to the United Nations and head of the
Arms Control and Disarmament Agency under President Reagan

"Imagine a member of Congress who helped bring down dictators, gave comfort to dissidents around the world, spent quality time with some of his era's most famous heroes and villains — and with lots of other interesting people in between. Then imagine that this former man has the pen of an angel, an eye for the extraordinary detail, and an ear for what people are really saying. That would be Steve Solarz, and that's why it's a blessing that he has given us this extraordinary memoir."

E. J. DIONNE JR.

columnist, *Washington Post*

"In the American scheme of government, the House of Representatives is not supposed to have a major role in foreign policy formulation. Steve Solarz, by the force of his intellect, personality and passion for a just and peaceful world defied that set of rules and was, during his tenure, one of the major forces for a rational American foreign policy. His story is an example of how politics can be practiced at its highest level for the common good."

CONGRESSMAN BARNEY FRANK

"As a youngster, Steve Solarz knew he wanted to accomplish something worthwhile with his life and he was granted a Brooklyn size portion of chutzpah to give him the confidence to go for it. This book is a wonderful read, a life's tale told with humor and candor. He takes you through his Congressional career, introducing you to the titans and common folk he encountered around the globe. His saga could only have happened in America."

DAVID STEINBERG

President, Long Island University and author of
The Philippines: A Singular and Plural Place

"*Journeys to War and Peace* is many things: powerful, candid, humorous, and more. But most importantly, it is evidence of the profound positive contribution Congressional representatives can make to America's engagement with the world. Steve Solarz's passionate and informed commitment to international affairs, detailed in this book, should be an inspiration to members of Congress and private citizens alike."

LEE H. HAMILTON

President and Director of the Woodrow Wilson
International Center for Scholars

"Steve Solarz has written a classic account of congressional diplomacy, filled with the wit of a practical politician and the wisdom of one of the nation's leading experts on American foreign policy. Political scientists and historians who teach about Congress, the Presidency, and foreign policy-making should assign this book to their students, who will discover that individual legislators can change the world for the better, that knowledge makes a huge difference in making policy, and that it is possible to be a both a realist and an idealist while trying to defend democracy at home and extend it to oppressed peoples around the world."

RICHARD M. PIOUS

Adolph and Effie Ochs Professor, Barnard College;
Graduate School of Arts and Sciences, Columbia University

"When I retired from Congress and was asked what I felt were some of the most important things I had done, I invariably referred to my sponsorship with Steve Solarz of the first Gulf War resolution. There was no question but that the willingness of Steve Solarz to take the lead on the Democratic side was a key to our winning the issue. He showed real courage in standing up against the overwhelming opposition of his fellow Democrats. For an inside account of how it came to pass, I strongly recommend *Journeys to War and Peace: A Congressional Memoir.*"

BOB MICHEL

former Republican leader of the House of Representatives

"The Honorable Stephen J. Solarz's memoir reflects not only an incredible depth of thought and feeling about world affairs, but also compellingly demonstrates the benefits of official travel by responsible Members of Congress. His energy and accomplishments while in the House earned the profound respect of his peers and serve as a reminder of the enduring value of bipartisan cooperation."

CHARLES W. JOHNSON

former Parliamentarian, U.S. House of Representatives

"This remarkable journey of Steve Solarz in his quest for people empowerment, democratic governance, and servant leadership is a 'must-read' for persons responsible for others. Because of his vast experience, global reach and unswerving advocacy for peace in the world, this book can be a powerful 'Weapon of Mass Upliftment' (WMU) everywhere."

EDDIE RAMOS

former President of the Philippines, 1992–1998

JOURNEYS
· TO ·
WAR & PEACE

JOURNEYS TO WAR & PEACE

A Congressional Memoir

Stephen J. Solarz

with a FOREWORD *by* NORMAN ORNSTEIN

✦ BRANDEIS UNIVERSITY PRESS ✦

WALTHAM, MASSACHUSETTS

BRANDEIS UNIVERSITY PRESS

An imprint of University Press of New England

www.upne.com

© 2011 Brandeis University

All rights reserved

Manufactured in the United States of America

Designed by Eric M. Brooks

Typeset in Adobe Jenson Pro by

Passumpsic Publishing

University Press of New England is a member of the
Green Press Initiative. The paper used in this book meets
their minimum requirement for recycled paper.

For permission to reproduce any of the material in this book,
contact Permissions, University Press of New England, One Court
Street, Suite 250, Lebanon NH 03766; or visit www.upne.com

Library of Congress Cataloging-in-Publication Data
appear on the last printed page of this book.

5 4 3 2 1

TO NINA

*without whom none of this
would have been possible*

**TO LEAH, ARIANA,
BENJAMIN, & JED,**

my hope for the future

CONTENTS

FOREWORD

Norman Ornstein

In 1986, as a Fulbright Fortieth Anniversary Scholar, I embarked on a lecture tour in Southeast Asia, including a stop in the Philippines. In Manila, I visited Malacanang Palace, the posh home of Ferdinand and Imelda Marcos when they ran the country with an iron hand. After their overthrow, it had been turned into a museum of sorts where the couple's greed and high living were on display, including room after room devoted to Imelda's shoe collection and other jaw-dropping extravagances (including several *five-gallon* containers of Chanel No. 5 perfume, which sells for roughly $400 an ounce; each container would be enough for a battalion of women).

I spoke both to Philippine government officials and to Filipino graduates of the Fulbright program, who made up a major share of the elite in the country. Nearly everyone, it seemed had the same question for a Washington insider: did I actually know Steve Solarz, who had been instrumental in saving the country from the authoritarian, dictatorial Marcoses and their excesses? It was not just members of the elite who were curious. One Sunday afternoon in the summer of 2010, when my wife and I were going to visit Steve and Nina Solarz, we mentioned our plans to my father-in-law — and his caregiver, a woman from the Philippines, said, "You mean the Congressman Solarz who helped save my country?"

In 2007, I traveled to Cambodia for a conference of the Asia Society that brought together a number of Americans and Asians from various countries. At a banquet in Siem Reap, the home of Angkor Wat and other mesmerizing ancient Hindu temples, I was seated next to a deputy foreign minister of Cambodia. He had one question for a Washington insider: did I know Steve Solarz, who had been instrumental in saving Cambodia from the murderous excesses of the Khmer Rouge?

To a reader of this remarkable book who is not an insider, it might seem as if Steve Solarz is exaggerating his role — portraying himself as a kind of Zelig who happened to be in multiple places in the world at key times when dictatorial governments fell or were toppled, or when human rights abuses were confronted, and taking credit for events that were well beyond the reach of more visible figures like secretaries of state or chairmen of the Senate Foreign Relations Committee. My personal experience suggests the opposite. In his eighteen years in the House of Representatives, Solarz had a profound impact on many countries and many movements, as well as on the foreign policy of the United States. His influence was unique for a single member of the House.

As a student of Congress for more than four decades, I have often marveled myself at the sweep and depth of the role Solarz was able to play. A part of the reason was timing. As he notes in the book, he came to Congress at a time of dramatic upheaval, after the 1974 "Watergate" election that brought in a huge class of seventy-five freshman Democrats who acted en bloc to precipitate major reforms in the House, decentralizing power from a coterie of senior committee chairs to a much larger group of subcommittee leaders as well as rank-and-file members. The Class of '74 had many remarkable members, including Henry Waxman, who still exerts enormous power over policy as chair of the House Energy and Commerce Committee; George Miller, powerful chair of the Education and Labor Committee; and current senators Chris Dodd, Tom Harkin, and Max Baucus, chairs of three of the most influential committees in the Senate. It also included the late John Murtha, a longtime powerhouse, and Tom Downey, a New York colleague of Solarz's who was the youngest member of the class. But in a group that had dozens of accomplished politicians and policy wonks, Solarz stood out because of his intellect, drive, and mesmerizing, articulate way of speaking.

He also stood out because of his area of interest and his work ethic. To be sure, many members of the Watergate class were interested in the world — theirs was the era of the Vietnam War, not just of Nixonian scandals — but most turned their focus and time to domestic policy and to devising innovative ways of connecting with constituents back home to ensure that they could also be lawmakers after the 1976 elections. As Solarz says in this book, he decided for practical political, as well as intellectual, reasons to seek a seat on the House Foreign Affairs Committee and to develop a deeper specialty in foreign policy. For most lawmakers, a

focus on foreign policy is an electoral liability: voters want their representatives to spend their time on issues close to home. But in Steve's district,
a focus on foreign policy was an asset because the district's overwhelmingly Jewish population had a strong interest in Israel. At the same time,
the high level of information and engagement in his district, along with its
ideology, meant a strong opposition to the Vietnam War, also an asset for
an antiwar liberal Congressman making foreign policy his specialty.

Other New York delegation members also had constituency reasons to
focus on America's place in the world, such as Ben Rosenthal of Queens
and Lester Wolff, whose district (which he won after being redistricted
into it) also included parts of Queens but who lost his seat in 1980 in large
part because of charges that he had taken too many foreign junkets.

Fortunately for Solarz, his Brooklyn district did not object strenuously
to its representatives traveling around the world. That was partly because
Solarz eschewed the usual "Codels" — foreign trips by congressional delegations that mixed official business with some sightseeing and shopping.
Solarz preferred to travel alone and keep the focus on his work. And as
this book details, and many former Solarz staffers have confirmed to me,
his schedules on these trips were punishing, with eighteen-hour days devoted to seeing officials, meeting with dissidents or other leaders, getting
briefings on what was really going on, and traveling around a country to
see for himself.

Along the way, Solarz picked up immense knowledge of the dynamics
of a wide range of countries and became acquainted with an even wider
range of political actors. He became known as one who would not cod-
dle dictators, and whose office door in Washington was open for freedom fighters and human rights activists. That latter characteristic added
to his aura and clout. For example, for years oppressed Kurdish leaders
from Saddam Hussein's Iraq knew they had a friend in Steve Solarz —
and when those leaders became the governing powerhouses in Kurdish
Iraq after Saddam's downfall, Steve was high on their list of heroes.

I suggested above that a non-insider would be surprised by Solarz's
clout and reputation around the world. So too would many insiders. By
Washington standards, many of the things he was able to do as a rank-
and-file member of the House, even as a subcommittee chair, seem trivial
or merely symbolic: congressional resolutions, letters signed by members,

statements made on the House floor and printed in the *Congressional Record*. But as Solarz perceptively points out in this book, Americans, including most of the members of Congress, do not realize the clout and reach of the United States in the world, its impact as a moral force and a superpower. From Burma to Cambodia to Nepal, things that Solarz did resonated with the countries' leaders or with their liberation movements in ways that had real consequences, even if they were unnoticed or dismissed by the sophisticates and cognoscenti in Washington. And because Solarz followed up, by urging additional US action such as aid or the denial of aid, and by pushing hard and consistently on the diplomatic front, his "symbolic" moves resonated even more.

This is not to suggest that Steve Solarz was a prophet without honor at home, inside the Capitol. In my four decades immersed in the politics of Congress, I have witnessed a small, select number of lawmakers who are able to command broad respect from their colleagues — people who, when they get up on the House or Senate floor to speak cause others in both parties to stop schmoozing, reading, or writing and pay attention. Solarz was one of these select few, in part because of his ability to speak in perfectly parsed, grammatically correct, and consistently eloquent sentences, but largely because what he had to say was compelling and was based on a combination of logic, precision, and deep personal experience.

There was another reason as well: Solarz was generally a political liberal, fitting well his district's predilections. But as he says, he was an "idealist without illusions." He came in as an anti–Vietnam War candidate, but he also understood that military force is sometimes necessary to protect America's national interest and to promote its values. His worldview had elements that resonated with members of both parties and across ideologies. That combination of intellect, integrity, knowledge, and credibility helps to explain his pivotal role in 1990 in the highly emotional congressional debate on the resolution authorizing the use of force in Kuwait to repel Saddam Hussein's invaders. President George H. W. Bush had requested congressional authorization, but it was no sure thing. The Democratic majority was divided, with strong antiwar sentiment from such opinion leaders as Senator Sam Nunn of Georgia, chairman of the Senate Armed Services Committee. There was substantial expert opinion that going to war in the Persian Gulf could result in horrific American casualties.

The debate on the floors of both houses was riveting—even if it was not really a debate, but more a series of emotional and often personal expressions of views by a majority of members preparing to cast the most consequential vote they can, to send young Americans into harm's way. But no speech was more riveting or significant than the one Solarz made. He offered compelling reasons for the United States to authorize force, using history and logic to make the case for American action in America's interest. Many members who had been on the fence told me afterward that Solarz had made a big difference in their decision.

It has been thirty-six years since Steve Solarz came to Congress, and eighteen years since he left public life—eons in our media age. Chances are that if Solarz walked down K Street in Washington at lunchtime today, he might be recognized by one or two grizzled veterans. But if he walked down Quezon Avenue in Manila, he would probably be mobbed. If he visited Phnom Penh in Cambodia, or Erbil in Iraqi Kurdistan, he would be treated as a hero. His impact on the world remains huge. And his insights about power, values, politics, and foreign policy remain as pointed and insightful today as they were when he influenced the course of events in these and other countries.

Solarz's book is valuable as a memoir, and as an inside slice of eighteen years of history involving America and the world, and the dynamics and role of Congress. But it is also important for the lessons he distills from his time on the national and world stage. Given the other changes that have taken place in American politics and Congress in the eighteen years since he left, it is unlikely that there will be another like him for a very long time, if ever. Congress has become much more partisan and ideologically polarized. No lawmaker can get up on the House floor in this era and grab the undivided attention of colleagues from his or her own party, much less get the time of day from those on the other side of the aisle. That unfortunate fact makes *Journeys to War and Peace* worth savoring for yet another reason: to remember, with nostalgia, how valuable it was to have real opinion leaders who could both talk and act, and change the world for the better.

August 31, 2010

PREFACE

If I am not for myself, who will be for me?
But if I am only for myself, what am I?
If not now, when?

The Ethics of Our Fathers

"Depend upon it, sir, when a man knows he is to be hanged in a fortnight, it concentrates his mind wonderfully," Samuel Johnson said. I can testify to the enduring truth of this observation. For several years after my involuntary departure from Congress in 1992, I thought about writing a memoir describing my experiences as a member of the House of Representatives. But for a variety of reasons, some good and some bad, I never quite got around to it.

It wasn't until the summer of 2006, when I was diagnosed with esophageal cancer — a particularly virulent form of this disease — that I realized it might soon be too late to embark on such a project. So, like Ulysses S. Grant, who undertook to write a memoir about his experiences in the Civil War after receiving a cancer diagnosis, I resolved that the time had come to write mine.

My purpose here is to describe how an individual member of Congress can have an impact on American foreign policy and even on developments in faraway countries. Most people assume that foreign policy is primarily, if not exclusively, the prerogative of the executive branch. Yet as the great constitutional scholar Edward Corwin wrote, the Constitution "is an invitation to struggle for the privilege of directing American foreign policy." For much of American history, Congress tended to defer to the president on matters involving foreign policy. There were exceptions, of course, such as the rejection of the Treaty of Versailles after World War I and the passage of neutrality legislation before World War II. But after the debacle in Vietnam and the Watergate scandal, the assumption that the president always knew best how to handle foreign policy was no longer politically tenable.

I was elected to Congress at precisely the moment in American history when Congress decided it would no longer abdicate its constitutional authority for foreign policy to an executive branch that had lost its claim to presidential infallibility. Congress has the ability to shape America's response to events abroad through hearings, speeches, legislation, resolutions, appropriations, confirmations, and ratifications. This book illustrates how such legislative mechanisms can be used to promote our national values and protect our national interests. It also describes how a third-generation American, a Jewish boy from Brooklyn for whom a trip into Manhattan was a daring venture, became known as the Marco Polo of Congress, traveling to over a hundred countries around the world.

Above all it tells of my encounters with some of the world's greatest statesmen and most terrible tyrants. Among the former were Anwar Sadat, Lee Kuan Yew, Indira Gandhi, Nelson Mandela, Norodom Sihanouk, Menachem Begin, and Oscar Arias. Among the latter: Saddam Hussein, Kim Il Sung, Fidel Castro, Mobutu Sese Seko, and Robert Mugabe. Here too are detailed descriptions of the role I played in facilitating the triumph of people power in the Philippines, the establishment of democracy in South Korea and Taiwan, the peace agreement in Cambodia, the abolition of apartheid in South Africa, and the adoption of the resolution authorizing the use of force in the first Gulf War.

The fabled American jurist Oliver Wendell Holmes once said: "It is required of a man that he should share the passion and action of his time at peril of being judged not to have lived." During my eighteen years in Congress, I was indeed privileged to participate in the "passion and action" of my time. But I would like to think that I was also fortunate enough to have influenced some of its events as well.

Stephen J. Solarz
August 31, 2010

JOURNEYS
· TO ·
WAR & PEACE

PROLOGUE

The Making of a Congressman

It is not the critic who counts; not the man who
points out . . . where the doer of deeds could have done
them better. The credit belongs to the man who is actually
in the arena . . . who strives valiantly; who errs, who comes
short again and again . . . but who does actually strive to do
the deeds; who knows great enthusiasms . . . who spends
himself in a worthy cause; who at the best knows in the
end the triumph of high achievement, and who at the
worst . . . at least fails while daring greatly.

♦ THEODORE ROOSEVELT ♦
"The Man in the Arena"

Who can say for sure what factors determine someone's destiny in life?
My path to Congress was neither predictable nor easy. There were several
contributing factors: a father with an intense interest in politics; a broken home that left me with wounded self-esteem; a group of friends and
classmates who gave me confidence in myself; a drive to seek validation as
early as sixth grade, when I discovered in myself a capacity for leadership;
and a desire that my life should make a difference. But my trajectory also
involved a series of fortuitous coincidences and opportunities that could
never have been predicted.

I was born September 12, 1940, at the height of the London Blitz — a
brutal battle mirrored in a small way by the fighting between my mom
and dad in our apartment on the West Side of Manhattan. My parents
divorced a few months later; they had been married less than two years.
Among other grievances, my mother apparently resented my father's
spending almost every evening campaigning on the streets for President
Franklin Roosevelt. For reasons I didn't discover until many years later,
my mother decided not to keep me and the court awarded custody to my

father. My birth mother disappeared from my life and was never spoken of again in the family. It would be twenty years before I met her for the first time.

A few years later, my father married Laura Sussel, a refugee from Nazi Germany, and I grew up loving her deeply. But it was a troubled marriage. My father often shouted at my stepmother. She would lock herself in the bathroom while he stood outside, banging angrily on the door. For a young child it was a traumatic experience. My father and Laura divorced when I was ten, and she too completely vanished from my life. I tracked her down about three decades later and was deeply disappointed to discover that she had no interest in reestablishing a relationship with me.

After my father's second divorce, I went to live with my Aunt Beattie, my father's older sister, in Brooklyn. She was widowed and had two sons, Howard and Billy, both in their early twenties. Meanwhile, my father moved in with his parents, who also lived in Brooklyn. I spent weekdays with my aunt and cousins in the Midwood section of Brooklyn and weekends with my father and grandparents in Flatbush. For the first time, my life became relatively normal. My Aunt Beattie clearly loved me, and I was grateful to her for taking me in. I idolized my cousin Billy, a great athlete who charmed virtually everyone he came in contact with. My cousin Howard, much more subdued, was handicapped by a pronounced and persistent stutter, though he had a certain sweetness.

On my aunt's tree-lined block lived about a half-dozen boys my age. My life growing up with friends like Mark Groothuis, Ross Brechner, Howard Siegel, Bennet Perlmutter, Elliot Puritz, Johnny Plaskow, and Warren Kronenberg was joyful: an endless round of softball, stickball, stoopball, football, basketball, and slapball. The boys on the block became a kind of family for me, a genuine band of brothers. Sixty years later, we still get together for annual reunions.

I have never quite sorted out how this unconventional upbringing affected me. My father, an attorney with his own practice, was very intelligent and had a good sense of values. I was the center of his universe. He passed on to me his love of books. He took me to my first theatrical productions, *An Enemy of the People*, about a courageous doctor who discovers that the healing waters that constitute the major tourist attraction in his Norwegian town are infected with disease and must be closed down, and *Inherit the Wind*, about the titanic clash between Clarence Darrow and William Jennings Bryan at the Scopes monkey trial, in which Tennessee's right to prohibit the teaching of evolution was at stake. These plays had an enormous impact. The first instilled in me a lifelong admiration for those courageous enough to speak truth to power and willing to take principled even if unpopular positions. The second inspired me to consider a career as an attorney, championing the cause of the downtrodden and deprived. My father, who was politically active in the Tammany Hall Democratic organization in Manhattan, also took me to my first political event, a Tammany Hall beer and pretzel gathering in 1956, at which Senator Albert Gore Sr. delivered an eloquent speech about the need for a nuclear test ban treaty.

My relationship with my father was troubled, however. His darker side resurfaced even in his worship of my boyhood accomplishments. I often felt he was more interested in living vicariously through my achievements than he was in my actual well-being. When I lost a race for senior class president in high school, instead of consoling me he berated me; he was angry that I had diminished the reflected glory he derived from my achievements. I also could never forget or forgive the way he had treated my stepmother. To this day, I find it painful to listen to a person shout at someone else.

I had been interested in politics since elementary school, when I was elected president of my sixth-grade homeroom class. In eighth grade I was elected vice president of the student council and in ninth, president of the student council. My first (but not last) electoral loss occurred when I ran for p.m. coordinator during my sophomore year at Midwood High School. But I made a comeback shortly afterward when I was elected president of the P.M. Council. A year later, I won the race for "mayor" of Midwood, which made me the leader of the student government of this huge public school in a predominantly Jewish neighborhood filled with bright, ambitious kids. I used to joke that it was a terrible thing to reach the peak of my career at seventeen! And I was only half joking, because getting elected and then serving as "mayor" was tremendously exciting and fulfilling and substantially enhanced my self-esteem.

One day, visiting my father's apartment, I came across a letter to him from a woman who was apparently related to my birth mother. I never asked my father about my mother for fear of hurting his feelings. I didn't feel for her the yearning that had motivated my search for my stepmother, but I was curious about her and very much wanted to meet her if she was still alive. I used the return address on the letter to get the sender's phone number from information, called her, and learned that my mother had married a man named Ben Robin and was living with him somewhere in Brooklyn. The letter writer gave me my maternal grandfather's name and number so I could find out where my mother lived. But my grandfather's response to hearing from me was brusque: everyone had a cross to bear in life, he said, and mine was that I would never know my mother. Then he hung up. So I looked Ben Robin up in the phone book and found one listing: for a law office in the Bedford-Stuyvesant section of Brooklyn.

Since I had no idea whether Ben Robin knew my mother's past history, I was reluctant to call him and possibly upset someone else's life. So I went with my friend Johnny Plaskow to see his office, which turned out to be a storefront with a big bay window. Johnny called the office and asked to speak to Mr. Robin, while I looked inside to see who answered. When Robin came to the phone Johnny hung up, but I had seen enough to identify him. The next day we went back around closing time and followed him to his home in the Kings Highway neighborhood.

Now I could get my mother's phone number from information. A few days later, I called, told her who I was, and suggested we get together. She said she had always suspected she would receive such a call and agreed to meet me the next day at a nearby luncheonette. For her this was a much more emotional encounter than for me. She explained that her father had persuaded her not to seek custody of me because it might hurt her chances for remarriage. She had never come to see me, she claimed, because she had been very unhappy with my father and did not want to have anything to do with him again. Now, though, she very much wanted to become a part of my life and urged me to meet her husband, who did know about me, and her two sons by her second marriage. A few days later I met them. Ben turned out to be as warm and understanding as one could possibly imagine, and the two boys, Avy and Seth, were both delightful and intelligent. Although I had never expected to establish a relationship with my mother, over the next several years I came to regard myself as part of their family.

I was now a student at Brandeis University in Waltham, Massachusetts, where again I got involved in student politics and by sophomore year
was vice president of the student council. That summer of 1960, I hitch-
hiked to the Democratic convention in Los Angeles, where I witnessed
a dramatic moment in American politics. On the night of the balloting
for the presidential nomination, I sneaked into the convention center and
managed to climb up on the TV platform about thirty feet in front of the
podium. Just below me was the Wyoming delegation. By the time the roll
call reached them, near the end of the first ballot, it was clear that Senator
John Kennedy needed only two more votes than the Wyoming delegation
had planned to give him to lock up the nomination. I saw the delegation
chair turn his back to the podium to face the delegates. "I need two votes,"
he pleaded. "I need two votes." Their faces reflecting their fear of losing this
chance to make history — and of the consequences of passing it up — the
delegates leaped to their feet, raised their hands, and shouted, "Take me,
take me!" So it was that Kennedy clinched the nomination.

In my junior year I decided not to run for president of the student
council and instead became editor in chief of the student newspaper, *The
Justice*. That was a challenging but also gratifying experience. We got immediate feedback on what we printed, creating a real sense of community
and communication. Brandeis students were politically sophisticated and
engaged, ranging from socialists on the left to Democrats on the right.
Many were involved in the struggle for civil rights and the movement to
ban the bomb. Their progressive leanings helped shape and reinforce my
own liberal views and values. I left Brandeis feeling strongly that civil rights
was a moral imperative and the pursuit of peace a strategic necessity.

One of my Brandeis professors was Max Lerner, a nationally syndicated columnist and author of *America as a Civilization*, a widely admired
account of life in the United States from sociological, political, and cultural perspectives. During my senior year, I had the job of driving Professor Lerner to and from the campus and got to know him well. He was
a role model of the politically engaged intellectual, and it was from him
that I learned the importance of ideas in politics. My first job after graduation, during the summer of 1962, was as his research assistant. That fall,
I enrolled at Columbia Law School. I had always assumed I would go
to law school — my father certainly expected me to do so — after which

I envisioned a career as either a latter-day Clarence Darrow or an appointed or elected government official. But I found the work uninteresting and onerous. The whole emphasis at Columbia seemed to be on serving the corporate establishment. But helping the rich get richer wasn't what I had in mind, and I began to wonder if I really wanted a career in the law.

One day, a Brandeis friend doing graduate work at Columbia showed me the reading lists for his courses in American government. My eyes lit up. These were books I would have wanted to read even if I didn't have to read them for school. It struck me that I didn't need to be a lawyer to have a career in politics and government. Woodrow Wilson, John Kennedy, and Lyndon Johnson hadn't been lawyers, and while I had no aspiration to become president, I began to feel that if they could succeed in politics without a law degree, I might be able to as well. I left law school and in fall 1963 enrolled in Columbia's graduate school of Public Law and Government. My courses on international Communism with Zbigniew Brzezinski, the American presidency with Richard Neustadt, and American history with Bill Leuchtenburg were far more interesting than my law school classes on contracts and civil procedure.

In fall 1965, a chance meeting with an old friend set the stage for my introduction to professional politics. This encounter triggered events which led to my marriage to the remarkable woman I have shared my life with for forty-three years. It also made possible my subsequent career in Congress.

At lunch at a kosher restaurant during the Rosh Hashanah holidays, I ran into Johnny Levine, a close friend in junior high and high school. We had lost touch, and I did not recognize him with his full beard. But he recognized me and came over. We revived our friendship and began having dinner together once a week. Johnny was studying to become a Conservative rabbi at the Jewish Theological Seminary. He had become involved in the civil rights movement, where he met Mel Dubin, a well-to-do businessman and political progressive who had decided to run for Congress in 1966 against Congressman Abraham Multer in Brooklyn. A twenty-two-year incumbent with a history of using his public office for private gain, Multer was also a strong supporter of the war in Vietnam. By this time, with several hundred thousand American troops in Vietnam, the war was becoming a major political issue, and Dubin's candidacy was one of the first antiwar campaigns for Congress.

Johnny (who apparently remembered my successful campaign for "mayor" of Midwood seven years earlier) somehow convinced Dubin to hire a young, inexperienced graduate student to be his campaign manager. To my amazement, Dubin, who had already gone through two campaign managers, offered me the job, and I accepted. I had become increasingly unhappy with our deepening involvement in Vietnam, but I hadn't been actively involved in the growing antiwar movement. Now I welcomed the opportunity to register my concerns about the war in a meaningful way. What made Dubin's offer even more attractive was his willingness to pay me $200 a week, a princely sum for an impecunious student paying his own way through graduate school. In February 1966, I moved into a Brooklyn apartment that Dubin, who actually lived in Queens, was using as his official address.

We were running against an entrenched incumbent in a district that had no legacy of insurgency to build on. It was overwhelmingly Democratic, and there had been no challenge to Multer for the Democratic nomination in two decades. We had to build a campaign virtually from scratch. All I found when I arrived at campaign headquarters were 25,000 campaign buttons with the puzzling slogan, "Yes he can, if you will." I threw them away. (It took a far more sophisticated American politician than me to discover the potency of that slogan forty-two years later.)

I began to accumulate lists of people who had worked in Brooklyn on previous campaigns for citywide candidates whose politics and liberal views were similar to Dubin's. We contacted them and invited them to join our campaign. By primary day we had over a thousand volunteers, attracted not by the nonexistent charisma of our candidate, but by his opposition to the war and the opportunity his candidacy offered to express their discontent with American policy.

One of the people who responded to our recruitment efforts was Nina Glantz. She sent in our return postcard with a note that said, "Tell Mel I'm Jackie Levine's sister." Nina's sister was a prominent activist in the American Jewish community who ultimately became president of the woman's division of the American Jewish Congress and then president of the National Jewish Community Relations Advisory Council. In later years, as

I traveled all around the country speaking to Jewish communities, I used to say to great applause that my major claim to fame was that I was Jackie Levine's brother-in-law.

I vividly remember the day Nina came to our headquarters wearing a white vinyl raincoat with black diagonal stripes, accompanied by one of her students at Brooklyn College, where she taught political science. He was tall and handsome, and I used to tease her that he was probably more than her student. But when I got to know her I learned that, after fourteen years of marriage, with children aged nine and two, she was actually in the midst of a divorce she hadn't expected and hadn't wanted.

Eager to enlist Nina in the campaign, I asked her to serve as a captain, which meant being responsible for canvassing the registered Democrats in an area of a few square blocks. I soon recognized her considerable talents and promoted her to area coordinator, supervising several captains. Once again she distinguished herself. After about a month, she agreed to serve as deputy campaign manager. Not long after, we went on our first "date": a demonstration outside a neighborhood production of *Fiorello* where Dubin volunteers held up signs saying "Dubin for Congress: No More Politics and Poker." Later the two of us went for coffee and, during a long conversation, discovered we had much in common, not least that we shared many views and values and both had a deep interest in politics.

Since Nina was several years older than me, I suspect that under other circumstances we never would have gotten married. She would have seemed unattainable and untouchable to a young graduate student like me. And I would probably have seemed at most a likable kid to her. But working together for many hours a day in a common enterprise to which we were both deeply committed and then going back to her house for delicious dinners that she cooked late in the evening gave us an opportunity to know each other. I had gone out with my share of girls, but Nina was an incredibly impressive woman. Attractive, intelligent, and elegant, she excelled at whatever she did. I could hardly believe she was interested in me. As it turned out, politics became a lifelong interest for her, giving our marriage the added dimension of a political partnership. Whenever possible, Nina traveled with me, sagely advising me, smoothing my rough edges, and—as she put it—always watching my back.

Another important strategy for the Dubin campaign was to recruit can-

didates for the lesser positions, including state assemblyman, state senator, and district leader. If each candidate on our ticket could bring in a
dozen or more volunteers, I believed we could amass an army of people
who would work not only for their candidate but for Dubin as well. This
strategy worked reasonably well, but it was not without its drawbacks.
One day I got a call from Larry Simon, one of our Assembly candidates,
who said he had just the kind of guy we were looking for as a candidate
for the state senate from Bensonhurst. "His name is Abe Cohen," Simon
said, "and he is the president of a local B'nai B'rith chapter. He's also on the
community board, and well thought of in the neighborhood." He didn't
have Cohen's phone number but told me to look him up.

I got a number for Abe Cohen in Bensonhurst and reached him on the
phone. He was surprised to hear that he'd been recommended for office,
but he seemed impressed when I told him that Dubin was prepared to finance his campaign. A few days later, he showed up at headquarters wearing dungarees and a T-shirt, with tattoos on his arms. I was a bit taken
aback but thought I shouldn't hold his bizarre body art against him. Besides, I reasoned, when he's campaigning he'll wear a tie and jacket, and no
one will see the tattoos. I explained we were asking only that he recruit at
least a dozen volunteers to ring doorbells for him and Dubin. He said he
would. We shook hands, and the deal was sealed.

A month went by, and he had produced only two volunteers. So I asked
him to come to campaign headquarters. Pointing to a big map on the wall
with each election district marked off, I said, "Abe, look at the map. There
are lots of different colored thumbtacks. Each color represents the volunteers brought into the campaign by one of our candidates. Your volunteers
are the white thumbtacks and, as you can see, there are only two. You're
supposed to produce at least a dozen volunteers. You simply have to do
better."

"You want thumbtacks, I'll give you thumbtacks!" he exclaimed, grab-
bing a bunch of white thumbtacks and sticking them on the map.

By now I had realized he was the wrong Abe Cohen. But I had read
somewhere that in politics the most valuable thing you have is your word,
and once you made a commitment you had to keep it. Having promised
to put him on the ticket, I felt I couldn't go back on my word. In the end,
though, keeping Cohen on the ticket might have cost us the election. He

was running against a very popular state senator, Bobby Brownstein, who didn't really like Congressman Multer. If we hadn't opposed Brownstein, he would probably have sat on his hands and done nothing. But because he now had an opponent whom Dubin was financing, he went out and campaigned far more than he otherwise would have. The extra votes Brownstein brought out undoubtedly accounted for more than the narrow margin — 950 votes out of 41,000 — by which Dubin lost the election.

The other reason I think we lost the primary was that Dubin ran a half-hearted campaign, tending to his business during the day and only showing up for coffee klatches in the evenings. It's clear to me in retrospect that if Dubin had become a full-time candidate and a part-time businessman, he would have won. But I was a twenty-five-year-old kid managing the campaign of a millionaire businessman, and it didn't occur to me to tell him to find someone else to manage his business for a while.

Two incidents from the campaign will give a sense of Brooklyn politics in those days. The first occurred during a debate that was supposed to be between Dubin and Multer. But Multer didn't show up; he sent Morris Stein, a local city councilman, in his place. Dubin began by detailing the many ways that Multer had profited personally from his position as a congressman. When Stein's turn came, he said: "All Dubin talks about are the deals where Congressman Multer made money. He never tells you about the deals where he lost money!" We Dubin people shouted, "Tell us! Tell us!" But Stein did not elaborate.

The second incident happened the weekend before the primary. I was summoned to the home of Hy Wohl, a local supporter who worked for the United Jewish Appeal. Wohl told me he thought we were on the verge of victory but needed something special to "put Dubin over the top." "We should spread a rumor that Multer has an Arab mistress," he said. Somewhat taken aback, I asked how we could do that. "I've been thinking about that too," Wohl said, "and I think the way to do it is to send Nina into a luncheonette on Kings Highway and have her tell some of the ladies there about Multer's affair with an Arab woman." Perhaps if I had taken his advice Dubin would have eked out a victory. But as Richard Nixon once said in another context, "that would have been wrong," so I declined.

The Dubin campaign attracted notice, both because of the closeness of the race and because it was an early indicator of the politically toxic effects of our escalating involvement in Vietnam. As a result, I came to the attention of William Fitts Ryan, a congressman from the West Side of Manhattan who had sought the Democratic nomination for mayor in 1965; Nina had been one of his volunteers. He offered me a job in Washington as his administrative assistant. I was strongly inclined to take it. I was interested in politics, Ryan was a courageous and charismatic congressman whom I admired, and it seemed like a terrific opportunity.

This was summer 1967, and Nina and I were already married. I told her about this job offer during a walk on the beach in Fire Island, a beautiful stretch of sand along the Atlantic Ocean. Kicking up some sand for emphasis, she exclaimed, "Why would you want to do that?" Then she asked, "Why don't you run for office yourself?" I had always wanted a career in government, although I thought more in terms of an administrative appointment than electoral politics. And at twenty-seven, I thought I was a bit young. Still, the prospect of actually running for office — and even more, being elected — was too enticing to pass up. So we consulted a close friend and mentor, Stanley Lowell, a former deputy mayor of New York, who had run a number of political campaigns. With his encouragement we started looking at various political offices that would be significant enough for a youthful, aspiring politician, but not beyond my reach. We came up with the legislative seat occupied for thirty-two years by Max Turshen, who was dean of the New York Assembly, having served longer than any other member of the state legislature. He had been elected before I was born, but for most of his time in office he had represented an entirely different part of Brooklyn. A reapportionment a year earlier had moved his district further south, to an area wholly within the congressional district in which Dubin had run against Multer. Not only had Nina and I grown up there, but through the Dubin campaign we were known to hundreds of newly minted political activists.

With the primary scheduled for June 1968, my campaign began in February. In that overwhelmingly Democratic district, whoever won the primary was certain to win the general election. During a typical campaign day, I got to a subway station at 7 a.m. and stayed until 8:30, greeting as many as a thousand people on their way to work. There were six stations in the district, and I went to a different one every day. For the rest of the day I campaigned at shopping centers, parks, and wherever else people congregated. In the evening, I canvassed apartment buildings with a group of volunteers. By the end of the campaign, I had been to each subway station several times and had rung every doorbell in 200 of the 300 apartment buildings in the district.

One campaign technique I pioneered was to stand during the morning rush hour on the empty subway platform serving trains going to Brooklyn, across from the crowded platform where commuters waited for trains to Manhattan. In between trains, a new influx of people would gather on the platform, and I would give them my little spiel through an electronic bullhorn, standing next to a big sign that said "Steve Solarz for Assembly." One effective argument I used was that my opponent had been in office for thirty-two years, but nobody knew his name. I offered $10 to anyone who could tell me who he was. Of course, nobody could, so I responded, "If you don't even know who he is, how good a job can he be doing?" The one time somebody got it right, I presented him with the $10, pointing out that out of thousands of people, this was the first man who knew our assemblyman's name.

After a while, going up to perfect strangers saying, "I'm Steve Solarz and I'm running for the Assembly" got tedious, so I decided to give street-corner speeches on why I was running. This was a lot closer to my idea of what a campaign should be like. One day, I went with my bullhorn to a corner in the busiest shopping area in the district and began my speech, but nobody stopped to listen or even look. I mean nobody. After a few minutes of shouting into the wind, I gave up and slunk back to headquarters. Still, I figured this was just bad luck and tried again. My second foray onto the mean streets of Brooklyn was no more successful, and once again I retreated. Everybody has an absolute minimum beneath which their dignity will not permit them to sink. For me it's talking to an audience when nobody is listening.

It's been said that you can't keep a New Yorker down. That goes in spades for a Brooklynite. And so, about a week later, I tried once more — and again felt more like a crackpot than a candidate. Just as I was about to pack it in, though, somebody began to heckle me. Sure enough, a crowd gathered. I realized people are drawn to conflict and drama, and I needed a heckler to attract an audience. I called Dick Pious, a friend from Columbia, and asked him to become my designated heckler. Dick — now a distinguished professor at Barnard and leading authority on the American presidency—agreed. We were doing well, drawing crowds (the only problem being that Dick often got the better of me in our exchanges). One day, a big guy—about 200 pounds, rippling with muscles—informed Dick that he was Turshen's nephew and would like nothing more than to punch me in the nose. Thinking quickly, Dick responded, "That's just what he wants you to do!" The bruiser grumbled and shuffled away, leaving my nose and campaign intact.

Another problem was brought to my attention by Mabel Gold, the wife of the president of Young Israel of Avenue U, an Orthodox Jewish congregation, and one of our volunteers. "Steve," she said, "everybody on my block has met you. They've seen you at the subways. You've rung their doorbells. They've met you in the supermarkets. Some of the women have even met you in the beauty parlors. But nobody is voting for you. With your name, they all think you're Puerto Rican." In that predominantly Jewish district, religion and ethnicity often trumped politics and ideology. Somehow or other we had to communicate to the voters that I was a member of the tribe.

We changed our literature to emphasize that I was active in the Zionist Organization of America and the American Jewish Congress, and a member of Temple Beth El in the Manhattan Beach neighborhood. We also hit on the idea of printing and distributing several thousand copies of Nina Solarz's recipe for gefilte fish. I took a sheaf of them to the boardwalk at Brighton Beach, went up to the first elderly, obviously Jewish lady sitting on a bench, and said, "I'm Steve Solarz. I'm running for the Assembly, and I'd like to give you a copy of my wife's recipe for gefilte fish." The woman looked at the recipe, then looked at me, and said, "So what's the matter? You don't think I know how to make gefilte fish?" I went up to another lady on the boardwalk and repeated my line. She looked at me uncomprehendingly—as if to say, what's this all about? So I told her that the recipe was handed down in my family from my great grandmother, a *rebetzen* (rabbi's wife) in Romania. A flash of recognition appeared in her eyes, and she exclaimed to no one in particular, "Oh, he's Jewish. He's Jewish."

Two weeks before the primary, Gary Grossman—my bunkmate in camp, my roommate in college, and one of my very best friends—took a leave from work to organize our get-out-the-vote operation. We had a couple of hundred friends, relatives, and volunteers, and like a general deploying his forces, Gary sent them out with lists of favorable voters to make sure these people went to the polls. Thanks to him and so many others, I won the primary with 58 percent of the vote and was formally elected a few months later to the New York State Assembly, at the age of twenty-eight. It was enormously exciting.

But I soon realized the humbling limits of my influence—symbolized by the fact that, in a legislature of 150 members, I was given New York State Assembly license plate 152! It wasn't long before I learned that the Assembly was the closest thing to a parliamentary institution in the United States. All the decisions were made by the Republicans, who were the majority party, and there was little we minority Democrats could do except heckle. It was even considered inappropriate to offer amendments to legislation on the floor of the Assembly. If someone had offered the Ten Commandments as an amendment to the Code of Criminal Procedure, it would have been interpreted as lack of confidence in the leadership and immediately voted down. As a "reform" Democrat, I found myself a minority within the minority, which further limited my capacity to influence legislative events.

There were, however, other ways of establishing one's political presence. I made my first appearance as the "Quote of the Day" in the *New York Times*—a significant event for a New York politician—when I was in the Assembly. I had gone out to dinner with Franz Leichter, one of my closest friends in the Assembly, who represented a district on the Upper West Side of Manhattan. As a refugee from Nazi-occupied Austria, ten-year-old Franz had arrived in New York on the same day I was born. As his ship steamed into the harbor it collided with another vessel, and the *Times* reported the event. I used to kid Franz, who was not oblivious to press coverage, that even then he was getting more media attention than me.

Returning from dinner, we discovered to our surprise that the Assembly was in session debating the welfare budget. Copies of this hefty document had been placed on members' desks, but there was none on mine. So I asked the clerk of the Assembly for a copy. He said none were left. I asked him how I could possibly vote on the bill if I didn't even have a copy of it. "It's your tough luck," he responded. I exclaimed, "My God, what kind of a place is this? What's going on here?" Bill Kovach, the *Times'* Albany correspondent, overheard this exchange. The next day "My God, what kind of place is this?" was the Quote of the Day.

It was a place where I was unable to do really worthwhile work, and where much that went on was uninspiring, to say the least. Prevented from having any real impact on the legislative process, and unable to convene official hearings because we were in the minority, Franz and I decided to hold what we described to the media as a series of ad hoc hearings on victimless crimes, for which thousands of people were incarcerated, although no one was really being hurt by their transgressions. Mario Procaccino, a former city comptroller who had lost the mayoral race to John Lindsay in 1969 and perhaps hoped to run again, heard about the hearings and arranged to testify before us. He denounced the "pimps, prostitutes, and pornographers" he claimed were taking over New York and demanded legislation to rid the Big Apple of this scourge. I asked if this meant that he disagreed with St. Thomas Aquinas, who had said that simply because something is immoral, it shouldn't necessarily be made illegal. Procaccino thought for a moment and said, "Well, St. Thomas was way ahead of his time." I then asked whether he felt the law should prohibit fornication between competent and consenting adults. "I'm against all these unnatural sex acts," he replied.

The Assembly was also the venue for some classic malapropisms. One day in the midst of a debate, Stanley Steingut, the minority leader, got up and said, "If this bill passes, the sword of Damocles will fall into the Pandora's box." A Brooklyn assemblyman, Peter Mirto, once introduced a bill making it a crime to read the name of an American soldier killed in Vietnam as part of any demonstration against US policy. With American casualties mounting into the thousands, reading the names of the fallen at rallies was a standard practice of the antiwar movement. Some of us objected that the bill violated the First Amendment guarantee of free speech — presumably one of the principles for which we were fighting. Mirto responded: "If this bill is defeated, there will be joy in Hanoi tonight. They'll distribute sake to the troops." It was the wrong drink in the wrong country. But that was what passed for parliamentary repartee in Albany.

Another big project in Albany in those years was driven by Governor Nelson Rockefeller. He pushed for construction of fallout shelters throughout the state, to protect New Yorkers from a nuclear attack by the Soviet Union (then considered a real danger). The day before we were scheduled to debate the state budget for the coming fiscal year, which included a line item appropriation for Rockefeller's civil defense program, Franz Leichter and I decided to inspect the fallout shelter in the basement of the state capitol. The next day I reported to my colleagues that in this shelter — a huge, dingy, poorly lit basement — we found a bunch of metal barrels on whose tops were stenciled the words "water container and convertible commode." But when we pried one open and looked into it, we couldn't tell whether it was still a water container or had become a commode!

We then made a motion to strike the money for civil defense and, amazingly, succeeded. But much to our surprise and chagrin, when the budget came up the next year, we discovered the civil defense funds once again included. Franz reminded the majority leader, Jack Kingston, that we had abolished the program last year and asked what the money for it was doing in the budget this year. "Well, just because we eliminated the program didn't mean we eliminated the budget," the majority leader retorted.

There was, however, one unambiguous legislative achievement that gave me considerable satisfaction. In 1970, we became the first state to pass a bill legalizing abortion. Since it passed by only one vote and I voted for it, it had a special meaning for me. It also provided one of the most dramatic political moments I ever witnessed. At the end of the roll call, but before the final vote was announced, the bill was down by two votes. George Michaels, a Democrat from upstate New York who represented a predominantly Catholic district, had initially voted against the bill, as he had promised his constituents he would. Now Michaels rose and asked to speak. What he was about to do, he said, would probably mean the end of his political career, but he couldn't live with himself if it was his vote that defeated the bill. Then he switched from nay to aye, creating a tie. The Speaker, Perry Duryea, a Republican from Long Island, had previously indicated that he would vote for the bill if his vote was needed. He now said "aye," and the bill passed. The debate was reported on national television, and Michaels received thousands of letters from women across the country thanking him for his political courage. Unfortunately, his prediction came true and he was defeated in the next election.

Although frustrated by events in the Assembly in general, I could still find gratification in the opportunity that public service gave me to make a difference in people's lives. Two unrelated events stand out in my memory. One day, I received a postcard from a constituent named Abe Heller. Now that City University offered open enrollment to high-school graduates, he suggested, there should be a similar program for senior citizens who wanted the intellectual stimulation of taking a college course. I thought it was a great idea. It seemed to me that the life of the mind didn't end when you reached retirement age, and that many senior citizens would be eager to participate.

I contacted the chancellor of City University, Bob Kibbee, who agreed to call a meeting of all the university's deans where I could present the proposal. They all opposed it, claiming it would create bureaucratic problems and overcrowded classrooms, and detract from the main mission of educating undergraduates. But the chancellor, to his great credit, overruled them, saying, "I think this is what the university should be all about." As a result of the program that Kibbee established, based on an average citizen's suggestion to his representative, thousands of senior citizens have enrolled in courses on a space-available basis on the many City University campuses. Eighty-four-year-old Bertha Farmer, a resident of Manhattan's Lower East Side, read that I had been responsible for initiating the program and proudly wrote me that she had taken history and Spanish and gotten an A in both.

The second event involved an earthquake in Nicaragua — not something that normally fell under the jurisdiction of a Brooklyn assemblyman. One Sunday morning my home phone rang. The caller, an extremely agitated constituent, told me about the earthquake and said she couldn't reach her daughter, who was nine months pregnant, and her son-in-law in Managua. She asked for my help in finding them. At first I was stumped. But before hanging up, I asked what her son-in-law did for a living. It turned out he worked for United Fruit, and by chance, through my childhood friend Johnny Levine, I had gotten to know Eli Black, the president of United Brands, which owned United Fruit. I reached Eli at his weekend residence and explained the situation. He said he would try to help and called back in about ten minutes. "We were able to establish radio communications with our Managua office," he reported, "and you can tell your constituent that her daughter and son-in-law are okay and she's now the grandmother of a new baby." I was thrilled. Only half an hour after she had called me, I called her back with the good news, anticipating some words of praise. But all she said was, "Is it a boy or a girl?"

Holding public office did afford opportunities for political involvements I might otherwise not have had. In the last week of the 1972 presidential election, for example, I was asked to escort Senator George McGovern's daughter on a campaign excursion through my district. As we entered an appetizer shop, I started to explain that the bagels and lox in the display case were a Brooklyn Jewish specialty. "You don't have to explain bagels and lox to me," she said. "My husband is Jewish and comes from Brooklyn, so I know all about them." I told her that in New York ethnicity and religion were the beginning (if not also the end) of politics. "If I didn't know your father's son-in-law was a Brooklyn Jew," I said, "you can be sure no one else knows it either." She agreed that if I thought it would be helpful to spread the word about this, I should do it. So at our next stop, I approached an elderly Jewish woman sitting on a crate in front of a shop. "I'm Assemblyman Solarz," I said, "and I'd like to introduce you to Senator McGovern's daughter, who just happens to be married to a nice Jewish boy from Brooklyn."

"So what difference does that make?" she responded. Not only was she right on the substance, but her reaction indicated that the campaign was in even more trouble politically than I had thought.

Although I had been enormously gratified and excited by my election to the legislature in 1968, by 1973 much of the thrill had worn off. I was increasingly frustrated over my inability to have an effect on any of the issues I really cared about. As a backbench member of the minority, my influence in the Assembly was somewhere between negligible and nil. I had already met the challenge of consolidating my position in my Assembly district. Having won renomination with 88 percent of the vote in the Democratic primary in 1970 against a fairly vigorous opponent, I was somewhat surprised to find that I faced not one but two opponents in the 1972 primary. This time I managed to win renomination with 80 percent of the vote. So I now began to consider other offices I might run for. I lacked the financial resources for a state- or city-wide race, and Bertram Podell, the congressman from the district where I lived, was a popular incumbent who seemed unbeatable. The only position left that I had a chance at seemed to be Brooklyn borough president — at that time the borough's chief representative in city government — which was up for election in 1973.

The incumbent, Sam Leone, a machine Democrat from Bensonhurst, was a perfectly decent fellow, but he was also the embodiment of old-line politics. I thought I had a chance to defeat him by running the same kind of reform-oriented insurgent campaign that had carried me to victory in my first Assembly race. A win would position me for a future city- or state-wide race, since Brooklyn was the most populous of the five boroughs of New York. But my calculations were faulty. In a three-way race for the Democratic nomination, I came in second with 33 percent of the vote, compared to Leone's 46 percent and 21 percent for Ruth Lerner, another reform candidate. If Lerner hadn't run, I might have won, since most of her votes would probably have gone to me. But even then I would most likely have lost. I had given the campaign everything I had. By the time it was over, I had shaken the hands of 300,000 people, but my best was clearly not good enough.

I was at a loss about what to do next. A city- or state-wide race was out of the question, a congressional campaign appeared unrealistic, and remaining in the Assembly as part of what seemed a permanent minority wasn't attractive either. As much as I loved politics, I began to consider leaving public life.

As I licked my wounds and contemplated this bleak political future at our summer home on Fire Island, I got a call from Josh Howard. Josh, who was only eighteen, had been my press secretary in the borough presidency campaign. I had first met him in 1966, when I appointed him my eleven-year-old deputy press secretary in the Dubin campaign. Josh, who later went on to a distinguished career as a television producer at CBS, was a precocious and extremely likable youngster whom Nina and I came to think of as our second son.

Josh reported he had just heard on the news that Bert Podell had been indicted for bribery, conspiracy, conflict of interest, and perjury. Here was an opening for me to run for his seat in the primary next year. "Don't dance on his grave," I said — since he hadn't yet been convicted — but Josh responded, "Well, I don't think we should sit shiva, either." It was true that there was no reason to mourn for Podell. But the fact that he might be

convicted and forced to resign certainly opened up a political possibility
for me.

I assumed that everything would depend on what happened at his trial,
since if Podell was acquitted, he would have no problem winning renomination and election. If he were convicted, on the other hand, I would have
a realistic chance of filling the vacancy. So I waited, convinced that one
way or the other, there would be a verdict well before the September primary. But Podell kept getting the trial postponed. By spring 1974, it became clear that the trial wouldn't be held until after the primary. Now I
faced a dilemma. If I waited until the trial was over and he was convicted,
his successor would not be elected in a primary, where I would have a good
chance of winning, but by the Democratic County Committee, which was
dominated by the regular Democratic organization, where my chances
would be zero. Challenging Podell in the primary, however, meant relinquishing my seat in the Assembly, since I couldn't run for both Congress
and the legislature in the same election. Feeling as I did about remaining
in the Assembly, and seeing no other electoral possibilities, it was easy to
decide to put my future on the line and enter the race.

My first move was to conduct a survey of voter attitudes toward Podell.
Many voters, it turned out, were unaware that their congressman had been
indicted. Two-thirds of these favored his renomination. Among those
who did know, two-thirds were against his renomination. It didn't take a
rocket scientist to figure out that in order to defeat him, I had to make the
charges that the US Attorney, Rudy Giuliani, had leveled against him the
main issue. We also had to deal with the presence of a third candidate, Bob
Chira. With no record of political or community involvement, he had little
chance of winning, but I feared he might split the anti-incumbent vote.

So we ran a single-issue campaign. All our brochures and mailings
prominently featured the fact that Podell had been indicted for using his
public office for private gain. I insisted that our literature also contain a reminder that in our system of government everyone was entitled to be pre-
sumed innocent until proven guilty. Josh Howard suggested (as a joke, I
think) that we add "even Bert Podell, no matter how unlikely that may be."
But of course we didn't.

In those days, television ads and even radio spots were virtually unknown in New York congressional campaigns. So we had none. Instead we

had "Abbate's Army," about a hundred mostly teenage boys and girls under the direction of Peter Abbate, who put our campaign literature under doors and in mailboxes throughout the district. This required enormous organizational talent, since we had to make sure our modestly paid workers actually distributed our fliers where they were supposed to, rather than dumping them down a sewer so they could go home early. But Abbate, who had been my aide-de-camp in the borough president campaign and later worked on my congressional staff, was well up to the job. Many years later, having graduated from the school of bare-knuckle Brooklyn politics, Abbate was elected to the State Assembly himself, where he continues to serve with distinction.

On primary day, after the polls closed at 9 p.m., a hush fell over our campaign headquarters, as we waited for our polling place volunteers to phone in the results. At about 9:01 p.m. the phone rang. It was picked up by my extremely able campaign manager, Mike Lewan, who said someone by the name of Congressman Phil Burton was on the line. I had never heard of Congressman Burton, but of course I took the call. Introducing himself as a California congressman and future colleague, Burton exclaimed, "Congratulations, Steve!" How he knew I had won when we had yet to receive a single return was beyond me. But he was right on the mark. When the votes were counted, I had 46 percent, Podell had 33 percent, and Chira had 21 percent. It wasn't until I arrived in Washington and came to know and admire Congressman Burton that I appreciated what a consummate politician he was, with a seemingly unparalleled grasp of the politics of virtually every congressional district in the country. And so it was this man of encyclopedic political knowledge who ushered me into the 94th Congress and the life I would lead for the next two decades.

One of my first tasks was to decide what congressional committees I wanted to serve on and then persuade the Democratic leadership to give me those assignments. I knew that my impact in the House would be exercised largely within the framework of these committees. If I had had my druthers, I would certainly have chosen either Appropriations or Ways and Means, the two most powerful committees. But New York already had three members on Ways and Means and two on Appropriations. There was little chance that the leadership would agree to add another New Yorker to either panel, let alone a freshman member. So, after consulting with some senior members of the New York delegation, like Jonathan "Jack" Bingham and Ed Koch, I opted for Foreign Affairs. Bingham, a man of great integrity and stature whom I came to admire and even revere, pointed out that at a time when the war in Vietnam still raged on, and in the aftermath of the 1973 Yom Kippur War between Israel and Egypt, this assignment would give me an opportunity to play a role in shaping American policy toward the Middle East and Southeast Asia, not to mention other trouble spots around the world. He added that whenever foreign leaders came to Washington, they usually met privately with the members of the committee. For a kid from Brooklyn, this seemed like a very attractive opportunity to get to know the movers and shakers from around the world who were influencing the course of history.

I was, after all, deeply committed to the security and survival of Israel, whose establishment in the aftermath of the Holocaust I considered a political miracle. I had also begun my career in politics running one of the first antiwar congressional campaigns in the country. I concluded that an appointment to the Foreign Affairs Committee would combine my personal commitment to Israel and to ending the American military involvement in Vietnam with considerable political benefits in a district with a large pro-Israel and antiwar constituency.

My district had the largest number of Jews (about two-thirds of my constituents were Jewish), and the most Holocaust survivors, of any in the country. This reality was brought home to me one summer day, on a walking tour of the Bensonhurst area of the district. I encountered a woman in her sixties wearing a short-sleeved dress that revealed the tattooed number on her arm. When she said she had been in Auschwitz, I told her I had just read Martin Gilbert's book *Auschwitz and the Allies*, which describes the debate over whether the Allies should bomb the camp. Many people had objected that the bombing would kill the very people we wanted to save. So I asked this woman how the prisoners would have felt had the Allies carried out the bombing. "It would have been our finest hour," she responded (perhaps inadvertently paraphrasing Churchill). "We all assumed we were going to die anyway, and at least some Nazis would have died as well." To me, the Holocaust was the greatest evil in human history, and I believed we had an obligation to those who lost their lives in the gas chambers and killing fields of Nazi-occupied Europe to do everything we could to make sure their suffering and sacrifice was not in vain and that such a thing never happened again. (This belief played a decisive role in my later efforts to bring an end to the genocide in Cambodia, for example.)

I knew that whoever represented New York's Thirteenth Congressional District had to be seen as a strong supporter of Israel. I expected that anyone who ran against me in the future would also support Israel. But as a member of the Committee on Foreign Affairs, which had jurisdiction over the foreign aid budget, I would be able to argue that I was in a position to actually make a difference in the level of American support for Israel. Similarly, given the many antiwar activists among my constituents, a seat on this committee would enable me to potentially influence issues ranging from arms control to peace in Southeast Asia. It was a process of reasoning similar to that of newly elected members from rural constituencies who sought an assignment to the Committee on Agriculture.

Thus I decided to seek the support of the Democratic leadership for an appointment to the Foreign Affairs Committee. I persuaded Abram Sachar, the president of Brandeis, to write his congressman, Tip O'Neill, then the House majority leader, urging him to support my candidacy. I also got a number of Jewish leaders in Pennsylvania to write to Thomas "Doc" Morgan, the chairman of the Foreign Affairs Committee, who represented a district in that state, asking him to back my candidacy as well. In the end, the Democrats on the Steering and Policy Committee, who made the committee assignments, voted to give me the appointment.

I arrived in Washington for the organizational caucus of the House Democrats that December, along with seventy-four other freshmen Democrats elected that year. We were the Class of 1974, collectively known as the "Watergate babies" and destined to have a major impact on the new Congress even before it was officially convened in January. Sensing that such a large group could have a significant influence on how the House functioned, we resolved as our first order of business to take a crack at changing the seniority system. Most of us thought that this system, which made seniority the basis of advancement to positions of power and influence, was a root cause of Congress's sclerotic ineffectiveness.

We were significantly aided by legislative reforms adopted in 1971 and 1973. Nominations for committee chairmanships, which technically had to be approved by the Democratic caucus, were no longer based solely on seniority, and 20 percent of the caucus could demand a secret ballot in the election of any committee chair. As a practical matter, when committee chairs were elected in those years, seniority invariably prevailed. But these earlier procedural reforms had created an opportunity for change that our class eagerly seized.

Before the caucus meeting at which all the committee chairs would be elected, we invited the returning chairs to address our class and answer our questions. When the time came to vote on the chairmanship recommendations of the Steering and Policy Committee, we were able to insist on secret ballots and managed to defeat three incumbent chairmen whose appearances before our class had convinced us that they simply were not up to the job. So it was that we replaced seventy-five-year-old W. R. Poage with forty-five-year-old Tom Foley as chairman of Agriculture; eighty-one-year-old Wright Patman with sixty-two-year-old Henry Reuss as chairman of Banking and Currency; and seventy-three-year-old F. Edward Hébert with a chipper seventy-year-old Melvin Price (who himself was deposed a few years later) as chairman of Armed Services.

Far more important than these leadership changes, however, was the message sent to all the other committee chairmen. It was now clear that their chairmanships no longer depended on seniority alone, and that arbitrary, dictatorial, and ineffectual behavior would jeopardize their positions. A Subcommittee Bill of Rights that had been enacted in 1973 also limited the power of the full committee chairmen in several significant ways. It gave the "Democratic caucus" on each committee the power to choose subcommittee chairmen and members; gave the subcommittees the right to meet, hold hearings, and act; and guaranteed them independent budgets and staff. Committee chairmen could still influence the course of legislative events. But they were now more like the first among equals than feudal barons who held virtually undisputed sway over the congressional serfs. Together, these changes meant that individual members who were neither committee chairs nor part of the leadership were now in a much better position to have an impact on the legislative process than ever before.

I didn't realize it at the time, but these developments were to have a significant impact on my own congressional career. At first, they didn't seem to make much difference. Thomas "Doc" Morgan, the genial chairman of the Foreign Affairs Committee, who wasn't in any case inclined to push his considerable weight around, remained chair. And as a freshman member, I had to suffer the frustrations inherent in my lowly status. When we held hearings, for example, as a new committee member I had to wait for all the more senior members to ask their questions before I got the allotted five minutes to ask mine. By that time most of the other members had already left, as had the reporters covering the hearing, if there were any there at all. Since I had no additional staff (only available to the full committee and subcommittee chairs) and could not convene hearings on issues of special interest to me, my influence on the committee's work was sharply limited. But this changed during my third term in the House, when the chairman of the Subcommittee on Africa, Charles Diggs, had to resign because of a payroll padding scandal. As the most senior member of the committee without a subcommittee chairmanship, the "Democratic caucus" approved me to succeed him. Thanks to these various reforms, I was able to hire additional staff, set the agenda for subcommittee hearings and legislation relating to Africa, and play a leadership role on these issues.

Aside from the relationships I developed with the members of the Foreign Affairs Committee, my closest associations in Congress were with the other members of the New York delegation, especially the Democrats. And what a delegation it was. When I arrived in Washington it included Bella Abzug, the feisty, hat-wearing feminist agitator and liberal lion from Manhattan's West Side; Shirley Chisholm, the sharp-tongued congresswoman from Bedford-Stuyvesant who became the first credible black candidate for a presidential nomination; Ed Koch, the brash and self-confident militant moderate from the East Side; Otis Pike, the bow-tied patrician from Long Island who chaired the Select Committee on Intelligence that probed and revealed the CIA's misdeeds; Jack Bingham, the courtly progressive from the Bronx who embodied an unassailable integrity; Elizabeth Holtzman, the stern Cassandra from Brooklyn who had defeated the venerable Emanuel Celler, chairman of the Judiciary Committee, and who in her freshman year played an important role in the impeachment of President Nixon; Tom Downey, the brash wunderkind from Suffolk and youngest member of the House, whose combative intellectual activism belied the old notion that new members should be seen and not heard; Charlie Rangel, the genial, avuncular legislator from

Harlem who had unseated the legendary Adam Clayton Powell and was to become chairman of the powerful Ways and Means Committee; Ben Rosenthal, the consummate legislative craftsman from Queens who lent his brilliance to the proposition that human rights deserved a more important role in American foreign policy; Herman Badillo, the first Hispanic congressman from New York City, whose main preoccupation was becoming the first Puerto Rican mayor of New York; Matt McHugh, the quiet but solid former district attorney from Ithaca who, more than most, was always inclined to do what was right rather than what was expedient; and Sam Stratton, the outspoken champion of national defense who was an articulate supporter of a more hawkish foreign policy.

The delegation met for lunch twice a month—once just the Democrats and once Democrats and Republicans together—to discuss matters of special concern to the city and state. Jim Delaney, the dean of the delegation, who also chaired the powerful Rules Committee, presided. When several members clamored for recognition at the same time—which happened often among this talkative collection of unabashed political prima donnas—Delaney would shout out, "One fool at a time!" restoring some measure of order.

During my eighteen years in Congress, however, most of my time was spent on the various committees I served on: Education and Labor, Post Office and Civil Service, Budget, Merchant Marine and Fisheries, Intelligence, and Joint Economic. As much as possible, I attended their hearings and participated in their legislative markups. But the Foreign Affairs Committee was the primary vehicle for my efforts to have an impact on the legislative process, as well as to influence the course of American foreign policy. I had no idea that during the next two decades my position on that committee would lead me on fact-finding missions to over a hundred countries, where I would meet with dozens of heads of state and opposition leaders, or that it would enable me to advance the cause of democracy and human rights in countries ranging from South Korea to South Africa and from Poland to Pakistan. How this came to pass constitutes the story of my career in Congress.

I

CONGRESSIONAL TRAVEL
Boon or Boondoggle?

How's this for an understatement? Foreign travel by members of Congress doesn't have a very good reputation. The media tend to portray such trips as junkets and boondoggles — essentially vacations at taxpayers' expense by legislators more interested in sightseeing and shopping than in fulfilling their oversight responsibilities regarding foreign policy, foreign aid, and other government programs. Many members shy away from foreign travel specifically to avoid adverse media coverage that could jeopardize their reelection campaigns.

By contrast, I acquired a reputation as the "Marco Polo" of Congress. Perhaps the best account of how I came by that moniker is a story told by Joe Moakley, a genial, portly colleague from Massachusetts who was chairman of the Rules Committee. Early one Monday in the 1980s, Joe arrived at the gate for a flight from Boston to Washington with barely a minute to spare. As he searched for an available seat, his glance fell on me, just as the flight attendant slammed the door shut. Unable to get off the plane, Joe reported, he had a panic attack, thinking that if I was on it he must have gotten on an international flight by mistake.

Overall, I traveled to 140 countries, and based on this extensive experience, I would like to dissent from the conventional view. I certainly understood my colleagues' reluctance to go abroad. They were well aware of the fates of Senator Dee Huddleston of Kentucky and Congressman Lester Wolff of New York. Huddleston was the subject of a hilarious television ad showing someone with a pack of hunting dogs searching all over Washington but unable to find him because he was (presumably) not in the country. Another TV spot featured Congressman Wolff getting off an Air Force plane in some distant country as a group of bare-breasted African women welcomed him on the tarmac with a native dance. I was branded with the scarlet "J" (for junket) on several occasions myself. In January 1981, for example, as the war in El Salvador was heating up and it looked like the

Reagan administration was going to provide significant military assistance to the government, I decided to go there to get a better sense of the implications for American foreign policy. Since the Foreign Affairs Committee would be deeply involved in shaping the congressional response to the challenge posed by the FMLN guerrilla movement, I thought it important to see the situation at first hand.

When I arrived in San Salvador, the capital, to make the rounds of government officials, opposition leaders, human rights activists, and foreign diplomats, our embassy gave me a security detail that included a dozen armed guards, each with a bulletproof vest and an Uzi. A story in the *New York Post*, however, was headlined "Solarz Abandons New York for the Sunnier Climes of the Caribbean." It focused not on the dangerous and deteriorating conditions in the country, nor on my investigation into the escalating violence and its implications for the United States, but on my supposed vacation at the taxpayers' expense.

Certainly some members of Congress do treat foreign travel as a paid vacation. And there was a time, long since gone, when traveling Congressmen could use "counterpart" funds — money owed the United States that could only be spent in the countries that owed it — to purchase luxury items such as artwork and furniture. But just because some members have abused the privilege doesn't mean that those who really do want to inform themselves about the complexities and challenges that face us abroad should not travel on legitimate missions.

Whatever people may have thought about my own trips, they weren't paid vacations. Most journalists who called about my travels were more interested in portraying a given trip as a junket than in finding out why I went or what I learned. I used to tell them that if they were going to write about congressional travel, they ought to do a story about the Foreign Affairs Committee members who never went on fact-finding missions. I also pointed out that journalists rarely question or write negative stories about Health Committee members who visit hospitals, Education Committee members who visit schools, or Agriculture Committee members who visit farms. But foreign travel is portrayed as junketeering and deplored. Unfortunately, this tendency has not changed since I left Congress in 1993.

The truth is that there is no better way to get an understanding of the foreign policy challenges we face as a nation than to go to the places where these problems exist. With issues of war and peace hanging in the balance, and billions in foreign aid under consideration, it seemed almost willfully derelict of my responsibilities, especially as a member of the Foreign Affairs Committee, not to take the opportunity to speak directly to those who were most knowledgeable about such matters. Before leaving, I always prepared diligently. Typically, I got briefings from the Departments of State and Defense and the CIA. Interestingly, I often found that the CIA briefing gave me the most illuminating insights. This was probably because State and Defense had a policy line to defend, while the CIA analysts were just providing an intelligence assessment. I also had my staffers who set up the trip prepare briefing books on the foreign policy issues involved, which included newspaper and magazine articles as well as government and nongovernmental organization reports.

I traveled only when Congress wasn't in session, because I wanted to be there for votes. I knew that missing a lot of votes while on fact-finding missions abroad would be a potential source of criticism in my reelection campaigns, and I believed that a good attendance record would be the best defense against the charge that I was ignoring my responsibilities in Washington and to my constituents in Brooklyn. As a result, I was present for over 90 percent of the votes that took place during my congressional career.

As a further precaution against the charge of junketeering, I made a point of going back to my district in Brooklyn almost every weekend when Congress was in session. In those days Congress generally met from Monday to Friday, so on weekends I attended the many breakfasts, dinners, and other functions that were an important part of the community life of the neighborhoods I represented. I also maintained three district offices and sent out reams of mail that generally focused on local issues. I wanted to make sure that if someone charged in a future campaign that I had abandoned my district for foreign travel, I could make it abundantly clear that I was actively engaged in community affairs.

Since my purpose in traveling was indeed fact-finding, it seemed that the best way to get a handle on the problems we faced was to visit not only the country where the problem existed, but other countries in the region that were affected by it. I found it useful to meet with leaders and others — diplomats, journalists, and academics — who were a lot closer to the problems than we were and had insights I could benefit from. For example, Israel was a priority for me and I visited it frequently, but I also visited Arab countries to get their perspective on the situation in the Middle East.

On each mission, I tried to make maximum use of my time because I didn't know when I would be back. My schedule usually had me going from 7 a.m. to 11 p.m., mining as much information as I could in as much time as I could find. Every meal was a working meal, and I often had two working breakfasts, one at seven o'clock and another at eight. Generally, I allotted about an hour for a meeting, then allowed some time to get to the next one. I thrived on such back-to-back meetings, but they took a lot out of the people who made them possible. On one trip to India, my schedule was particularly hectic. The Foreign Service officer at the US consulate in Mumbai responsible for handling logistics had to work hard. After the trip, he had buttons made for the Indian staff members of the Foreign Service who helped organize it. They read: "I survived CODEL Solarz" (CODEL was the acronym for "congressional delegation").

Whenever possible, I met first with our ambassador and his country team to get their take on the politics and problems of the country. Generally these briefings were quite useful in giving me a picture of the state of play of the issues I had come to explore. But I had to be on guard against our diplomats' tendency to reflect the views of "their" country. The worst example of this "clientitis" occurred in Tokyo in the early 1980s. I asked our embassy personnel why Japan wasn't importing more American cars. Instead of giving me their own judgment about this contentious issue, they handed me a fact sheet put out by the Japanese Ministry of Trade and Industry. I also learned that I could often find out more about what was really going on by meeting with junior officers alone. Unobserved by the ambassador, they felt free to express their opinions without fear of being chastised for contradicting the official line.

In every country, I tried to see most of the key people, including the president, prime minister, or king, the foreign minister, the leaders of the opposition (where there was an opposition), foreign diplomats assigned there, international civil servants, American and local businessmen, foreign correspondents, and local journalists, as well as professors and students in the country's institutions of higher learning. In dictatorships where the penalty for speaking the truth could be severe and sometimes fatal, I often learned more from refugees who had fled the country than from people who remained inside it.

A main benefit of foreign travel was that it enabled me to focus intensively on the country I was visiting from early in the morning until late at night. In Washington, life was a kaleidoscope. On any given day, I would hurry from a hearing on one issue to a hearing on another, interspersed with meetings with my staff, constituents, and lobbyists, plus casting votes on sundry matters on the floor of the House. As I jumped from subject to subject, prolonged concentration on any of them was difficult if not impossible.

I was always amazed by how much access I had to the key people in most countries I visited, even as a junior member of Congress. This reflected their recognition that Congress, particularly after the Watergate scandal and the Vietnam War, was playing an increasingly important role in American foreign policy. Meeting with me offered foreign leaders an opportunity to present their assessment of the problems they confronted and influence Congress on matters of concern to them.

As a rule, I preferred to travel just with someone from my staff to assist with note taking and logistics, or at most with one or two colleagues, as opposed to going with a large congressional delegation. I did go on a couple of trips with larger delegations, but they were the exception. When such a delegation met with a foreign leader, for example, every member in order of seniority had a chance to ask a question. If the group had an hour with the leader, each member could ask only one or two questions and there was rarely time for a follow-up. I also found that several members generally had a limited knowledge of the issues under discussion. As a result, I usually got far less out of such meetings than when I had a senior official or other interlocutor all to myself. Solo travel enabled me to accomplish a good deal more. To mitigate the loneliness of long-distance travel, Nina accompanied me (at our own expense) when she could take time off from her own job.

At times, however, the presence of one or more colleagues was a real benefit. When I went to Singapore in 1981 with Congressman Joel Pritchard of Washington, for example, I had just become chairman of the Subcommittee on Asian and Pacific Affairs, and Pritchard had just become its ranking Republican member. At a meeting with Lee Kuan Yew, the prime minister of this bustling city-state and one of Asia's fabled wise men, Pritchard asked Lee one of the best questions I ever heard from a member of Congress: How did Lee explain the fact that in Singapore, Hong Kong, Taiwan, and elsewhere in Southeast Asia, the Chinese were very rich, but in China they were all poor? Lee responded that the best answer to that question came in a conversation he had recently had with Deng Xiaoping, the Chinese supreme leader, during a visit Deng made to Singapore. After paying tribute to Lee for facilitating the transformation of Singapore from an impoverished backwater into a thriving city-state, Deng went on, "Just think what I could accomplish if all I had to deal with was Shanghai." Lee recalled that he didn't "have the heart to say to him that with his system, even if all he had was Shanghai, it wouldn't make a difference."

Traveling with other members also provided an opportunity to create new friendships and a better understanding of my colleagues, which supported my efforts to have an impact on policy. Personal relationships were sometimes just as important as mastery of the issues—if not more so—in influencing the legislative process.

My desire to concentrate my travel on issues of real importance to our country, where Congress had some role to play, led me to turn down a number of opportunities to go to places that were nowhere near the top of the foreign policy agenda. In one case, this focus on top-burner issues probably saved my life. In November 1978 California Congressman Leo Ryan, who sat next to me on the Foreign Affairs Committee and with whom I was friendly, invited me to come to Guyana with him. His purpose was to investigate charges that some of his constituents were being held there against their will by the Reverend Jim Jones, a religious cult leader who had established a commune called Jonestown deep in the Guyana jungle. Since many of Leo's constituents were living in Jonestown, this trip was important to him, but it wasn't for me, and I explained that I planned to travel elsewhere during the coming recess. The outcome of Leo's trip is well known: the mass suicide of Jones's brainwashed followers and the cold-blooded murder of Leo himself, along with nine others, at the jungle air strip as they were about to depart. Had I accompanied him, I probably would have been killed as well.

Meeting with a broad range of unforgettable foreign leaders—from courageous democrats to absolute tyrants—was fascinating, and at times exhilarating. Overall, the foreign leader who impressed me most was Nelson Mandela, whom I met a week after he was released from prison. The word "greatness" is thrown around carelessly, but it fits Mandela well. He played an absolutely crucial role in the peaceful transition from apartheid to majority rule in South Africa. There is no doubt in my mind that without his towering presence, the fight over political power between whites and blacks in South Africa would have been a blood bath. After twenty-seven years in a grim prison on Robben Island, he emerged not only as a larger figure than before he was incarcerated, but without any apparent resentment toward his captors. He had a quiet charisma that bespoke enormous self-confidence and strength of character. And unlike so many other political leaders, he seemed not to need the adulation of a crowd.

Another impressive leader was Lee Kuan Yew of Singapore. He had a profound grasp of the strategic realities in Asia and a sophisticated appreciation of geopolitical realities elsewhere. I met with him often and invariably felt he was one of the truly great statesmen of our time. Somebody once remarked that it was Lee's unfortunate fate to preside over a city-state. He would undoubtedly have cut an even larger figure on the international stage if he had led a bigger, more significant country. Still, he was a man of great wisdom, and I benefited greatly from his understanding of the political dynamics of the region.

Anwar Sadat too left a lasting impression on me. His courage in undertaking his historic journey to Jerusalem, where he addressed the Israeli people from the Knesset, made possible an astounding diplomatic and psychological breakthrough, leading to a peace treaty between Israel and Egypt. Unfortunately, he paid for it with his life at the hands of some Egyptian fanatics. Sadat had a warm, even effervescent personality and a good sense of humor. Once I couldn't resist giving him a little lecture about the problems created by the ineptitude and inefficiencies of the Egyptian bureaucracy. After I finished he looked at me with a bemused expression and said, "Have you ever tried dealing with USAID?" I had to acknowledge that he had a point.

Most charismatic of all was Fidel Castro. Incredibly intelligent and extremely articulate, he was also a tyrant and an ideologue who ran his country into the ground and created the most repressive regime in the hemisphere. Captivated by the sound of his own voice, and seemingly in-toxicated by his own eloquence, he could go on for hours expressing his views on virtually any subject under the sun. But the fog of his rhetoric could not obscure the tragedy brought about by his revolution.

A striking, sad note to my foreign travels was that well over twenty for-eign leaders I met were subsequently assassinated, most from developing countries. If nothing else, this fact underscores the extent to which poli-tics is really played for keeps in large parts of the world. This group in-cluded Indira Gandhi, murdered by her Sikh bodyguards; her son, Rajiv Gandhi, blown up by a Tamil terrorist; Anwar Sadat, gunned down by rogue Egyptian soldiers in a military parade in Cairo; Yitzhak Rabin, shot to death by a Jewish fanatic who opposed his efforts to make peace with the Palestinians; Park Chung-hee, murdered by the chief of his own in-telligence apparatus; other South Korean officials killed by a bomb placed by North Korean agents in a Buddhist temple they were visiting in Ran-goon; several Sri Lankan political leaders, including President Ranasinghe Premadasa, murdered by Tamil terrorists at a May Day rally; Velupillai Prabhakaran, the Tamil Tiger leader, killed by the Sri Lankan army; Ziaur Rahman, president of Bangladesh, murdered by soldiers under his com-mand; Muhammad Zia-ul-Haq, president of Pakistan, killed together with Arnie Raphel, the American ambassador, in a plane crash; Benazir Bhutto, the charismatic Pakistani leader, blown up by a Pakistani funda-mentalist; William Tolbert, president of Liberia, his son, A. B. Tolbert, and his foreign minister, Cecil Dennis, killed by the plotters of a coup; Bashir Gemayel, killed by a bomb shortly after being elected president of Lebanon; and Benigno Aquino, the Filipino opposition leader, murdered by Filipino soldiers as he stepped off a plane on his return from exile in the United States.

In the final analysis, however, it was what I learned on my foreign jour-neys that constituted their real benefit, as the following chapters demon-strate. In the Middle East, I got an appreciation of the possibilities for peace between Israel and the Arabs, and the importance of resisting and reversing Iraq's annexation of Kuwait. In the eastern Mediterranean, I learned about the strategic importance of Turkey and the need to improve the relationship between Ankara and Washington. In Eastern Europe, I was encouraged by the leaders of Solidarity in the mid-1980s to work toward repealing US sanctions imposed against Poland after the establishment of martial law in 1981 and to provide additional assistance to its fledgling democracy. In Central Africa, I was able to expose corruption in our agricultural assistance program in Zaire. In Southeast Asia, I discovered the utter futility of a Potemkin-like antipiracy project in Thailand and the depth of opposition to the Marcos kleptocracy in the Philippines, and I came up with the idea for a UN-supervised election that made it possible to end the conflict in Cambodia and marginalize the Khmer Rouge. In South Korea and Taiwan, I learned the importance of consulting with those leading the struggle for human rights in determining how best to advance the transition from dictatorship to democracy. In South Africa, I got an idea that led to the establishment of a scholarship program providing educational opportunities in the United States for South African blacks who would play an increasingly important role in their country's future.

These are just a few examples of how my foreign trips, and what I learned from them, enabled me to influence American foreign policy and, in the process, promote our values and protect our interests. Other congressmen have had — and can have, and ought to have — the same experience. Foreign travel by members of Congress should not be discouraged and denounced, but encouraged and praised. With billions of dollars of foreign aid at stake, and issues of war and peace hanging in the balance, the more fully congressmen and senators understand the challenges that confront us around the world, the more likely they are to develop and support sound policies for dealing with them.

CROSSING THE ALLENBY BRIDGE

Israel, the Arabs, and the Peace Process

When people asked me to describe my congressional district, I often responded that it was the most Jewish in the nation, with more Jews than Jerusalem. But I also pointed out how diverse its population was. I represented Hasidic Jews, Orthodox Jews, Conservative Jews, Reform Jews, secular Jews, Russian Jews, Syrian Jews, and Polish Jews.

Obviously, such a constituency created some compelling political realities. One was the importance of being a strong supporter of Israel and the unique relationship between that country and the United States. Since I shared the commitment most of my constituents had to Israel's security and survival, this was a morally and politically easy position to take. Fortunately, my personal interest as an American and a Jew blended with my political interest in demonstrating that I could make a difference on this issue.

Over the course of my eighteen years on the Foreign Affairs Committee, I championed a long list of legislation for Israel. In 1977 and 1978, I supported amendments earmarking $1 billion in military credits and $785 million in security assistance for the Jewish state. In the late 1970s, I played a key role in securing the passage of legislation prohibiting American participation in the Arab boycott against Israel. In 1980, I was instrumental in adding $200 million to the administration's aid request for Israel. In 1981, I helped secure adoption of an amendment adding $312 million in aid for Israel. I also opposed the sale of AWACS (airborne warning and control system) aircraft to Saudi Arabia. As a result of these and many other actions, the pro-Israel American Israel Public Affairs Committee gave me a near-perfect voting record.

After the Yom Kippur War in 1973, American aid to Israel reached a base level of $3.5 billion a year in economic and military assistance. At United Jewish Appeal dinners in my district, when attendees were asked how much they were prepared to contribute, I used to say, "I've already given $3.5 billion at the office." Then in honor of the evening's honoree, I would personally add another $1,000. From a political perspective, my advocacy was not unlike congressmen from agricultural districts getting farm subsidies or congressmen from coal mining districts getting money for black lung disease. While foreign aid might have been unpopular in much of the country, in my district it was considered essential for the security and survival of a friendly nation to which my constituents were deeply attached. At the same time, I believed that American aid to Israel enhanced the prospects for peace in the Middle East by giving that beleaguered democracy the sense of security it required in order to make the territorial concessions to the Arabs that were essential to any agreement. I was convinced we were not only helping a democracy that shared our values but were advancing our strategic interests in this critically important part of the world.

So it was natural that my first official trip as a member of Congress, a month after I was sworn in, was to the Middle East, and that my first stop was Israel. I arrived at Tel Aviv's Ben-Gurion airport dressed comfortably in dungarees, sneakers, and a short-sleeved shirt and joined the long line heading slowly toward the Israeli immigration inspectors. I was like one of Mark Twain's innocents abroad, with no idea that standard operating procedure was for someone from the US embassy to meet official visitors and whisk them through the arrival procedures. As we inched along, I noticed a man dressed in a tie and jacket going up and down the line, clearly looking for someone. When he came within earshot, I heard him say, "Is Congressman Solarz here?" I guess I didn't look much like a congressman, so I raised my hand to get his attention.

Later that day, Nick Veliotes, the US chargé d'affaires (the top embassy official when the ambassador is out of the country), invited me to dinner at the ambassador's residence in Herzliya, a city near Tel Aviv named in honor of Theodor Herzl, the father of modern Zionism. I arrived about seven o'clock and peppered Nick and his "country team" with questions until at least midnight. I suspect that most of the embassy staffers there preferred the cuisine to the conversation. But for me the food for thought, rather than the food on the table, was the main attraction. (That remained true throughout my years of travel.) In later years, I met Nick several times in his capacity as American ambassador to Jordan and Egypt. We became

With Moshe Dayan in Washington during the 1970s.
Congressman Silvio Conte is in the middle.

good friends and tennis partners, and I came to admire his insights into the region's politics as much as I appreciated his tenacity on the court. As I soon found out, our Middle Eastern ambassadors in general made up an all-star diplomatic team.

As my visit progressed, I met virtually all the top Israeli leaders. Privately I was amazed that a lowly freshman congressman had such access. But I soon learned that the Israelis had a sophisticated understanding of the American political system and went out of their way to make friends with members of Congress, no matter how far down on the congressional totem pole they were.

I also met with Israeli opposition leaders. Most visiting congressmen didn't bother to meet with them because the ruling Labor Party had dominated politics since Israel was founded, and the Likud minority appeared consigned to the role of permanent opposition. But on that first trip abroad I learned how valuable it was to meet with opposition leaders — not only in Israel, but everywhere — because they offered a different per-

Shimon Peres at my house in Virginia during the 1980s.

spective that helped illuminate the domestic political considerations that shaped the government's foreign policy. When a country had no organized opposition because it was either prohibited or in jail, I met with exiled dissidents. Indeed, I came to realize that in some times and places the best way to understand a country was to meet with refugees who had fled to other lands and were free to speak the truth about it.

In Israel, of course, there were many opposition political parties, and no one hesitated to criticize the government. The leading opposition leader at the time was Menachem Begin, whom I saw regularly whenever I visited. Begin, a small, scholarly looking man, wore thick glasses and had a mild, unassuming demeanor. But appearances can be deceiving. Before Israel became a state, Begin had been the leader of the Irgun, a militant Zionist group that had blown up part of the stately King David Hotel in Jerusalem, where British forces were headquartered. In the context of

With Menachem Begin in Washington during the 1970s.
Congressman Ben Rosenthal is in the middle.

Israeli politics, Begin was a hard-liner. He believed that for both religious and security reasons, Israel needed to keep control of Judea and Samaria (otherwise known as the West Bank), as well as the Gaza Strip, the Golan Heights, and the Sinai desert. We often had lunch in the Knesset cafeteria, where a big bay window offered a view of the West Bank. Pointing out the 1967 border, only about a quarter-mile away, Begin would remind me that if Israel withdrew from Judea and Samaria, the Knesset would be within easy range of Palestinian mortars. In 1977, after years in the political wilderness, he became prime minister, ending three decades of Labor Party hegemony. Most observers of the Israeli political scene felt that his election had diminished the prospects for peace between Israel and its Arab neighbors. Yet when the moment of truth came at Camp David in 1978, much to my surprise but even more to my gratification, Begin made the concessions necessary for peace with Egypt.

I was struck by the high caliber of Israel's leadership in general. Golda

Meir, Abba Eban, Yitzhak Rabin, Shimon Peres, and Yigal Allon — all part of Israel's founding generation — impressed me deeply. I admired Golda, as everyone called her, for her unassuming demeanor and deep commitment to the Zionist cause; Eban for his extraordinary eloquence and memorable formulations, like his observation that the Yom Kippur War was the "first military conflict in history in which the losers are celebrating their defeat while the winners are mourning their victory"; Rabin for his ability to transcend his ideological convictions, as he did in reaching agreement at Oslo with Yasser Arafat and the Palestine Liberation Organization; Peres for his wit and wisdom, often expressed in Delphic aphorisms; and Allon for his charismatic presentation of the Israeli point of view. Aryeh "Lova" Eliav, the gentle apostle of peace, recognized long before most Israelis the need to negotiate with the PLO if a final agreement on the status of the Palestinians was to be achieved. In some ways the most impressive of all was Yehoshafat Harkabi, a former chief of military intelligence, who had a profound understanding of the changing Arab attitudes toward Israel. He was no longer a government official when I first met him, but I found his analysis of the conflict between Israel and the Arabs so compelling that I made it a point to meet with him on every trip. In a discussion of terrorism during the 1980s, Harkabi remarked, "I fear that mankind has not yet exhausted its capacity for satanic invention." It was a tragically prescient analysis of what was in store on 9/11.

Determined to find out how the Arabs perceived the conflict, I decided to go to several Arab countries after leaving Israel. My first stop was Jordan. It was my first visit to an Arab country, at a time when it was relatively rare for American Jews to go to the Arab world. I remember experiencing some trepidation as I approached the famed Allenby Bridge over the storied Jordan River. What a disappointment! The bridge was a rickety wooden structure, and the Jordan at this point more a creek than a river. But together they constituted a formidable political obstacle. My car halted at the Israeli end, and I had to carry my luggage to the middle of the bridge, where I was met by a driver from our embassy in Amman. He picked up my suitcase and took me to his car for the one-hour drive there.

I vividly remember my first night in Jordan. The embassy had arranged for me to give a talk entitled "A Congressional Perspective on the Middle East" at a local library. Rather than tell people what I thought they wanted to hear, I decided to give them an unvarnished view of the conflict from my perspective. At that time, I completely shared the Zionist point of view that the only thing necessary for peace was an Arab willingness to accept Israel. But like most American supporters of Israel, I thought that what the Arabs really wanted was to drive the Israelis into the sea — a perspective shaped by my attendance at countless United Jewish Appeal and Bonds for Israel breakfasts and dinners in New York. So long as the Arabs were unwilling to live in peace with Israel, I argued in my talk, Israel could hardly be expected to withdraw from territories that would then be used as a springboard for further acts of aggression against it. And since the Arabs refused to recognize or even negotiate with Israel following their humiliating defeat in the 1967 Six-Day War, the fault lay with them. My talk didn't go over well. The next day's *Jordan Times*, an English-language paper in Amman, said in an editorial, "If Congressman Solarz is at all representative of the new members of Congress, then God help us."

I also met with King Hussein. I arrived at the king's palace, which is on a hill above Amman, accompanied by Thomas Pickering, then the youngest US ambassador in the Middle East, whose energy and charisma made him one of the most distinguished Foreign Service officers of his generation. He went on to serve as ambassador to Israel, Nigeria, El Salvador, India, Russia, and the United Nations, before becoming under secretary of state for political affairs in the second Clinton administration.

The king was about four hours late. Such is the prerogative of royalty. We waited patiently in the office of the chief of the royal court, who, to divert our attention from the king's tardiness, told us stories about the king and his kingdom. Perhaps the most memorable involved an unannounced visit from Idi Amin, the erratic military dictator of Uganda, during the 1973 war. Amin asked to see King Hussein's battle plan and pronounced it satisfactory. Upon which King Hussein told his entourage in Arabic, "If this idiot approves of our plans, we'd better review them immediately." Since Jordan managed to stay out of the war, however, the plans were never used.

The king finally arrived. He was a soft-spoken, dignified man whose cautious nature was no doubt formed when he witnessed the 1951 assassination of his grandfather, King Abdullah, who advocated peace with Israel. As we talked, King Hussein sat with his hands in his lap, addressing

With King Hussein of Jordan in Washington.

me as "sir" in a clipped British accent acquired at the Royal Military Academy in Sandhurst, England. I heard no talk about "driving the Israelis into the sea" but instead heard him voice a desire to find ways to live in peace with them. It was hard not to conclude that here was at least one Arab ruler who was prepared to make peace with Israel, particularly if other Arab leaders were willing to do so as well.

My next stop was Egypt, where the US ambassador was Hermann Eilts, a seasoned diplomat and one of the most impressive Foreign Service officers I ever met. He had an extraordinary relationship with Anwar Sadat, Egypt's president, and was able to explain Sadat's views of the country, the region, and the world more lucidly than Sadat himself.

Egypt was a country with enormous strategic significance. By far the most populous Arab country, and the one with the longest national history, it was key to preserving peace in the region, if only because the Arabs simply had no viable military option against Israel without Egypt's participation. I was therefore eager to find out what the Egyptian leaders thought about the conflict and whether they were prepared to consider a real peace with Israel. The key to understanding Egypt's attitude was Sadat, who had succeeded Gamal Abdel Nasser as president. Sadat had reclaimed at least

My first meeting with Anwar Sadat (right).
Hosni Mubarak (center) was then vice president of Egypt.

part of the Sinai during the 1973 war. In an effort to secure US diplomatic support to get back the rest of it, he had also kicked out thousands of Soviet military advisors on whom Egypt had depended. As a result, he was the country's dominant political figure.

I have to confess that initially I was not overly impressed by Sadat. I saw him as a man prepared for a long-term period of "nonbelligerency" with Israel but not willing to contemplate a real peace, including diplomatic recognition, trade, tourism, and the other accompaniments of genuine normalization, even in the context of an Israeli withdrawal to the 1967 border. He struck me as a somewhat conventional and uninspiring head of state — far from the charismatic, courageous leader he revealed himself to be when, by his historic journey to Jerusalem in 1977, he broke the political and psychological ice in which the Israel-Egypt relationship had been frozen.

On my last day in Egypt, I learned that a delegation of US senators visiting Cairo had been invited on a tour of the Suez Canal the following day for a briefing on the historic crossing that began what Egyptians call the "October War." The Arab world, and especially Egypt, hailed this action as a great victory. But following a successful counterattack by Israeli forces across the canal that left the Egyptian Third Army cut off from its supply line, the surprise offensive was stopped after eighteen days. By the time a cease-fire was put in place, as Abba Eban noted a year later, the Israeli army was closer to Cairo than it had been before the fighting began.

I was supposed to leave for Damascus that morning, but I switched my flight to the evening so I could join the senators. To save time, I packed my bags and left them at the reception desk in my hotel. Figuring that I didn't need to wear a suit and tie for a tour of a battle zone, I changed into dungarees, a casual shirt, and sneakers without socks. After a tour of the Bar Lev Line, a chain of fortifications built by Israel along the eastern coast of the Suez Canal, and other sites, I returned to my hotel at about six o'clock to pick up my luggage and catch my flight to Syria. I was met by John Craig, a US embassy official who was managing my trip. "I've got good news," he told me. "Foreign Minister Fahmy has agreed to see you at seven, which should give us enough time to get to your nine o'clock flight." That sounded fine to me, so I told him I would get my luggage, take a quick shower, and change.

But my luggage was nowhere to be found. I asked the hotel clerk to check every room to see if it had been left somewhere by mistake, but it had vanished. Just before seven, Craig insisted that we leave for our appointment with the foreign minister. I protested that I couldn't meet him in what I was wearing, but he warned that if we didn't show up it would trigger a diplomatic incident. Besides, he added, the foreign minister had canceled several appointments in order to meet with me. Reluctantly, I agreed, and we went to Foreign Minister Ismail Fahmy's elegant office, decorated with French provincial furniture, in the heart of the Foreign Ministry.

To say I didn't fit in with the décor would be a gross understatement. The foreign minister, who was wearing a three-piece business suit, was clearly puzzled by my casual attire, particularly the absence of socks. I realized an explanation was in order. "Mr. Minister," I said, "when I return to my congressional district in Brooklyn, I want to tell my constituents that I achieved something even more important than progress in the peace process."

"What could that be?" he asked.

"That I got my luggage back," I said. "My clothes, my notes, everything I have is in my luggage. They can't find it in the hotel. I'm lost. Please," I begged him, "you have to help me get my luggage back." Minister Fahmy put the Egyptian police on the case, and my luggage was discovered the next day in Luxor, an ancient city in Upper Egypt, where it had been sent by mistake with a tour group.

My clothing travails did not end there. Nine months later I was back in Egypt, arriving in Cairo at 5 a.m., dressed again in dungarees, sneakers, and no socks. The Foreign Service officer who met me at the airport said my first meeting would be at eleven, with the foreign minister. He suggested that my wife and I get some sleep, and he would send our luggage over to our hotel. Unbelievably, my suitcase got lost again, and I was forced once more to meet with Minister Fahmy wearing what he probably now thought was my customary garb! I didn't see him again until he came to Washington several months later, when the House Foreign Affairs Committee and Senate Foreign Relations Committee held a joint lunch in his honor in the Capitol. I got there early to greet him, and we embraced in the customary Arab fashion, with a kiss on both cheeks. As we did so, he leaned down and picked up my pants leg to see if I was wearing socks. This time I was, and we both had a good laugh.

Another example of the good humor characteristic of Egyptians occurred when I went to meet with a group of students from the American University in Cairo, an outstanding institution that tries to advance the ideals of American higher education. I tried to visit students there on every trip, in order to understand better what young Egyptians thought about the peace process with Israel and the future of Egypt. The meetings were held in the apartment of the dean of students, overlooking the Nile. On this occasion, the embassy driver dropped me off at the dean's building rather late in the day. My schedule listed apartment 2B as the place. I rang the bell and the door was opened by Mustafa Khalil, the prime minister. I was surprised—I wasn't expecting him to be at this meeting. But without blinking an eye, the prime minister said he was pleased to see me and invited me in for tea and sweets. We talked for about forty minutes. Eventually I asked when the students would arrive. "What students?" he responded. It turned out that I had the wrong apartment number. The

With King Fahd of Saudi Arabia in Washington.

prime minister, whom I had met on previous trips, thought his staff had forgotten to tell him that he had a meeting with me. When I explained, he told me the dean lived two floors above and graciously took me to the dean's door himself.

Whenever I went to the Middle East, I made it a point to visit Saudi Arabia. As the location of Islam's two holiest places, Mecca and Medina, and the wealthiest Arab nation, the kingdom would play an important role in any potential peace agreement with Israel, both to legitimate any agreement on Jerusalem and to help provide the substantial subsidies for refugee resettlement that would be required to make the agreement viable. After meeting with King Fahd, Crown Prince Abdullah, Foreign Minister Prince Saud, and the chief of intelligence, Prince Turki, I concluded that Saudi Arabia would support a peace with Israel acceptable to the

With Prince Bandar on the floor of the House, 1991.

Palestinians, Egypt, Syria, and Lebanon, but was not prepared to join in any meaningful efforts to achieve it. Caution rather than boldness was the chief characteristic of Saudi foreign policy.

On all my visits, I was struck by the fact that even though I was Jewish, the Saudi royals received me with great cordiality. On an early trip, I met Prince Bandar, then a major in the Saudi Air Force, who subsequently became a fabled, highly influential ambassador in Washington. I had dinner with him and a couple of his cousins in the Royal Air Force at his prefabricated palace in Dhahran. We dined beside a huge swimming pool with a fountain in the middle that sprayed colored water up and down. Music played in the background. I thought the décor was a bit tacky, but it was an amazing evening. Some years later, Bandar held a small dinner for Nina and me at his palatial though less spectacular home in McLean, Virginia. During the evening, Nina asked Bandar's wife, Haifa, what her father did. "He was the king," she replied. A faux pas, but a well-intentioned one.

Given that Saudi Arabia practiced the strictest form of Islam in the Muslim world, whenever I visited I felt there was something strange about the kingdom. After a while, I realized it was that I hadn't seen any women. Occasionally, an apparition draped in black from head to toe shuffled along the street. But when I visited the homes of Saudi officials, the women were always sequestered, and I never saw one in any of those palaces and mansions. Once I walked through the airport in Riyadh holding a copy of the *Economist*, whose cover featured a photograph of Margaret Thatcher in a short-sleeved dress. A member of the "morality police" saw the prime minister's naked arms and stopped me. He rapped me on the knuckles with his baton and confiscated the magazine. A couple of years later, I saw Mrs. Thatcher in London and told her this story, remarking that in Saudi Arabia it appeared she was thought of as a porn star! I had the impression that although this wasn't a comparison she often heard, she did fleetingly enjoy it.

I made it my practice to travel at least once a year to Israel and a number of Arab countries. Much to my surprise—based on what I had heard and believed before actually visiting the region—I found a residual willingness on the part of most Arabs to live in peace with Israel, if agreements could be reached between Israel and the Palestinians, as well as with Egypt, Jordan, and Syria, that were compatible with Arab dignity and honor. I sensed that the Arab world was ready to accept Israel as a reality, at least partly because the Arabs were not in a position to eliminate it militarily. With the Arab mainstream—Egypt, Jordan, Syria, Saudi Arabia, and some of the Persian Gulf and North African states—having come to this conclusion, it seemed to me that there was a better prospect for peace than many thought possible.

Given that the Arabs had rejected the establishment of the Jewish state in 1948 and then gone to war against it three times, I tried to understand what had brought about this change in their thinking. I concluded that three main factors were responsible. The first was the magnitude of their military defeat in the 1967 Six-Day War, in which Israel destroyed the Egyptian and Syrian air forces in the first hour of combat and came into possession of the Sinai desert, the West Bank, and all of Jerusalem, as well as the Gaza Strip and the Golan Heights. The second was Israel's presumptive acquisition of nuclear weapons, which convinced the Arabs that even if they could defeat Israel with conventional weapons, it would be a costly victory hardly worth the ensuing nuclear destruction of their own countries. The third was the massive US arms airlift to Israel during the 1973 war, making it clear that America was not prepared to permit the Arabs to wipe Israel off the map—even if they got the upper hand on the battlefield, as they did in the early days of that war. As time passed, the impact of these events was reinforced by the end of the Cold War and the collapse of the Soviet Union, which meant the Arab states could no longer rely on Moscow to resupply them with the weapons they lost in their periodic conflicts with Israel.

I believe that these factors had an enormous political and psychological impact in the Arab world and were responsible for the emergent sense of realism on the part of most Arab leaders. I do not suggest that the Arabs came to believe that the establishment of Israel was morally or historically justified. Almost half a century after its declaration of independence, few Arabs considered it legitimate. For the most part, they saw Israel as an unfair and unwarranted Jewish intrusion into the Muslim Middle East. But they recognized that, for better or worse, it was a reality and here to stay. After four wars and the loss of innumerable amounts of blood and treasure, the mainstream Arab leaders had concluded that, if they could get back the territory they had lost in 1967 as well as obtain justice for the Palestinians, peace with Israel would be a price worth paying.

At the same time, I perceived a certain insularity in much of the Israeli leadership, whose views of Arab attitudes toward Israel didn't square with what I observed myself. Despite their military might, the Israelis had a sense of relative insecurity. Most Israeli leaders were firmly convinced that the Arabs were determined to "throw them into the sea." From their perspective, territorial concessions in the interests of peace made no sense, since the Arabs would only use them as a launching pad for new attacks.

When I reported my experiences with Arab interlocutors to the Israelis I met with, they invariably objected that I needed to distinguish between what the Arabs were whispering in my ear in English, and what they were saying to their own people in Arabic. They are just telling you what you want to hear, the Israelis insisted repeatedly, but not what they really believe. Yet I heard this message from a broad cross section of Arab society. If it had come only from President Sadat of Egypt, or King Hussein of Jordan, or one of the Saudi leaders, I might have been willing to dismiss it, but I heard it from people who ranged from the very top to the very bottom of society in these and other Arab countries. I heard it too from foreign diplomats and journalists posted to the countries I visited. The subsequent willingness of both Egypt and Jordan to sign peace treaties with Israel demonstrated that what my Arab interlocutors told me was a more accurate reflection of reality than the Israeli dismissal of those Arab statements as fantasy at best and propaganda at worst. There was, in fact, a fundamental disconnect between Arabs and Israelis that resulted from decades of not communicating with each other.

However, any attempt to move from the abstract willingness to make peace to the particulars of a peace agreement made the real challenges apparent. The differences between Israelis and Arabs over what would constitute an acceptable agreement, including the degree of territorial withdrawal, the establishment of a Palestinian state, the future status of Jerusalem and the Golan Heights, and the fate of the Palestinian refugees, were profound. A breakthrough seemed exceedingly unlikely. The Israelis weren't prepared to go back to the 1967 borders as the Arabs demanded. They considered Jerusalem their indivisible and eternal capital, while the Arabs insisted that East Jerusalem become the capital of a Palestinian state. The Israelis were unwilling to completely withdraw from the Golan Heights, while the Syrians wanted it all back. Finally, Israel was certainly not prepared to agree to a "right of return" for the Palestinian refugees that could change the demographic character of the Jewish state, while the Palestinians insisted that all refugees should have that right to return to the homes from which they fled or were evicted. Moshe Dayan, the hero of the Six-Day War, once famously summed up the problem by saying that he would rather have Sharm el-Sheikh, a strategic location at the tip of the Sinai Peninsula, without peace than peace without Sharm el-Sheikh. Yet once it became clear that Egypt was prepared for a real peace, Israel agreed to return Sharm el-Sheikh and the rest of the Sinai to Egyptian control. This diplomatic flip-flop indicated that, under the right circumstances, a peace agreement might be possible after all.

Yet bridging the gap between Arabs and Israelis would be very difficult. When I returned from my initial trip, I reflected the pessimism I felt in my maiden speech on the floor of the House of Representatives on March 4, 1975. I told my colleagues I had come away with the feeling that the prospects for peace in the Middle East were dim indeed. The major obstacle, I believed, was that even though Arab states were taking the first small steps toward accepting Israel's existence in their midst, they still refused to offer any tangible manifestations of their alleged desire for peace. This reluctance to move forward worked against the Arabs' own interests. Without peace, impoverished Egypt would probably have to continue spending close to 40 percent of its national budget on preparations for war rather than on economic development. The same was true for other Arab states. And the result was that the Palestinians would remain in squalid refugee camps scattered among a number of Arab countries without the dignity of a state they could call their own.

Indeed the status of the Palestinians was the thorniest issue by far. A few months before my trip, Arab heads of state meeting in Rabat, Morocco, voted unanimously to give the Palestine Liberation Organization, rather than King Hussein, the authority to represent the Palestinian people in any subsequent negotiations concerning the future of the West Bank. That was a formula for frustration. During many conversations in the region, it was evident to me that among Israelis there was strong opposition to any dealings whatsoever with the PLO, which they considered a terrorist organization bent on the destruction of Israel. Their concerns were not without justification. In addition to its hijacking of planes, attacks against nursery schools, and the massacre of Israeli athletes at the Munich Olympics in 1972, the PLO was formally committed to the elimination of Israel and the removal of all Israelis who had not come to Israel before 1917. In the absence of any indication whatsoever that the PLO was prepared to accept a resolution that required Palestinian recognition of Israel, the Jewish state could hardly be expected to acquiesce to the PLO's demands.

One night in Amman during my initial trip there, I met with a number of Palestinians who insisted, "If Israel went back to the 1967 borders, it might satisfy the Egyptians and the Syrians, but it wouldn't satisfy us." What they wanted was an initial Israeli withdrawal to the borders embodied in the partition resolution adopted by the UN in 1947, followed by the establishment of a secular democratic state in the whole of what had been Palestine. Since the Palestinian population between the Jordan River and the Mediterranean Sea greatly outnumbered the Jewish population, this was clearly a nonstarter for Israel. It would have meant political suicide. Other, more moderate Palestinians had a firmer grip on political reality. Men such as Elias Freij, the mayor of Bethlehem; Sari Nusseibeh, the president of Al-Quds University in Jerusalem; and Rashad al-Shawa, the mayor of Gaza, made it clear to me that they were prepared to recognize and live in peace with Israel if a Palestinian state could be established based on the 1967 borders, with East Jerusalem as its capital.

Interestingly, there seemed to be a convergence between the views of Palestinian moderates and conservatives. The latter were represented by the Village Leagues, an organization of rural, tribally oriented West Bank Palestinians established by the Israelis in the hope that it would become a counterweight to the more radical PLO. Interested in learning their position, I met with their leader, Mustafa Dudeen, who looked like an Arab version of Vito Corleone in *The Godfather*. When I asked Dudeen under what circumstances he thought the Palestinians should be willing to make peace with Israel, he replied that peace would only be possible if Israel went back to the 1967 borders and agreed to the establishment of a Palestinian state with East Jerusalem as its capital. As it turned out, the views of the moderates and conservatives were a more accurate reflection of overall Palestinian sentiment than those I heard from the refugees in Jordan. When, more than a decade later, the PLO repealed the provisions of its charter calling for the elimination of Israel and signed the Oslo agreement calling for a two-state solution, it seemed that a peace treaty between Israel and the Palestinians was more than just a theoretical possibility.

Many Israelis moderated their views as well. When I first met Ariel Sharon, one of the hardest of the Israeli hard-liners, he pulled out maps of the West Bank to demonstrate why, purely from the point of view of security, Israel could never risk relinquishing control over that territory. His solution was "peace for peace": that the place for a Palestinian state was the East Bank of the Jordan River, not the West Bank. He saw Jordan, whose population was 75 percent Palestinian, as the appropriate location for this state. This view that "Jordan is Palestine" was shared by most right-wing Israelis, such as future Prime Ministers Binyamin Netanyahu and Ehud Olmert. But in time it became clear that such a solution was acceptable to neither Jordan nor the Palestinians and had no international support whatsoever. Furthermore, more and more Israelis came to realize that permanent Israeli control over the West Bank and Gaza would mean creating an Arab majority between the Jordan and the Mediterranean. That meant Israel would eventually have to choose between remaining a democracy — which would require giving the Palestinians the vote and losing the Jewish character of the state — and remaining an occupying power in perpetuity, which was antithetical to Jewish values. As a consequence, many Israeli leaders — including Sharon, Olmert, and Netanyahu — who had once categorically rejected the establishment of a Palestinian state in the West Bank and Gaza came around to accepting it.

Even in the absence of an agreement, there were sound moral and strategic reasons for continued US support of Israel. Morally, it was the only genuinely democratic state in the region. Strategically, it served as a bastion against the advance of radical movements and regimes strongly sympathetic to the Soviet Union. Without the presence of Israel, I concluded, the pro-Western governments of Jordan and Lebanon, as well as other Arab states, probably would have fallen a long time before. In 1970, for example, when a Syrian division crossed into Jordan, it is doubtful King Hussein could have survived if the Israelis hadn't made it clear to the Syrians that Israel was not prepared to accept the overthrow of the Hashemite regime. And to the extent that any possibility existed for a peace agreement between Israel and the Palestinians, which would clearly be in the interests of the United States, the prospects for it would be greatly diminished if the Arabs concluded we had abandoned the Jewish state to its fate. Their incentive to accept a two-state solution would likely be trumped by the belief that they could now establish a Palestinian state in the whole area from the river to the sea.

As it happened, the key development in the peace process was an unexpected twist — the treaty signed between Egypt and Israel in 1979, after Sadat's courageous and historic journey to Jerusalem. It was a beacon of hope, demonstrating that Israel would make territorial concessions it otherwise wouldn't have contemplated if the Arabs recognized it and agreed to a real peace. But before long this achievement was shadowed by a darker message: Sadat, a peace advocate like King Hussein's grandfather, was also cut down by an assassin's bullet. Other Arab leaders necessarily had to recognize that they could suffer the same fate if they made peace with Israel. The subsequent assassination of Yitzhak Rabin by a right-wing Jew indicated that the Arabs had no monopoly on fanatics determined to derail the peace process.

Meanwhile I attempted to generate sympathy and support for Israel among Washington decision makers in a number of ways. One was to invite some non-Jewish members of the administration who were in a position to influence American policy in the Middle East to our yearly Seders on the first night of Passover. I hoped to show them that the conflict between Israel and the Arabs didn't begin in 1948 but had ancient antecedents. Among our guests over the years were Vice President Walter Mondale, National Security Advisor Zbigniew Brzezinski, Secretary of State Cyrus Vance, CIA Director Stansfield Turner, and two chairmen of the Joint Chiefs of Staff, William Crowe and Colin Powell, whom I presented with camouflage yarmulkes for the occasion. Another guest was the ambassador from a Persian Gulf state whose name I won't mention, lest it prejudice his chance of one day becoming the ruler of his country. Our Seders were conducted by Johnny Levine, the rabbi who had started my political career by arranging for me to manage the Dubin campaign in 1966, and who had married Nina and me in 1967.

Perhaps the most memorable Seder was the one at which Brzezinski was our guest of honor. As the ceremony progressed, he got repeated phone calls from the situation room of the White House, which was managing a crisis created by the unauthorized intrusion into our coastal waters of a Soviet fishing trawler. Returning to the table from one such call, Brzezinski reported it had been from President Carter, calling from the home of Bob Lipschutz, his White House counsel, whose Seder he was attending. Why was the president's Seder on step twelve of the Haggadah (the Passover prayer book from which the Seder is conducted), while we were only on step six? Brzezinski asked. Rabbi Levine explained it was because of his constant calls, which kept us waiting for him to return to the table!

Ironically enough, my efforts to help Israel were not always appreciated by the Jewish organizations whose support for that country was the main justification for their existence. When Phil Crane, a Republican congressman from Illinois, offered a nondebatable amendment on the floor of the House to cut off all funding for the US embassy in Israel unless it was moved from Tel Aviv to Jerusalem, there were only a few members on the floor besides me. One was Ben Rosenthal, a Democrat from Queens, like myself a staunch supporter of Israel. When a record vote on this surprise amendment was called, Rosenthal and I decided to vote "no." It was obvious to us that the administration, fearing that such a move would bring an end to the peace process, would never relocate the embassy to Jerusalem. Thus passing the amendment would have meant the closing of our embassy in Israel. We also hoped that our votes would help legitimize a politically difficult "no" vote for most of our colleagues and give them a rationale for it that they could use when they were criticized, as many surely would be, for their opposition. Our opposition was sufficient to convince a majority of members, and the amendment was defeated. Afterward I received a good deal of criticism from my district and from elements of the organized Jewish community for this vote. But I felt it was more important to keep the peace process going than to curry favor with the friends of Israel by voting for a purely symbolic amendment.

On another occasion, I felt compelled to take an action that didn't generate criticism from the organized Jewish community—which was unaware of it—but did result in a protest from the Israeli ambassador, Simcha Dinitz, who came to my office to personally and privately register his concern. I had drafted a letter to Prime Minister Begin that was signed by several other leading supporters of Israel in Congress, including Jack Bingham, Millicent Fenwick, and Ben Rosenthal. In the aftermath of the Israeli invasion of Lebanon in 1982, a Maronite militia had entered two Palestinian refugee camps in Beirut, Sabra and Shatila, and over two days had slaughtered about a thousand Palestinians. This massacre took place within view of Israeli soldiers at posts overlooking the camps, raising questions about Israel's responsibility. The letter urged the prime minister to establish an independent commission to look into the affair and to hold accountable any Israelis who might have been responsible.

Ambassador Dinitz urged me not to send the letter on the ground that even a suggestion that Israel was involved could undermine support for Israel in the United States. I responded that as friends of Israel, we were deeply concerned that if Israel didn't establish such a commission American support for his country could be jeopardized. It was precisely because of our commitment to Israel that we felt obligated to share these concerns with the prime minister. I also said we had no intention of publicizing the letter, which we saw as a purely private communication. Finally, I pointed out that a few days earlier, 500,000 Israelis had demonstrated in Tel Aviv in support of such a commission. We were merely suggesting a course of action supported by a majority of his own people.

We sent the letter anyway. As I had promised, it was kept private and never found its way into the media. The Israeli government did establish a commission, although I cannot say what, if anything, our letter had to do with its decision. The commission ultimately concluded that Israel had had no direct involvement in the massacre, but that it bore indirect responsibility for not stopping it. As a result, Ariel Sharon, then minister of defense, was obliged to resign.

Politics isn't always about keeping your ear to the ground. At its best, it's about looking ahead and leading. Given the large number of Jews in my district, wading into a controversial issue concerning Israel meant taking risks. But there were times when I felt I had to do what I thought was right, even if that meant going against the tide of public opinion. If I wasn't willing to do this, why had I sought public office in the first place? I fully agreed with the British statesman Edmund Burke, who said, "Your representative owes you not his industry only, but his judgment; and he betrays instead of serving you if he sacrifices it to your opinion."

· 3 ·

A JEWISH AGENDA
Rescue Abroad and Relief at Home

Representing my constituents often involved me in efforts to help distressed Jewish communities around the world. I undertook this work not
just to curry favor at home, but out of a deep commitment to human rights
and from my sense of obligation as a Jew to help other Jews in distress.

The best example of this confluence of interests is my role in easing
the plight of Syrian Jewry. When I came to Congress in 1974, Syrian Jews
were perhaps the most oppressed Jewish community in the world. This
ancient, once-flourishing community, numbering about 45,000 in 1948,
had dwindled to a tenth of that size. Their life became particularly harsh
after Israel was founded, since the Syrian government regarded them as
a potential fifth column in the Arabs' unending war against the fledgling
Jewish state.

Syrian Jews were required to carry identification papers indicating that
they were Jewish. They were barred from employment in the public, or
nationalized, sectors of the economy. They were not permitted to have
telephones in their homes or to own automobiles. Nor could they travel
within Syria without first receiving government permission. Most important, they were denied the right to emigrate, in direct contravention of the
Universal Declaration of Human Rights adopted by the UN General Assembly in 1948.

I represented 25,000 Syrian Jews, a tight-knit community in the Ocean
Parkway and Midwood neighborhoods of Brooklyn who constituted a no-
table American success story. Many had amassed substantial fortunes in
the import-export trade and were known for their exceptional business
skills. They had preserved their religious faith and culinary traditions.
Most were Orthodox, and they had created a network of synagogues, yeshi-
vas (religious schools), and mikvahs (ritual baths for women) throughout
their neighborhoods. Many spent summers at an oceanfront community
in Deal, New Jersey, where they built spacious, beautiful homes.

The burning issue that worried and motivated these people was the future of the 5,000 Jews still in Syria, who were under tremendous pressure from the Syrian government. Around 1974, four young Jewish men attempted to escape from Syria but were murdered by the Syrians. In another instance, four Jewish women from Damascus trying to escape were caught and raped by their Syrian captors. These events, of course, caused great consternation in Brooklyn. The fate of the Syrian Jews hadn't been a major issue in my campaign, but after I was elected, I realized that this important community cared deeply about their fate. I shared my constituents' concern, just as I cared about the status of other beleaguered Jewish communities in the Soviet Union, Iran, Yemen, and Ethiopia.

In the early twentieth century, Isaac Shalom was the first really successful businessman in the community of newly immigrated Syrian Jews in Brooklyn. A man of great stature and integrity, he became the community patriarch and often lent money to other community members to start their own businesses. He was a great philanthropist, responsible for the establishment of a network of Jewish schools throughout the Arab world at a time when hundreds of thousands of Jews still lived there.

His son, Stephen, had inherited his role as the secular leader of the community, and shortly after I was elected, I reached out to him as I prepared for my first trip to the Middle East, which included a visit to Syria to see what could be done to secure the freedom of the Jews there. I had no idea what to expect, but I asked Steve if the community would be prepared to finance the departure of the Syrian Jews on chartered flights if Syrian President Hafez al-Assad agreed to let them go. He assured me that money was not a problem. Even if it took millions, funds would be available.

Arriving in Damascus at 3 a.m., I was met at the airport by Richard Murphy, another distinguished career diplomat who was our ambassador to Syria. I thought it was an extraordinary gesture on his part, and I also appreciated his invitation to stay at his residence in Damascus, which made me feel more at home than I would have in a hotel.

I met with the leaders of the Syrian Jewish community, including Rabbi Abraham Hamra, who officiated at the main synagogue in Damascus; Salim Totah, the elderly patriarch of the community; and Maurice Nusari, one of the leading Jewish businessmen in the city. They made it clear that the entire Jewish community wanted to leave but recognized it was un-likely that this would be allowed. Unlike the Egyptian pharaoh who bade good riddance to the Israelites after ten plagues had been inflicted on his people, the Syrian dictator was not about to let these people go.

The Jewish leaders told me their most pressing problem was that sev-eral hundred single Jewish women in their late teens and early twenties had no one to marry. Most of the single young men, they explained, had ei-ther already surreptitiously departed or didn't want to get married because that would make it more difficult for them to escape in the future. In their community, it was a social disaster for a girl not to be married by her early twenties. If it wasn't possible for everyone to emigrate, they said, I should try to get permission for the single women to leave.

I met with President Hafez al-Assad, who turned out to be a tough, formidable interlocutor. I told him that I represented a community of 25,000 Syrian Jews in Brooklyn who cared deeply about the fate of their co-religionists in Syria, and that his willingness to let the Jews leave would be greatly appreciated in the United States and undoubtedly improve his relations with America. Assad explained that if he let them leave, he wouldn't be able to persuade the Soviet leaders to resist the pressure to let Soviet Jews emigrate as well. Most of the Soviet Jews would go to Israel, he argued, strengthening his enemy, which was unacceptable. I told him I didn't think the Soviet leaders' decision about whether to let their Jews leave had anything to do with whether he let Jews leave Syria. But I argued in vain. He was unwilling to accede to my request. I made several other trips to Syria but was unable to move this stubborn Syrian pharaoh off his position. Meanwhile, the leaders of the Brooklyn Syrian Jews emphasized their desire to help the single women depart.

Then in May 1977, President Jimmy Carter was scheduled to meet with President Assad in Geneva. I arranged to talk with Carter in the White House the day before his departure to ask him to intervene. I was ac-companied by Steve Shalom, who was staying at my house in suburban McLean. Our meeting was set for 9 a.m., and I allotted an hour to travel to the White House. It should have been more than enough time. But it was raining, and being a relative newcomer to Washington, I hadn't yet learned that when it rains in the capital of the world's mightiest nation, the traffic slows to a crawl. To my growing horror, at about five to nine we

*The hallway meeting with President Carter. Zbigniew
Brzezinski is between us and Steve Shalom is at left.*

were stalled in traffic on 14th Street, several blocks from the White House.
What I did then was totally out of character. Whether it was my anxiety
about missing a meeting with the president on which the fate of the single
Jewish women in Syria might depend, or a residual memory of the exciting chase scene in *The French Connection,* I noticed there was no traffic in
the opposite direction, so I pulled out of my lane and raced up 14th Street
against traffic at about sixty miles an hour.

Miraculously, we got to the White House safely, shortly after nine
o'clock. The president had already left the Oval Office for another meeting, and for a moment I thought my dash to the Executive Mansion was
for naught. But at that moment I ran into Carter in a White House hallway talking with Zbigniew Brzezinski, his national security advisor. I
quickly told the president about the young Syrian women and asked him
if he would raise the issue with President Assad.

On his return, Carter called to report that he had spoken with Assad
about what the president referred to as "the Jewish maidens." Assad had

The Syrian brides at Kennedy airport. At the table:
Steve Shalom, Rabbi Hecht, and Rabbi Dweck (far right).

said he would be willing to let them go on a case-by-case basis, providing they had marriage proposals. I wasn't in the business of marriage broker-ing, but this seemed too good an opportunity to pass up, so I turned to Steve Shalom. He got two dozen yeshiva students from the Syrian com-munity to write marriage proposals to single Jewish women in Syria whose names the Damascus community leaders provided. Steve had the propos-als notarized by city and state officials, and they looked very "official." Of course, these young men were not actually planning to marry their pre-sumptive fiancées. But there was no reason to let Assad in on that fact.

The proposals were hand carried to Syria by Steve Shalom and Mi-chael Lewan, my chief of staff, in August 1977. Since Syrian law required the women to be married before they could leave the country, a proxy wedding ceremony was arranged on a sweltering summer day in Damas-cus, with Michael serving as substitute husband for sixteen of them. The event prompted a huge celebration in the Jewish community, after which the women left for the United States. I met them at Kennedy airport, along with Steve Shalom and two Syrian rabbis from Brooklyn and Deal, Rabbi Abraham Hecht and Rabbi Israel Dwek. It was an extraordinarily emotional encounter. The next day the *New York Times* ran a front-page story, with a photo of me with the women. Though I doubt he appreciated it, this coverage was the best publicity Assad ever got in the American press.

As a result of the *Times* story, I began to get letters from men all over the United States who wanted to marry these women. One fellow wrote that he had twenty choice acres of riverfront property in Washington State available as a dowry. Another said he was tired of American women who were willing to have sex only when they wanted to. He preferred a traditional Jewish woman who would be content to have sex when he wanted it. I even got a letter from a woman in my district, who wrote: "Dear Congressman Solarz: I am not Jewish but I am single. Having read what you did to find husbands for these Jewish women from Syria, I would like you to find a husband for me too." I also received a call from a woman in my district who wanted my help in finding a husband for her daughter. It turned out that she wanted me to fix her daughter up with Mayor Ed Koch, whom I was friendly with. I replied: "Madam, assuming I can persuade Mayor Koch to ask your daughter out, what should he say if she asks, 'Mr. Mayor, how did you, the most eligible bachelor in New York, happen to call me up for a date?'" She thought a minute, then responded, "Why don't you tell him to say he met her at a singles weekend at Grossinger's [a hotel in the Catskills]?" I told the mayor about the phone call but wasn't surprised when he declined to ask my constituent's daughter out. I used to joke that as a result of my efforts on behalf of the Syrian women, I became the leading *shadchen* (Yiddish for matchmaker) in Congress. Eventually, all the Syrian women were married, although not to the young men who had sent them the proposals. One, whose parents were still in Syria, asked me to give her away at her wedding. Over time they all had children and grandchildren as well.

Once I had created this opening, Steve Shalom made several trips to Syria, where he was greatly revered in the Jewish community. He clandestinely brought in money — up to $50,000 at a time — to take care of the community's religious and other needs. He was also the first American Jew to visit the fifty-person Jewish community in Qamishli, a small Syrian town on the border with Turkey, about a fourteen-hour drive from Damascus. His visit was a huge event in the history of that community. As a mark of their appreciation, they slaughtered a sheep in his honor and stayed up all night celebrating. His appearance showed them that they hadn't been forgotten, and that the larger Jewish community outside Syria cared about them.

Over the next decade or so, I got resolutions adopted expressing the sense of Congress that the Syrian Jews should be permitted to leave. Various letters were sent to presidents and secretaries of state, asking them to raise the issue with the Syrian leadership. Assad eventually gave permission for all the Jews to leave, and by the 1990s virtually all had done so. The ancient Jewish community in Syria, which dated back to biblical times, ceased to exist. But the Syrian Jews were now free. About half came to Brooklyn, and the rest settled in Israel.

Among other struggles on behalf of oppressed Jewish communities, the most prominent was the massive effort to liberate Soviet Jews from their captivity in the Soviet Union. I was only one of many trying to advance their cause. Every major American Jewish organization took up the struggle. There was also an umbrella group, the National Conference on Soviet Jewry, that included representatives from all the established Jewish organizations in the United States. As part of this effort, I made a trip to Moscow for the first time in 1980 and met with some of the Refuseniks, as the Soviet Jews denied permission to leave were called. I strongly identified with their cause and supported the Jackson-Vanik amendment, the main legislative vehicle for putting pressure on the Soviet government. It made the granting of most-favored-nation trade status conditional on freedom of immigration. By granting MFN status, the United States offers a country trading advantages equal to those it gives its most favored trading partners. The denial of MFN status made it clear that Moscow would pay a heavy economic price for its refusal to let the Jews emigrate.

Natan Sharansky, a diminutive but tremendously courageous man, was an icon of the Soviet dissident movement. In 1973, he applied for an exit visa for Israel but was rejected on "security" grounds. He refused to remain silent and became a prominent protester. In 1977, the Soviets arrested him, precipitating a global protest that became a huge problem for Moscow. He was released in 1986, left Russia, and settled in Israel. On May 11, 1986, he came to the annual rally for Soviet Jewry on East 42nd Street in New York. It was a stirring moment. Some 75,000 people attended, including Mayor Ed Koch, New York Governor Mario Cuomo, and the future Israeli Prime Minister Binyamin "Bibi" Netanyahu.

I had the privilege of speaking on that occasion. I praised Sharansky as "a man who has returned from the Gulag, where souls are crushed and bodies broken, but whose indomitable spirit enabled him to survive a horrible ordeal." I used the Hebrew word *dayenu* to punctuate my speech. This word comes from the Passover Seder celebrating Jewish liberation from bondage in Egypt and means, roughly, "It would have been enough." As I told the crowd, "To have survived at all in the face of such cruelty, *dayenu*; to have remained faithful to his ideals under such conditions, *dayenu*; to have emerged after almost ten years, not only alive, but with his spirit intact, and his sense of humor undiminished, *dayenu*." So, "even as we honor Mr. Sharansky, we reflect upon the fate and renew our commitment to the over two million Jews for whom liberty is a fading illusion and unrestrained religious observance a faraway ideal . . . and so we must raise our voices now for the Jews who are still trapped in the Soviet Union." In time the Jackson-Vanik amendment did the job; Moscow eventually lifted its ban on immigration, and over a million Soviet Jews left for Israel.

I also became active in an effort to protect Ethiopian Jews. For centuries, the world was unaware of this ancient Jewish community, whose members lived in thatched huts. In 1991, however, in the face of military successes by rebel groups, the government of Mengistu Haile Mariam began to unravel. Some Jewish organizations, as well as the state of Israel, grew concerned that amid the chaos the sizable population of black Ethiopian Jews, who called themselves Beta Israel ("the house of Israel"), might be at risk. Along with several other members of Congress, I supported early efforts to "free Ethiopian Jewry."

Senators Rudy Boschwitz and Alan Cranston, along with Congressmen Ben Gilman and Barney Frank and I, established an Ethiopian caucus that got Congress focused on the need to help the Ethiopian Jews. It produced some practical assistance, such as getting student visas to help people leave and us college admissions for those who had visas. I also wrote a letter for a member of the board of the American Association for Ethiopian Jews, a grassroots group, requesting that the us ambassador in Sudan, William Kontos, assist private relief groups on the ground providing aid. American pressure also helped pave the way for a modern miracle. Later that year Operation Solomon, involving thirty-four Israeli aircraft in thirty-six-hour nonstop flights, transported 14,325 Ethiopian Jews to

Israel. Giving new meaning to the word "airborne," two women gave birth during the flights.

Another beleaguered Jewish community lived in the remote reaches of Yemen, one of the oldest centers of civilization in the Middle East. Although Jews had been there for centuries, they weren't treated equally. Since the beginning of the nineteenth century, they had been forbidden to wear new or good clothes or to ride on a donkey or mule. They were also barred from engaging in monetary transactions. Between June 1949 and September 1950, virtually the entire Jewish population, some 50,000, left for Israel in what was called Operation Magic Carpet. My concern was for the 1,500 Jews who had chosen to remain and were reported to be living under difficult circumstances near Sa'dah in the north of the country. I had tried to go there during my first visit to Yemen in the early 1980s, but the Yemeni government had refused permission. When I returned in the summer of 1990, however, the government relented and allowed me to meet with the leaders of the community in Sa'dah. I was flown there on a government helicopter, over some of the most mountainous and rugged terrain to be found anywhere in the region. During this one-hour flight, I read Maimonides's "Epistle to the Jews of Yemen," written 800 years earlier by this renowned Jewish sage in response to a request from the community for his views on how to distinguish the real from a false messiah. It gave me a vivid sense of being part of the long historical saga of a community that lived, as I discovered upon arrival, in circumstances similar to what they must have been in biblical times. People's homes were mud huts that lacked electricity, indoor plumbing, and running water, and they dressed in flowing robes, a style that I imagined had not changed for millennia.

Accompanied by two very good friends from New York, Jay and Diana Goldin, as well as my subcommittee chief of staff, Stanley Roth, I was introduced to the community leaders and taken to one of their homes. Some young boys were brought before us to recite by heart sections of the Bible as a way of showing us that the community still took seriously the rituals and obligations of their faith. I came away convinced that most of the remaining Yemenite Jews would leave the country if given the opportunity. A few years later, as a result of constant prodding and pressure, the government of Yemen agreed to let them depart. Most left for Israel and the United States. Though I rejoiced, my satisfaction was tinged with regret

Meeting the Yemeni Jews.

over the disappearance of a community that had lived in Yemen for thousands of years.

As I think back now on these battles, big and small, a unifying theme
emerges. My view of history was shaped profoundly by the destruction
of European Jewry in the Holocaust, and the failure of the United States
and other countries to come to their assistance when this could have made
a difference. I believed that wherever there were people in distress, as a
congressman I had a responsibility to do whatever I could to relieve their
suffering. That is why, whether it meant protecting the right of people to
practice their religion, to freely emigrate, or to express themselves without fear of persecution, I kept my office door open to Timorese, Baha'i,
Vietnamese, Cambodians, Filipinos, Taiwanese, Pakistanis, South Africans, Bangladeshis, and anyone else in harm's way who sought help from
the US government.

Sadly, there is nothing historically unusual about the slaughter of innocents — Armenians by Turks, Poles by Russians, Biafrans by Nigerians,
Cambodians by other Cambodians, Kosovars and Bosnians by Serbs, and
Native Americans by white Americans. The list is long, if not endless. But
even amid such carnage, the destruction of European Jewry by the Nazis

stands out. The systematic slaughter of six million human beings, for no other reason than that they were Jewish, is an especially shocking indication of the depths of depravity to which the human spirit can sink.

One of the moral monsters in the Nazis' production line of death was Kurt Waldheim, who brazenly became secretary general of the United Nations and president of Austria while hiding his Nazi past. I'm proud to have played a role in disclosing the sins of his earlier life. My involvement began in 1980, when I wrote a letter to then Secretary General Waldheim asking him about allegations that had been brought to my attention by Hillel Seidman, a constituent of mine who wrote an article in the *New Republic* about Waldheim's dark past. The article reported that he might have participated in war crimes on the eastern front during World War II, although it did not name any specific actions he engaged in. In my letter, I asked Waldheim to specify the units he had served in on the eastern front. I hoped that once they were identified, knowledgeable researchers might be able to determine if Waldheim had indeed engaged in war crimes while on active duty in the Soviet Union.

Waldheim did not name those units in his response. He simply asserted that the charges against him were "slanders." He explained that he had been wounded on the eastern front and sent back to Germany to recuperate, after which he went to law school. The clear implication was that he hadn't returned to active duty in the Soviet Union or anywhere else. At one point during my communications with him, he invited me to dinner at the secretary general's residence in New York. During the meal, he proclaimed his innocence and, in a palpably obsequious manner, tried to persuade me to drop my pursuit of his wartime activities. But I wasn't about to be bought off.

Gradually, the truth emerged. At the time that Waldheim claimed to have been studying law, he was actually serving in the Balkans under General Alexander Lohr, who was later hanged for participation in war crimes, including killing civilians. This discovery gave Waldheim's response to my letter the ominous implication that he had taken part in activities in the Balkans that he preferred not to disclose. It was like the Sherlock Holmes story in which the dog that didn't bark provided the main clue that enabled Holmes to solve the mystery.

In 1986, with controversy still swirling around him, Waldheim was elected president of Austria. Then an Austrian magazine revealed that his autobiography had omitted several of his activities during the war years. The United States officially declared Waldheim and his wife personae non gratae, and in 1987 they were put on a list of people banned from entering the country. During his tenure as Austria's president, Waldheim was not welcomed by any Western countries; he traveled mostly to the Arab Middle East, the Vatican, and some Communist states.

I devoted energy and passion to a number of other causes important to my Jewish constituents — and to me. I spent several years, for example, working to pass legislation that shouldn't have been necessary in the United States. Captain Simcha Goldman of the US Air Force was disciplined for wearing his yarmulke while in uniform, a violation of the Air Force dress code. Not one to supinely submit to what he considered unreasonable demands, Captain Goldman fought for his rights all the way to the Supreme Court, which in 1986 ruled 5–4 that the Air Force could prohibit this form of religious expression. I considered this a misguided decision, and it infuriated many of my Orthodox constituents. It seemed cruelly ironic that the Supreme Court would abridge one of the basic freedoms US soldiers were pledged to defend.

While the Court's rulings become the law of the land, Congress can reverse a Court decision that doesn't rest on constitutional grounds. So with the assistance of Nat Lewin, a prominent Washington attorney who had served as a law clerk to Justice John Harlan and had argued on behalf of Captain Goldman before the Court, I drafted legislation giving members of the armed services the right to wear "unobtrusive religious headgear" so long as it didn't prevent them from performing their duties.

It took a few years, but I was ultimately able to convince my colleagues in the House of Representatives to vote for my bill. Rather than trying to get it passed as stand-alone legislation, I offered it on the floor of the House as an amendment to the Department of Defense authorization bill. It provoked quite a debate. One member demanded to know whether my amendment applied to Sikhs, who are religiously required to wear a turban. I replied that the Sikhs were well known as a martial group whose bravery on the field of battle was legendary. The best thing we could do to redress the imbalance of conventional forces in Europe between NATO and the Warsaw Pact, I argued, would be to recruit and field two Sikh divisions. If my amendment made this possible, we would be more secure as a result. Charlie Wilson of Texas (who later became famous for his role in securing support for the mujahedin fighting the Soviet Union in Afghanistan) said he had a lot of Native Americans in his district and wanted to know if my amendment would permit them to wear war bonnets. It would depend, I answered, on whether they wore them for religious purposes and whether they were unobtrusive.

After adoption in the House, the bill with my amendment went to a conference committee to resolve the differences between the House and Senate versions. Since there was no comparable provision in the Senate bill, the Senate conferees had to be convinced to accept the House amendment. I knew it wasn't going to be easy when the Pentagon sent a platoon of generals and admirals to Capitol Hill to persuade the conferees to reject it. Their main argument was that it would impair military discipline and that if Orthodox Jews could wear yarmulkes on duty, Hare Krishna adherents would demand the right to wear saffron robes, and the military would soon dissolve into a hippie rabble unable to defend the republic against its enemies. To underscore the seriousness of their objections, one general warned that the Pentagon attached more importance to the defeat of the Solarz yarmulke amendment than to approval of the MX missile. When I heard this, I told the conferees, "If this is how much importance the military attaches to the MX missile, it's the best argument against it I've ever heard."

In an effort to make their task easier, I sent twenty camouflage yarmulkes to key senators to show that they could be designed to blend into the rest of a soldier's uniform. With the support of Senators Orrin Hatch, who was sensitive to the need of his fellow Mormons to wear temple garments, and Frank Lautenberg, who understood the importance to Orthodox Jews of wearing a yarmulke, the Senate conferees accepted my amendment, which shortly thereafter became law. So far as I can tell, its adoption has never impaired the effectiveness of our fighting forces, nor have the armed forces become an undisciplined rabble — just as the right to wear a yarmulke has not impaired the effectiveness of the Israeli, British, New Zealand, and other militaries either.

A few days after the legislation was adopted, I sent a letter and a camouflage yarmulke to Justice William Brennan, who had written an eloquent dissent in the Goldman case, inviting Congress to overrule the Court's decision. I was pleased to tell him that my colleagues had taken his advice. He later told me he was delighted to get the letter and promptly put on the yarmulke, then forgot to take it off when he left his chambers for the day, to the surprise of his wife when he got home. On a trip to Israel a year later, he wore it when he went to see President Chaim Herzog.

Another issue of particular concern to Orthodox Jews that I worked on began with a visit to my district office by Samuel Deitel and several other religiously observant constituents who worked for the federal government. Because Deitel observed the Sabbath, as well as Jewish holidays throughout the year, he had to leave work early on Fridays during the winter, when Shabbat arrives early, and stay out of the office all day on holidays when his religion prohibited him from working. The time lost was either deducted from his annual vacation or subtracted from his salary, leaving him with either a reduced income or very little time to spend with his family on vacation.

Mr. Deitel, who worked at a branch of the Internal Revenue Service, had approached his supervisor to ask if he could come in early and stay late on days when he had no religious obligations, to make up for the time lost. His supervisor rejected his proposal because it violated the Civil Service Law, which required that employees who worked more than eight hours a day be paid overtime. Deitel then came to my office seeking a solution.

Giving someone the opportunity to make up time lost for religious reasons made good sense to me, so I called Jerome Kurtz, commissioner of the Internal Revenue Service, and Alan Campbell, chairman of the US Civil Service Commission. Both said that under existing law nothing could be done. After reading the statute myself, I reluctantly concluded they were right — so the law itself would have to be changed. I introduced a bill in Congress, and the long, tedious legislative process began. Meanwhile, I enlisted support from various organizations, including the Anti-Defamation League of B'nai B'rith and the Agudath Israel of America, a national Orthodox organization. It soon became clear that passing the legislation would require support from the Carter administration. Again I enlisted the aid of Nat Lewin, the Washington attorney, who had become a legal champion of the rights of Orthodox Jews. He offered to help on a pro bono basis.

I also contacted Stu Eizenstat, President Carter's chief domestic policy advisor, himself an observant Jew. He arranged for us to present our case to the legal counsels from virtually every federal department and agency at a meeting in the White House. Unfortunately, every one of them opposed the measure, mostly on the grounds that it violated the First Amendment prohibition against the establishment of religion. After all the executive branch representatives had spoken, Eizenstat asked us for our response. Nat Lewin then spoke up. "I'm an Orthodox Jew," he said, "which means I have to be home before it gets dark on the Sabbath. When I worked as a law clerk for Mr. Justice Harlan on the Supreme Court, Mr. Justice Harlan, knowing of my religious obligations, used to let me leave his chambers early on Friday afternoons in the winter so I could get home before the sun set. And it never occurred to Mr. Justice Harlan that by letting me do this he was somehow violating the First Amendment." Slam-dunk for Lewin. Eizenstat was convinced the constitutional objections were without merit, the administration came out in support of my bill, and the legislation was enacted into law.

While my district was predominantly Jewish, I also represented significant numbers of Italians, Poles, blacks, and Hispanics. This was an added incentive to embrace causes with special relevance for these groups: earthquake relief for a stricken Italy, aid to Poland to facilitate its transition to democracy, sanctions against South Africa to put pressure on the apartheid regime, and human rights restrictions on our aid to El Salvador. Like most Americans, my constituents were primarily concerned about conditions at home. But given their ethnic diversity, they also had a special interest in foreign affairs, which dovetailed nicely with my own belief in my responsibility to help relieve suffering and distress abroad.

· 4 ·

AFRICAN ENCOUNTERS

Liberation Struggles, Civil War,
Corruption, and Tyranny

⤳

My first significant involvement in shaping American foreign policy in Africa began in 1976, when I took my first trip to South Africa. By the time I stepped down as chairman of the Subcommittee on Africa in 1981, I had become deeply involved in several major issues on the continent: the struggle against apartheid in South Africa; the liberation struggle in Rhodesia (as Zimbabwe was then called); the effort to deal with corruption in Zaire; the work to end the civil war in Angola; and the fight against tyranny in Ethiopia and Uganda.

As tempted as I was to participate in the bicentennial festivities in Washington and New York on July 4, 1976, I chose instead to go to Pretoria and Johannesburg. I felt that South Africa was where I could most meaningfully affirm the fundamental principle upon which our country was founded: "that all men are created equal, that they are endowed by their Creator with certain unalienable Rights, that among these are Life, Liberty and the pursuit of Happiness." At the time, an indigenous white minority governed South Africa, based on a body of racial laws known by its Afrikaner name, apartheid. Designed to perpetuate white rule, the apartheid system stripped blacks of citizenship in South Africa and arbitrarily assigned them citizenship in remote, impoverished tribal homelands. To live and work in South Africa, blacks needed to obtain a pass from the government. Without one, they could be arrested and deported to their homeland. Even though blacks constituted the great majority of people actually living in South Africa, they were denied the right to vote in elections. Prohibited from residing in white cities and communities, they were forced to live in poor, rundown, segregated townships. The opportunity this trip gave me to see precisely how apartheid deprived the black majority of its most fundamental human rights was the beginning of my deep and continuing involvement with South Africa and the struggle to end apartheid.

In 1979, when Congressman Charles Diggs was convicted of payroll padding and had to resign, I was the most senior member of the Foreign Affairs Committee who did not chair a subcommittee, so I took over his post as chairman of the Subcommittee on Africa. This put me in a position to set the agenda for congressional action on Africa. I could hold hearings, call witnesses, bring up legislation, and question administration representatives. I could also hire additional staff to help carry out these new responsibilities.

My new position significantly increased the amount of time and attention I gave to South Africa. I traveled there several times and held many hearings on the situation in that racist republic and its implications for American foreign policy. I also introduced legislation to impose sanctions on South Africa as a way of demonstrating that the United States was on the side of change rather than the status quo. Even though two years later I left the Subcommittee on Africa to chair the Subcommittee on Asia, I remained actively involved in the ultimately successful effort to pass sanctions legislation against the Pretoria regime.

My interest in South Africa emanated from my belief that apartheid embodied a monumental injustice. It didn't take much imagination for me, as a Jew and a strong supporter of the civil rights movement in our own country, to understand the psychological and political consequences of apartheid for the country's black majority. I couldn't help but notice the similarity between the treatment of blacks in South Africa and the treatment of Jews in Germany in the 1930s. To be sure, South Africa was not systematically killing blacks the way Nazi Germany exterminated the Jews in the 1940s. But the array of discriminatory provisions that relegated blacks to second-class status bore a strong resemblance to the anti-Semitic Nuremberg laws in Nazi Germany before World War II.

The reality of apartheid came across vividly on my first day in South Africa when a black woman who had come to clean my hotel room in Johannesburg addressed me as "Master." The fact that she presumably saw me as her superior simply because of the color of my skin was deeply disturbing. It helped drive home apartheid's moral horror.

As a youngster growing up in Brooklyn, I had been impressed by reports of the anti-apartheid activities of Helen Suzman. A feisty, indefatigable crusader for justice and human rights, Suzman was for many years

*With Helen Suzman,
July 4, 1976, at the US
embassy in South Africa.*

the only white opposition member of the South African Parliament. I first met her during this 1976 trip, at the Independence Day ceremony I attended at the US embassy. A photo of me with this courageous woman was taken that day, and I display it proudly in the library of my home in Virginia. Over the years, Helen and I became very good friends. In the 1980s, as a member of the Board of Trustees of Brandeis University, I arranged for her to receive an honorary degree at the graduation ceremony. As Helen was called to the podium, a small group from the graduating class stood, holding signs protesting the award on the ground that she opposed sanctions against South Africa — a position based on her belief that sanctions would do more to hurt the blacks than to pressure the whites. The several thousand other people present, however, recognized that her staunch opposition to apartheid over thirty years counted for far more than a tactical difference over sanctions. After thirty seconds of stunned silence, the entire audience and the rest of the graduating class rose to their feet to give her a standing ovation.

During my various trips to South Africa, I was deeply impressed by the quality and character of the black leaders I met. This was one reason I believed that if the whites could be persuaded to permit the blacks to fully participate in determining the destiny of their country, there were very good prospects for a successful transition to majority rule. I was amazed by the lack of rancor toward the whites that I found in most blacks I met. Like the Reverend Stephen Kumalo in Alan Paton's great novel *Cry, the*

Beloved Country, "My great fear was that by the time the whites turned to loving the blacks would have turned to hating."

Perhaps surprisingly, I also developed a great deal of sympathy and understanding for the white community in South Africa, whose achievements in building the country were impressive. I could understand, even if I didn't share, their anxieties about what might happen to them if they relinquished power. In the early years, however, I always came away from South Africa wondering why apartheid hadn't already been abolished. Virtually everyone I met in this strikingly beautiful and abundant land said it was an essentially unacceptable system that needed to be eliminated. Eventually I realized that the US embassy was arranging for me to meet a limited spectrum of people, ranging from black activists who favored the immediate abolition of apartheid to *verligte,* or "enlightened," Afrikaners who, while not prepared to abandon the system immediately, nevertheless recognized that it was ultimately unsustainable.

I began to understand that I had never met the so-called *verkrampte,* or hard-line, Afrikaners who constituted the core of support for the apartheid regime. As a result, I was not getting an accurate picture of the political dynamic that perpetuated apartheid. During a trip in summer 1980, I asked our embassy to arrange for me to meet with some rural Afrikaners who were more representative of the political base of the ruling National Party. The embassy arranged for me to stay overnight with a farming family in Warmbaths, about two hours by car from Pretoria. This couple invited some of their Afrikaner neighbors to have dinner with me at their home. They were all lovely people, but the underlying political reality of the country became clear to me during our discussion. They were convinced that the blacks in South Africa were incapable not only of ruling the whites, but of ruling themselves. They pointed to the killing and corruption in Uganda under Idi Amin and in the Central African Republic under Emperor Bokassa, as well as the economic stagnation that characterized most of sub-Saharan Africa.

These otherwise good and decent people had convinced themselves that if apartheid were abolished and majority rule established, chaos and conflict would ensue under a government dominated by blacks. One guest that evening was Fannie Hammer, the member of Parliament from Warmbaths. He was, naturally, a National Party member. It was clear to me that if I wanted to run for Parliament from Warmbaths with any chance of getting elected, I would have to express the views I had heard that evening. I came away understanding much better why apartheid enjoyed strong Afrikaner support.

The next day, I asked my hosts whether there were any Afrikaners in the vicinity who felt differently than they did about apartheid. They directed me to a fellow farmer who lived a few miles away. He was a strikingly handsome man who looked like a combination of Robert Redford and John Lindsay, the telegenic former mayor of New York. I explained why I was there and asked why he felt differently about apartheid than his neighbors. "I think apartheid is bad and has to go," he said. "I'm not a particularly religious man, but I do read the Bible and I think what we're doing is wrong, and I don't want to pass the problem on to my children." That response gave me great hope. I thought that if someone like this white farmer in the middle of rural South Africa could reach such a conclusion, perhaps over time, others might as well.

On a later visit, however, I came up again against Afrikaner intransigence, in the person of P. W. Botha, the president of South Africa. It was one of the most unpleasant encounters I ever had. The embassy hadn't been able to arrange a meeting with Botha for me, but I was traveling with my friend Stephen Shalom, who happened to know a rabbi in South Africa who knew Botha well and was able to set a meeting up. When I arrived at the South African version of the White House, Botha came out of his office to greet me. Dozens of reporters recorded our encounter. As we posed for pictures, I said in jest, "I seem to get more press coverage here than I do at home." He responded — not in a friendly way — "That's why you came, wasn't it?" It was not a good start.

During the meeting, I raised the issue of Nelson Mandela's status. Mandela, the iconic leader of the African National Congress, was serving a life sentence on Robben Island. I asked President Botha if it might be possible, since Mandela had already spent over twenty years in prison, to let him go as a gesture of national reconciliation. Botha replied that he would release Mandela "when the Western powers free that old man imprisoned in Berlin." This was a reference to Rudolf Hess, Hitler's deputy in the Nazi party, who had been sentenced to life imprisonment at the Nuremberg war crime trials after World War II. Stunned, I asked Botha if he was really comparing Nelson Mandela to a convicted Nazi war criminal. That, he answered, was exactly what he had in mind.

Asked how the meeting had gone at a press conference afterward, I replied, "It was like taking a cold shower." Botha hadn't shown the slightest hint of flexibility, and his comparison of Nelson Mandela to Rudolf Hess indicated how distant he was from most outsiders' perception of Mandela and his country. Nevertheless, I was grateful for my exposure to hard-line Afrikaner views. I realized that not having spoken to such people earlier had given me a mistaken impression of South Africa's political reality. That evening in Warmbaths and my meeting with President Botha helped me understand that the majority of white South Africans, particularly the Afrikaners, were determined to hold on to apartheid.

While there was little support for apartheid in the United States, in the late 1970s there wasn't much support for doing anything meaningful about it, even under Jimmy Carter, a big proponent of human rights. The Carter administration was, of course, rhetorically critical of the human rights situation in South Africa. But if it talked the talk, it didn't walk the walk. Nor were most of my own constituents particularly interested in the struggle against apartheid. I'm sure most were against racial separatism, but it wasn't their first or even fiftieth priority. Involvement in the anti-apartheid struggle wouldn't bring me any political benefit in Brooklyn. This became abundantly clear when I was invited to address a black church in Coney Island. If there was any place I might expect to get some political mileage out of my efforts to end apartheid, surely this was it. So I devoted my entire talk to the struggle against apartheid and what I was doing in Washington to advance it. As I left the church, accompanied by one of the deacons, he remarked: "Congressman, what you said about South Africa was very interesting, but I think most of the people here are much more concerned about what's going on in Coney Island. Next time you come, perhaps you should talk about that."

After the Reagan administration came into office in 1981, there was an overhaul of our policy toward South Africa. It was led by Reagan's assistant secretary of state for Africa, Chester Crocker, an experienced Africa hand. He espoused a policy of "constructive engagement," based on the belief that the key to change in South Africa, as well as southern Africa as a whole—where conflicts were ongoing in Angola, Namibia, and Mo-

zambique — lay with the South African government. Given the white monopoly on power, the only way to eventually abolish apartheid and achieve
regional peace, Crocker argued, was to establish a more cooperative relationship with the South African government. Such an approach would
give us more influence with the Pretoria regime and a better chance to encourage change. If the Carter administration wouldn't walk the walk, the
Reagan administration was unwilling to even talk the talk. Like the members of the anti-apartheid movement in the United States, I felt strongly
that constructive engagement not only wouldn't give us the leverage we
were seeking but would have the perverse effect of creating the impression
among South Africa's black majority, as well as in the rest of black Africa,
that we were sympathetic to the apartheid regime and quite comfortable
having it remain in power indefinitely.

In July 1980, I got a close-up view of the black world created by apartheid
when I arranged to spend a night in Soweto, the most populous black township in the country, at the home of Leonard Masala, a community leader.
Technically, it was illegal for white people to spend the night in Soweto. But
I wanted to get a feel for what life was like for the majority of South Africans and so blithely ignored the restriction. When I got up in the morning,
I saw a dense haze in the sky and concluded that it was a cloudy day. But I
soon realized that the haze was caused by the outdoor breakfast-cooking
fires that people were forced to use because none of them had electricity in
their homes. It wasn't until I left Soweto later that morning that I discovered the day was actually bright and sunny. Just outside the township, I noticed a huge power plant. It could have provided electricity to Soweto, but
all the power it generated was for Johannesburg, where only whites were
permitted to live. The black people of Soweto were, in effect, deprived of
something as fundamental as sunshine by the policy of apartheid. It was a
powerful metaphor for the inequities of systematic racial repression.

I was picked up that morning by a young black man who worked for
our consulate in Johannesburg. We got into a conversation, and he told me
he wanted to go to college in the United States but couldn't afford it. "Why
don't you establish a program to help people like me get a higher education
in America?" he suggested. I thought it was a terrific idea. In all my trips
to South Africa, it was the only genuinely creative policy suggestion I ever
heard from anybody associated with the US mission there.

I asked everyone I met, from *verligte* Afrikaners to black activists, what they thought of this idea. Everyone applauded it. They knew that the white universities in South Africa accepted very few blacks, while the black colleges were vastly under-resourced and their graduates spurned by employers. All my interlocutors understood that whether you supported apartheid or abhorred it, whether you thought it would be there forever or would be swept into the trash heap of history, the country had to have a significant number of educated blacks to be economically viable. I left feeling that establishing such a program would not only help prepare South Africa for the future but also generate a residue of goodwill for the United States.

Ready to push the idea on my return, I met with Chet Crocker and told him that such a scholarship program was very much in line with his policy of constructive engagement. Because the program would cost money, I thought it would have a much better chance of being adopted if the administration supported it, and I encouraged him to embrace it as an administration initiative. To my surprise and chagrin, he not only opposed the idea but fought it every step of the way. He argued that instead of bringing South African blacks to the United States, we should provide a comparable amount of money for black higher education in South Africa. I objected that this would not only strengthen the existing apartheid system of higher education but constitute an implicit and unacceptable endorsement of it.

Despite the administration's opposition, I was able to get my proposal adopted in the House as an amendment to the foreign aid bill, with a $10 million authorization to provide 100 scholarships over the next two years. The measure then went to a conference committee. Determined to throttle the baby in its legislative crib, Crocker persuaded the Republicans on the committee to oppose it. Even though all the Democrats supported it, the Republicans had a majority of one, so at least one Republican vote was needed for adoption. I contacted the Reverend Jesse Jackson, whose political base was in Chicago, and asked him to urge Senator Charles Percy of Illinois, chairman of the Senate Foreign Relations committee and one of the conferees, to support the House position. The strategy worked. Percy accepted the House version of the bill, and his vote created a majority for the scholarship program, paving the way for it to become law.

About a year later, Lawrence Eagleburger, then deputy secretary of

*With Desmond Tutu at his house in South Africa
during the 1980s. Nina is at right.* The Weekly Mail.

state, gave a speech on the Reagan administration's policy toward South
Africa, in which he cited the scholarship program as the jewel in the crown
of constructive engagement. I called Eagleburger and told him that the
program he was praising had been initiated by Congress and fought bit-
terly by the administration. "I don't mind that you didn't give me credit," I
said, "but how can you claim credit for a program the administration tried
to scuttle?" Eagleburger had no answer except to apologize for a speech
someone else had written for him.

Many years later, Princeton Lyman, who had been our ambassador to
South Africa, told me there had been a dinner in Johannesburg to celebrate the program's tenth anniversary. Bishop Desmond Tutu (future
Nobel Peace Prize laureate) had been named head of the committee to
select the scholarship recipients and presided over the affair. By the time
the program ended in 2001, nearly 1,700 students had received an education in the United States in such fields as education, business law, health
administration, and engineering. Almost all returned to South Africa,
and many today play important roles in the country's economic and social development.

I was able to provide an educational benefit for one other black South African. In the mid-1980s, I received a call from Benjamin Pogrund, the deputy editor of the *Rand Daily Mail*, the leading anti-apartheid newspaper in South Africa. A wise and gentle man, Ben was one of the most thoughtful and intelligent critics of apartheid I had gotten to know during my visits. He was also one of the few people permitted to visit Nelson Mandela in prison. Ben told me that he had just met with Mandela at Pollsmoor Prison, where he had been moved from Robben Island, and that Mandela had asked if Ben could possibly arrange for his daughter Makaziwe to get a college education in the United States. Since Mandela obviously had no money, Ben said, Makaziwe would need a full scholarship including tuition, room, and board. Was there anything I could do? I promptly called Joe Duffey, chancellor of the University of Massachusetts, whom I had met in 1968, before his unsuccessful campaign to become a US Senator from Connecticut. I described Mandela's request, and without a moment's hesitation Joe told me to consider it done. Altogether I secured scholarship offers from four American universities for Ms. Mandela, but the University of Massachusetts at Amherst was where she chose to enroll. After receiving master's and doctoral degrees in social work, she returned to South Africa.

Meanwhile, I was still working to pressure South Africa's leadership to abolish apartheid. In 1980 I introduced legislation that would have required American firms to comply with the Sullivan Principles. These principles had been promulgated by the Reverend Leon Sullivan, a civil rights activist who presided over the Zion Baptist church in Philadelphia and was known as "the Lion of Zion." They consisted of voluntary equal opportunity employment guidelines that American corporations operating in South Africa were encouraged to embrace. Unfortunately, most US companies doing business there didn't adhere to them.

My legislation also included a prohibition on loans to the South African government, as well as a ban on the sale in the United States of Krugerrands, gold coins minted in South Africa. Before including this provision, I consulted Cyril Ramaphosa, the leader of the black National Union of Mineworkers, during a trip to South Africa. Since such a ban could have potentially adverse economic consequences for the thousands of mineworkers Ramaphosa represented, I wanted his views on its advis-

ability. He made it clear that exerting pressure on the South African government to abandon apartheid was essential, even if this meant that some
of his union's members would lose their jobs, so I resolved to include the
prohibition.

Over the next few years, even though my subcommittee approved the
legislation, it languished without any strong support in the House as a
whole. Then in 1984, a black revolt burgeoned in Soweto and other black
townships, and American television showed scenes reminiscent of the
brutal repression of the civil rights movement in Birmingham, Alabama,
in the 1960s. Congress began to feel the pressure of public support for
strong action against South Africa, supplemented by a growing backlash
against the policy of constructive engagement, which made us seem to be
embracing a regime that was killing peaceful protesters in the streets. At
the same time, the Free South Africa Movement began a highly visible
campaign of civil disobedience at South Africa's embassy and consulates
around the United States.

Though I was no longer chair of the Subcommittee on Africa, I worked
with Howard Wolpe, who had succeeded me as chairman; Bill Gray, the
Democratic House whip; and a few other members, including Stuart Mc-
Kinney, a Republican from Connecticut, and Ron Dellums, a Democrat
from California, to put together a comprehensive sanctions bill. It contained all the provisions of the bill I had introduced a few years earlier as
well as some additional measures, including a prohibition on all new American investment in South Africa. When the bill came up for a vote on the
House floor in 1986, Ron Dellums put forward an amendment to prohibit
virtually all trade with South Africa, except for importation of strategic
minerals unavailable elsewhere and exportation of medical substances and
supplies. It also would have required American firms doing business there
to divest themselves of whatever assets they owned in South Africa.

During the debate on the Dellums amendment, Howard Wolpe, Bill
Gray, and I huddled at the back of the chamber, trying to figure out
how to vote on it. We were sympathetic to Dellums's attempt to maximize American pressure on South Africa and so were inclined to support
his amendment on the merits. But tactically we were concerned that its
adoption would jeopardize final passage of the bill. A prohibition on new
investment was one thing. A divestment requirement was quite another

and would be sure to arouse intense opposition from the business community. But before we could decide what to do, the Dellums amendment was put to a voice vote by the presiding officer, and the Speaker ruled that the ayes—who had clearly out-shouted the nays among the handful of members present—had it. We were stunned when Mark Siljander, the ranking Republican on the Subcommittee on Africa, who was managing the bill for the Republicans, failed to ask for a recorded vote (in which almost all 435 members of the House vote). Such a vote probably would have resulted in the defeat of the amendment, since most of the Republicans and the more conservative Democrats opposed it. We were thus overtaken by events, and the amendment was included in the final bill.

Siljander had made a major tactical blunder. The bill including the Dellums amendment was approved and sent to the Senate where, with the support of Senators Richard Lugar and Ted Kennedy, a sanctions bill very close to the original House bill was adopted. Compared to the House bill as amended by Dellums, the Senate bill looked much more moderate, which made it a lot easier for senators to support. When Senator Lugar, who then chaired the Foreign Relations Committee, insisted that the House accept the version of the legislation adopted by the Senate, the House agreed, and the legislation passed.

There was now one more hurdle to overcome. President Reagan, acting on Chet Crocker's advice, remained adamantly opposed to sanctions and decided to veto the legislation. From their perspective, the adoption of sanctions constituted a decisive repudiation of constructive engagement and would diminish rather than enhance our ability to bring about change in South Africa. But the pressure to take a strong stand against apartheid had reached unprecedented proportions. To a substantial majority in Congress, constructive engagement had not only failed to persuade the Afrikaner regime to repudiate apartheid, it had also alienated the black majority in South Africa—as well as much of the rest of the world. For the first time since 1973, Congress voted to override a presidential veto on a foreign policy issue. Since the Republicans controlled the Senate, this was an exceptional achievement that reflected broad public support for a much stronger American policy toward South Africa.

A few years later, South African President F. W. de Klerk entered into negotiations with Mandela and the African National Congress and agreed

*Meeting Nelson Mandela, one week after his release
from prison. Congressman Ron Dellums is at center.*

to abolish apartheid and establish majority rule. The peaceful transition in
South Africa was one of the great political miracles of our time. Few had
anticipated that the end of apartheid could be brought about so quickly
and with so little bloodshed. There was little doubt that sanctions played
a significant role in persuading the white regime that the future of their
country depended on adopting a new and genuinely democratic political
dispensation. But much of the credit belonged to Nelson Mandela, who
was so remarkably free of the rancor one would have expected in a man
who had been incarcerated for over a quarter of a century, and to de Klerk,
Botha's successor as president, who was wise enough to realize that the
whites would have a better future in a South Africa governed by the principles of majority rule and minority rights than in a country characterized
by racial repression at home and increasing isolation abroad.

As mentioned in chapter 1, I met Mandela a week after he was released from prison in 1990. Several years later, after he had capped his extraordinary life by being elected president of South Africa, I met him again quite by accident in the lobby of the Royal Guest Palace in Riyadh, Saudi Arabia, where we were both staying. "What are you doing here, Mr. President?" I asked.

"I'm on vacation," he replied.

"You must be the first person in history," I said, "who went to Riyadh on vacation."

"I came here because it's one of the few places where I can get some privacy," he responded. Perhaps because he remembered what I had done for his daughter, or the role I played in the anti-apartheid movement, he was kind enough to invite me to his suite, where we spent about an hour talking about the situation in South Africa.

While the struggle against apartheid was unfolding in South Africa, the struggle for liberation continued in white-ruled Rhodesia. During my initial trip to southern Africa I went to Mozambique, where I met Johnnie Carson — not the entertainer, but the US deputy chief of mission there (the second highest post in the US embassy). He and I arranged to see Robert Mugabe, who had recently been released from prison in Rhodesia, where he had been incarcerated for over a decade for his involvement in the rebellion against the white regime. We flew by chartered plane to the town of Quelimane on the northeast coast of Mozambique, where Mugabe was staying under the protection of the Mozambique government. He had become the leader of the Zimbabwe African National Union (ZANU), one of two guerrilla groups struggling to bring an end to white rule in Rhodesia. Mugabe is now internationally infamous for having brought Zimbabwe to the brink of ruin, but he was then little known outside his own country. I believe we were the first Americans Mugabe ever met. I found him impressive. He had gotten several degrees through correspondence courses while in prison. He spoke eloquently about the need for democracy and racial reconciliation once minority rule in Rhodesia had been eliminated. There was no sign, in that first of several meetings we had over the next few years, of the brutish dictator he later became.

Meanwhile, I was so impressed with Johnnie Carson that in 1979, when I became chairman of the Subcommittee on Africa, I asked him to become its staff director. He took a leave from his job at the State Department, and over the next two years we worked closely and constructively together to advance American interests in Africa. After his tour of duty on the Hill, Carson returned to the State Department and went on to serve as our ambassador to Zimbabwe, Kenya, and Uganda and then as assistant secretary of state for Africa.

During a subsequent trip to southern Africa, I met Joshua Nkomo, the leader of the Zimbabwe African People's Union (ZAPU), the other Rhodesian liberation movement, at a ZAPU guerrilla training camp in Zambia. Nkomo, a genial 300-pound giant of a man, asked if I would like to meet his people. Sure, I said, and he blew a whistle. Over the next ten minutes hundreds of trainees, most without shoes, came running to the assembly ground. It sounded like a stampede of cattle on a Hollywood soundtrack. They lined up, and Nkomo handed me a bullhorn and asked me to talk to them. I asked what I should say, and he answered, "Say Z." I did, and the crowd shouted "Z!" back. He then told me to say "I." We continued in this way — with me feeling more and more like a cheerleader at a football game at Midwood High School — until they all roared, "Zimbabwe!" Being a politician, I did manage to get in a few words about how I hoped the day would come when all the people of Zimbabwe would be able to determine their own destiny.

In 1979, Nkomo and Mugabe combined their respective movements (ZANU and ZAPU) in a common Patriotic Front, which continued the liberation struggle against the white-dominated regime. That same year they came to Washington to muster support for their movement. On an impulse, I invited them to lunch at my home, then hurriedly called Nina to tell her they were coming with twenty people from their official party. The only thing Nina had enough of in the house was tuna fish, so she made lots of it. After the meal, Nkomo pulled her aside and told her how much he appreciated her recognition that he was a vegetarian!

My major contribution to Rhodesia's transition from minority to majority rule came in the aftermath of the "internal settlement," in which Ian Smith, the white prime minister, reached an agreement with Bishop Abel Muzorewa, a black Protestant minister who was considered much more moderate than either Mugabe or Nkomo. The agreement renamed the country Rhodesia-Zimbabwe and provided for the establishment of a new

*Robert Mugabe (left)
and Joshua Nkomo (right)
at my home in Virginia
in 1979 after the tuna fish
lunch.*

government, with blacks entitled to vote for the first time since Smith's unilateral declaration of independence from Great Britain in the 1960s. But the Patriotic Front, which enjoyed the sympathy and support of most of the blacks, was excluded from participation. Since it was not on the ballot, Muzorewa was elected prime minister. Because the Patriotic Front did not recognize the "internal settlement," the fighting continued.

The election generated tremendous pressure in Congress to lift the existing economic sanctions against Rhodesia-Zimbabwe. This pressure came from conservatives such as Senator Jesse Helms of North Carolina. He argued that we had imposed the sanctions because of Rhodesia's unilateral declaration of independence from Great Britain and the establishment of white rule over a decade earlier. Now that a black prime minister had been elected with blacks participating in the election, maintaining sanctions was no longer justified. This argument was not totally devoid of merit, but accepting it would have been counterproductive.

Shortly after the internal settlement elections, President Carter called a meeting at the White House, to which he invited those of us in Congress who had supported sanctions, to decide what to do. Together with my colleagues Bill Gray and Cardiss Collins, a Democrat from Illinois, I argued strongly that it would be a mistake to recognize the result of the election, on the grounds that most Rhodesian blacks identified with the Patriotic Front, and that excluding the liberation movement from the election made the result inherently illegitimate. In our view, Bishop Muzorewa's government also lacked legitimacy among the black majority because it had not been part of the liberation struggle.

President Carter accepted our advice and indicated that his administration would not recognize the new government. But there was still considerable pressure in Congress to lift sanctions. I was able to negotiate an agreement with Paul Findley, a Republican congressman from Illinois and a senior member of the Foreign Affairs Committee, to introduce legislation that would preserve sanctions for a few months, in order to give the British time to make a last-ditch effort to facilitate a settlement between the Muzorewa-Smith regime and the Patriotic Front. It was hoped that such an agreement would lead to an end to the fighting and to new elections in which all the political parties, including the Patriotic Front, would participate.

While the negotiations were going on, the sanctions legislation I had introduced with Congressman Findley was brought up before the Foreign Affairs Committee. I argued that lifting the sanctions now would doom any chance for a political settlement, because Muzorewa and Smith would have no incentive to make the necessary concessions. If the negotiations failed, the fighting would inevitably continue and the rest of black Africa would continue to support the Patriotic Front. It would not be in our interest for virtually every African country to see us as propping up what to them was an illegitimate regime whose black façade masked the reality of continued white domination.

Most members seemed to feel that if a liberal Democrat like me and a conservative Republican like Findley agreed on what to do about sanctions, our proposal was probably a reasonable compromise between those who wanted to abolish sanctions immediately and those who wanted to maintain them indefinitely. Our legislation was adopted unanimously by the committee. It then went to the floor, where we were able to defeat an amendment to eliminate sanctions forthwith, put forth by conservatives who hadn't bought into our compromise. The fact that the Foreign Affairs Committee had adopted the bill unanimously gave it a legitimacy its opponents couldn't overcome, and it passed.

The importance of this vote cannot be exaggerated. The Senate had already voted to lift sanctions, and the administration would have been under irresistible pressure to do so if the House had gone along. Holding the line on sanctions made it possible for Lord Carrington, the British Foreign Secretary, to bring the negotiations to a successful conclusion, thus ending the war and making possible a new election in which the Patriotic Front participated. The result was the election of a Patriotic Front government with Mugabe as prime minister.

I was invited to be part of the American delegation to the independence ceremonies in Zimbabwe. The delegation was co-chaired by Andrew Young, US ambassador to the United Nations, and Averell Harriman, a former New York governor and one of the grand old men of the Democratic Party. On the Air Force plane to Zimbabwe, Harriman, whose longevity made him a walking history book, regaled us with stories about negotiating railroad concessions in the Soviet Union with Leon Trotsky in the 1920s.

During a reception before the independence ceremony, I had a long discussion with Lord Carrington about the Soviet invasion of Afghanistan. President Carter had called for an international boycott of the Moscow Olympics as a way of putting pressure on Moscow to withdraw its troops, but the chairman of the British Olympic Committee had rejected this proposal. I asked Lord Carrington, a charming man with a great sense of humor, if there was anything he could do to get Britain to support the boycott. He asked me if I had ever met the Olympic committee chairman, who would make the decision to participate in the Olympics or not. I hadn't. "Well," Lord Carrington said, "he's made of cement from the tip of his toes to the top of his head." In other words, immovable.

At the ceremony in a sports stadium in Harare, the British, known for their ceremonial splendor — and with lots of practice conducting independence ceremonies in the twilight of their empire — put on a marvelous show. Prince Charles, in military uniform, entered in a Rolls Royce convertible, preceded by a dozen lancers on white horses and followed by a dozen more, all circumnavigating the stadium. The Union Jack was lowered, to the mournful sound of bagpipes, and the flag of Zimbabwe raised. But in a harbinger of things to come, the celebration was marred by disorder and violence, with the police firing tear gas to disperse a raucous crowd.

Immediately after independence, Mugabe made several speeches in which he sounded like an African Abraham Lincoln, extending the hand of reconciliation to the white community. Over time, sadly enough, like so many others Mugabe was corrupted by the privileges and perquisites of power. Though he started out as a liberator, he ended up as a tyrant who massively abused his people's human rights and adopted policies that ruined his country's economy.

I have no regrets over having facilitated an end to the liberation struggle and the establishment of genuine majority rule. The alternative — a continuation of the armed struggle, with the United States at odds with the rest of Africa — would have been unacceptable. But I deeply regret the subsequent political, social, and economic tragedy inflicted on Zimbabwe by Mugabe's emergence as a tyrant far more interested in preserving his power and enriching his cronies than in benefiting his people.

If attempting to bring an end to apartheid in South Africa and colonialism in Rhodesia was uplifting, the effort to deal with corruption in Zaire was depressing. On my first visit there in the early 1970s, I discovered one example of that country's massive corruption. To be sure, uncovering corruption in Zaire was the equivalent of discovering that water flowed in the Congo River. The country's long-time dictator, President Mobutu Sese Seko, who had seized power in a 1965 coup, had become a billionaire by siphoning off much of his country's mineral wealth into his own pocket. In this particular case, I found that the government was taking rice that the United States provided to Zaire's people under the PL 480 Title I food aid program and sending it across the river into the Congo's Brazzaville, where it sold for ten times the price it brought in Zaire. PL 480 included Title I and Title II programs. Title II was free food; Title I food was supposed to be sold, with the proceeds being used to pay the United States back in local currency. Instead, the proceeds lined Mobutu's pockets, helping pay the upkeep on his many mansions and palaces.

On returning to Washington, I offered an amendment to eliminate the Title I rice program. I thought it would be easily adopted. To win House approval, I left all the other commodities in the Title I program alone. I was so convinced my amendment would pass overwhelmingly that I didn't bother to do any preliminary lobbying. How could anybody support such a corrupt program? To my amazement, the amendment was soundly defeated. This was my introduction to the power of the agricultural lobby. As the representative of an urban district, I had never known much about its existence. But the defeat of my amendment taught me a real lesson about the clout of the agricultural interests. Each commodity producer — of rice, wheat, corn, sugar, or cotton — supported the others. So when the rice program was threatened, all the congressmen who had other commodity producers in their districts opposed the amendment and defeated it.

The rice program survived for another two years until the Carter administration eliminated it, for the same reason I originally opposed it. But — somewhat like a latter-day Don Quixote, perhaps — I myself decided to do something about the massive corruption in Zaire. The looting of the country by Mobutu's hopelessly corrupt government had produced a standard of living that was, if anything, below the impoverished levels of the colonial era, and I became heavily involved in the effort to try to bring about change in Zaire by pressing Mobutu to make essential political and economic reforms. I consider the fact that he was still in power when I left Congress in 1992 to be one of my major failures.

I met Mobutu for the first time in my congressional office in 1978. Later I learned that he had paid $600,000 to a lobbyist whose main task was to neutralize me. That amount was small change for him. Over a quarter of a century he stole several billion dollars from the national treasury and acquired a sixteenth-century castle in Spanish Valencia, a thirty-two-room palace in Switzerland, an apartment in Paris worth at least a million dollars, and luxurious estates in Portugal and Italy, among other trophies. He made the famously greedy Ferdinand and Imelda Marcos look like penny pinchers. Certainly he had a much richer country to plunder. Zaire, the former Belgian Congo, is the second largest country in sub-Saharan Africa and the third most populous. It is spectacularly endowed with minerals, including copper, cobalt, diamonds, and tantalum.

After a brief period of economic and political stability in the early 1970s, bolstered by commodity prices, copper prices in Zaire plunged and Mobutu's economy tanked. At this point, what kept him in power (other than his North Korean– and Israeli-trained security forces) was the prospect of what would happen to giant, strategic Zaire without him. Mobutu survived by shrewdly playing the Cold War game. He became a key CIA "asset," receiving agency support under such covert operations as Project WIZARD and Project WIANCHOR and doing the CIA's bidding as a "pro-Western, anti-Communist force." He dispatched troops to Chad to pro-

*With Mobutu Sese Seko
in Washington, 1979.*

vide cover for joint French and American intervention against Libya. He aided an American-supported insurgency in Angola. He was the first African leader to resume relations with Israel after the 1973 war, an action that won him influential friends in Washington. Meanwhile, the Carter, Reagan, and Bush administrations all provided some military and economic assistance to Zaire, and the CIA helped Mobutu build his personal wealth and political influence. A 1990 State Department intelligence analysis found that Mobutu was draining off as much as 30 percent of government revenues for his personal use.

During a congressional hearing in 1990, I compared Mobutu to Nicolae Ceausescu of Romania, Erich Honecker of East Germany, the Marcoses in the Philippines, and Anastasio Somoza of Nicaragua. I warned that, sooner or later, Mobutu would go. And when that time came, it would not be in our interest to be perceived by the people of Zaire as having propped up this greedy dictator. Those who resisted efforts to pressure Mobutu to reform argued that he was the one force that held the country together. Unfortunately, their prediction of *après Mobutu, le déluge* turned out to be accurate. After Mobutu was forced from power and went into exile in Togo in 1997, Zaire was racked by foreign invasions and civil wars and descended into a Hobbesian maelstrom of death and devastation. Millions lost their lives, and the economy deteriorated even further.

There was, however, a lighter side to some of my trips to Zaire. On one occasion, I met with the Catholic cardinal of Zaire, who, somewhat to my surprise, was very supportive of Mobutu. Usually the Catholic cardinals I met who lived under repressive regimes were quite critical of the government's human rights abuses. When I raised this question with Maurice Tempelsman, an American businessman who had extensive investments in Zaire and knew Mobutu well, he explained that the cardinal had fathered nineteen children and was concerned that Mobutu might reveal this if he criticized him.

On my last trip to Zaire in December 1991, I told my staffer Eric Schwartz, who was handling the logistics, that I wanted to see the gorillas while I was there. Eric knew I always wanted to meet with the opposition leaders of whatever country I was visiting, so he naturally assumed I meant the leaders of the guerrilla movement. But he didn't know of any guerrilla movements in Zaire (there were none at that time) and was too embarrassed to ask what I meant. So he asked other people if they were aware of a guerrilla group in Zaire. No one was. Of course, I was talking about the real gorillas! Once we straightened that out, we made plans to hike for several hours deep into the jungle, where we crossed paths with a group of razorback gorillas munching on bananas about ten feet away from us. They looked up but then returned to enjoying their meal, ignoring us. I was pleased to get my wish on what was for me an unusual diversion (I suppose Eric's misapprehension reflected the fact that generally on my trips abroad, I was all business).

Other species of guerrillas roamed the halls of Congress, and some found sustenance there. Among the most memorable and successful was the Angolan rebel leader Jonas Savimbi, a hulk of a man with a bushy beard who made his rounds wearing olive-green military fatigues and a red beret. Savimbi became the darling of Washington conservatives because of his battles against the Marxist government of Angola, which was supplied with weapons by the Soviet Union, Cuba, and the Nicaraguan Sandinistas. To conservatives, Savimbi became the embodiment of an aggressive foreign-policy crusade not just to contain Communism but to "roll it back." During a 1986 visit, Savimbi was invited to the White House, where President Reagan proclaimed that his group, UNITA, the National Union for the Total Independence of Angola, was winning a victory "that electrifies the world." Savimbi also had backing from such influential conservative groups as the Heritage Foundation. Some of his US supporters visited him in his clandestine jungle camp in Jamba.

My interest in Angola went back to my years at Brandeis, when I edited the student newspaper. My first editorial for *The Justice* criticized the United States for voting with Portugal at the UN against a resolution calling for the independence of Angola, which was a Portuguese colony at the time. By the 1980s, of course, Angola was independent and the situation was vastly different, but once again I found myself disagreeing with the administration. Despite all his skillful public relations and support in Washington, I thought Savimbi was a charlatan. He had started out getting most of his aid from Communist China by espousing quasi-Marxist ideas—and then adroitly switched sides, proclaiming himself an anti-Communist. So I opposed efforts by the Reagan and Bush administrations to give him aid.

Throughout my congressional career, I never traded my vote on unrelated issues important to my colleagues for their votes on unrelated issues important to me. However, it happened once that my vote on an issue that a colleague considered critical enabled me later to secure his support on an issue that was critical to me. In this case, I was trying to pass legislation on Angola. I had previously been approached by Congressman Ralph Hall of Texas about a bill that was coming up before the Merchant Marine and Fisheries Committee, on which I served. The bill would have declared 75,000 acres in Ralph's district, where there was some kind of hunting club, as national wetlands. He pleaded with me to vote against the bill because his constituents cared a great deal about hunting, and the bill would have prevented the members of the hunting club from hunting on this land. Ordinarily I voted a straight environmental line, and I would have voted for this bill without thinking twice about it, but he made a heartfelt plea, and since the bill was not likely to be on the voting records kept by any environmental groups, I agreed to vote against it without asking for any quid pro quo.

Some time later, when a bill came up on the floor late one evening authorizing aid to UNITA, I proposed an amendment stating that the United States would cease military aid to UNITA if the Soviet Union refrained from providing military assistance to the Communist-dominated Angolan government, and if Angola committed to holding free and fair elections. As the roll call proceeded, my amendment was down by two votes. I saw Ralph on the House floor and reminded him how I had voted on his hunting club issue. "I really need this one, and your vote can make the difference," I told him. Ralph responded that if he switched his vote it would be a tie, and I would still lose because a majority was required to pass an amendment. But I told him that the Speaker, who by tradition rarely voted unless there was a tie, had agreed to support my amendment if his vote was needed. So Ralph reluctantly switched his vote. At this point, I heard later, the Speaker's staff woke him up from a nap he was taking in his office, and he somewhat grumpily came to the chamber to cast the tie-breaking vote for my amendment.

In 1992, after an agreement between UNITA and the Angolan government, the government did hold a seemingly free and fair election. Savimbi lost, and US assistance ceased. At the same time, the Cold War that had fueled the US-Soviet competition ended, taking Savimbi's leverage with it. Unwilling to accept his electoral defeat, Savimbi went back into the bush and resumed his war against the Luanda regime. He died in 2002 in a military clash with Angolan troops, and the conflict eventually petered out.

I also became actively involved in issues in Ethiopia and Uganda. After Haile Selassie, Ethiopia's longtime emperor, was assassinated in 1975, the new government of Mengistu Haile Mariam launched an extensive campaign of repression known as the "red terror." I successfully offered an amendment to the foreign aid bill cutting off military assistance to that country. Many years later, the Ethiopian driver of a Washington taxi recognized me and refused to accept payment as a way of expressing his gratitude for what I had done to support human rights in Ethiopia.

In the case of Uganda, I strongly supported the successful effort to impose sanctions against that country in response to the massive depredations and killings by Idi Amin, who was responsible for the deaths of tens of thousands of his own people. (As a congressman, Ed Koch once inserted an article in the *Congressional Record* titled "Idi, Short for Idiot.")

The sanctions didn't succeed in bringing Amin down. But shortly afterward, Tanzania invaded Uganda and forced Amin into exile. Initially I applauded this move. But Milton Obote, the ruler installed in Amin's place, turned out to be even more bloodthirsty than Amin. It was a cautionary reminder that the road to hell is sometimes paved with good intentions. Still, to have remained silent in the face of such depredations would have been morally unacceptable.

In both Ethiopia and Uganda, I thought it important to demonstrate that the United States was just as opposed to the repression of blacks by blacks in East Africa as it was to the oppression of blacks by whites in southern Africa. Unfortunately, the overthrow of Mobutu in Zaire, Amin in Uganda, and Mengistu in Ethiopia didn't lead to lasting or fundamental improvements in human rights in these countries, since their replacements were almost as bad, or worse, than they were.

There were other tyrants in Africa. One of the worst was Jean-Bedel Bokassa, president of the Central African Republic, who in December 1976 declared that from then on the country would be known as the Central African Empire. He had himself crowned emperor in a coronation ceremony that cost $20 million. I never visited that country, but one evening in the 1980s I found myself seated at a Washington dinner party next to a former American ambassador to Bokassa's fiefdom. I asked if there was any truth to the rumor that the emperor was a cannibal. "All I can tell you," the ambassador said, "is that every Sunday Bokassa had a dinner at his house for the members of his cabinet and a few foreign guests. One time, as they were passing the serving dishes around the table, the minister sitting next to me leaned over and whispered in my ear, 'Don't eat the veal.' You can draw your own conclusions."

All in all, my African encounters were among the most challenging and satisfying of my years in Congress. I learned a lot about a continent that had been too long neglected by Americans and met many impressive figures. Even more, my involvements there gave me an opportunity to influence US foreign policy on a range of issues with deep moral significance.

5

INDOCHINA

Bringing Peace to Cambodia,
Protecting Vietnamese "Boat People"

In the 1980 congressional election, Lester Wolff, who had chaired the Sub-committee on Asian and Pacific Affairs, was defeated, putting me in position under the seniority system to claim his spot. I decided to take it, even though this meant relinquishing the chairmanship of the Subcommittee on Africa. The decision wasn't easy, since I had gotten deeply involved in African issues. But I reluctantly concluded that both strategically and geopolitically, the issues we confronted in Asia were far more important to the United States. Chairing the Asia Subcommittee offered the opportunity to influence our policy on a number of them: what to do about Cambodia, which Vietnam had invaded in 1978; the struggles for human rights and democracy in the Philippines, South Korea, and Taiwan; continuing economic and military problems in our relationship with Japan; problems and possibilities generated by the normalization of our relationship with China; an incipient nuclear arms race between India and Pakistan; and the Soviet occupation of Afghanistan. These were among the most significant foreign policy challenges facing our country.

From a strategic perspective, Cambodia was not the most important of these issues, but it was the one on which I spent the most time and arguably had the greatest impact. While the Vietnam War raged, Hanoi and Saigon had consumed America's attention. Not much concern was directed toward Cambodia, whose place in the region was aptly expressed by the title of the journalist William Shawcross's book *Sideshow: Kissinger, Nixon, and the Destruction of Cambodia*. Eager to put the war in Indochina behind them, the American people had taken insufficient notice of the 1975–79 effort by the maniacal Cambodian Communists, known as the Khmer Rouge, to take the country back to "year zero" by destroying Cambodia's culture and traditions and executing all its non-Communist intellectuals. By the time they were driven from power by Vietnam in January

1979, perhaps as many as two million Cambodians, about 20 percent of the population, had been murdered or had died of sickness and starvation due to the autarchic policies imposed by the Khmer Rouge regime. After their victory, the Vietnamese installed some former Khmer Rouge cadres who had defected from the movement as the leaders of a puppet government in Phnom Penh, known as the People's Republic of Kampuchea (PRK).

I went to Southeast Asia for the first time in August 1975, several months after the establishment of Khmer Rouge rule over all of Cambodia. I arranged to visit Aranyaprathet, a border town in eastern Thailand, where a few thousand Cambodian refugees who had managed to escape were being kept by the Thai government. Charlie Twining, an American Foreign Service officer in Bangkok, accompanied me. Charlie had originally been scheduled to go to Cambodia as a political officer. He had undergone ten months of Khmer language training, but a couple of months before he completed his course, Phnom Penh fell to the Khmer Rouge and all foreigners were compelled to leave the country. He was reassigned to the US embassy in Bangkok as our Cambodia watcher, monitoring the Khmer Rouge radio broadcasts and interviewing refugees. But not much could be learned about the fate of the Cambodian people, who had become the victims of an Asian Auschwitz, in a country completely cut off from the outside world.

In Aranyaprathet, Charlie and I heard incredible stories: for instance, the Khmer Rouge were killing anyone they could find who wore eyeglasses, because that indicated they knew how to read. One of the Khmer Rouge's diabolical objectives was to eliminate all influence of the previous regime and all traces of the country's centuries-old civilization. For the first time, I began to appreciate the enormity of the evil that had descended on Cambodia. It generated a very strong feeling in me that somehow, some way, something had to be done.

My view of what that response should be was deeply influenced by my reactions both to the US failure to do more to rescue European Jewry from the growing Nazi threat in the 1930s and to the counterproductive consequences of our military involvement in Vietnam in the 1960s. The first demonstrated the consequences of indifference; the second, the limits of intervention. Together they underscored the imperative to prevent moral horrors within the framework of what was realistically possible. As the world awakened to what had befallen Cambodia, several books came out, including *Cambodia Year Zero*, by François Ponchaud, a French priest, who described what was happening there as "auto-genocide," the murder of a people by their own people. But just as the world had been seemingly indifferent to the tragic fate of the Jews, it now seemed indifferent to the "auto-genocide" in Cambodia.

When I returned to Washington, I urged Congressman Don Fraser of Minnesota, who chaired the Subcommittee on Human Rights and had authored the legislation that created the Human Rights Bureau in the State Department, to hold a hearing. It was the first of many hearings held over the next decade about the unfolding humanitarian and political tragedy in Cambodia, and it helped focus the administration's attention on the issue. I introduced a resolution, which the House adopted, calling on President Carter to consult with other world leaders to find ways to end the killings. The resolution didn't produce any concrete actions, but at least it constituted an expression of congressional concern, putting the issue on the political map.

Cambodia's former head of state, Prince Norodom Sihanouk, who had been living in exile since his overthrow in 1970 in a military coup led by Lon Nol, had embraced and endorsed the Khmer Rouge. This was a terrible mistake. Sihanouk decided to support the Khmer Rouge because they opposed Lon Nol. But by lending his name to their cause, he gave them a legitimacy, and an ability to recruit among the peasantry, that they would otherwise never have had. After the fall of Phnom Penh in 1975, Sihanouk returned to Cambodia and was placed by Pol Pot, the Khmer Rouge leader, under what the prince called "palace arrest." He was confined to his palace in the capital, from which the rest of the population had been forcibly evacuated to the countryside. In December 1978, the Vietnamese invaded and within a month overran Cambodia. Pol Pot fled to the jungles of southwest Cambodia, and from 1979 to 1991 he and his supporters launched attacks from the Cambodia-Thailand border region against the Vietnamese and the PRK. With the support of China, the Association of Southeast Asian Nations (ASEAN), and the United States, he also managed to keep the Cambodian seat in the United Nations, thereby securing international recognition as the legitimate government of the country he did so much to destroy.

I was very uncomfortable with the US position, which in effect put us on the side of the Khmer Rouge, at least in terms of UN representation. I would have preferred to keep the Cambodian seat vacant rather than let the Khmer Rouge have it. The administration, however, considered it important to act in concert with China and ASEAN, and since they wanted to prevent the Hanoi-dominated regime from getting the Cambodian UN seat, the administration went along with them.

During the Vietnamese invasion, Pol Pot agreed to release Sihanouk in exchange for his commitment to plead Cambodia's case before the United Nations in New York. Undoubtedly relieved to be out of the clutches of Pol Pot, who was responsible for the murder of several members of his immediate family, Sihanouk accepted the offer. I met with Sihanouk at the Palace Hotel in New York, where he was staying. We had never met before, but he opened the door to his suite and embraced me. He told me he listened every day to the Voice of America on the small shortwave radio that Pol Pot permitted him to keep. It was through the VOA that he heard of my efforts to focus attention on his country's tragedy, and he wanted me to know how much it meant to him to find out that the Cambodian people hadn't been forgotten.

This conversation made me realize that many things we did in Washington that attracted scant attention in the US media were big news overseas. People abroad learned of them through the VOA, the BBC, and the "jungle telegraph" operated by exiles and diaspora communities in the United States, which closely followed events in Washington. For those suffering from oppression in foreign lands, these manifestations of American concern were a source of tremendous encouragement.

I subsequently got to know Sihanouk well. He came several times to my home in Virginia, where we had small dinners with other members of my subcommittee. I once flew to Beijing, where he had sought refuge after his stay in New York, just to have dinner and a discussion with him in the former French embassy, where he was living. I flew back to Washington the next day, but the cuisine and the conversation made it worthwhile. Sihanouk was an engaging, enchanting character. His high-pitched voice and constant jumping up and down on couches he was supposed to be sitting on made him a dramatic and unforgettable figure. Despite his apparent flightiness, he was a man of considerable experience and shrewdness,

With Prince Norodom Sihanouk at his residence in Beijing.

who had met virtually all the key figures of the second half of the twenti-eth century. He was the only Cambodian leader who had both legitimacy in Cambodia and international recognition, and it soon became clear that if there was going to be a solution to the Cambodian conflict, Sihanouk would have to be part of it.

For ten years, the Vietnamese maintained 100,000 troops in Cambodia to deal with the resistance to their military presence and their client gov-ernment. Since any resolution of the conflict clearly required Vietnam's consent and cooperation, I made several trips to Hanoi to explore the prospects for a satisfactory solution. On one visit, I met the foreign minis-ter, Nguyen Co Thach, and asked why the Vietnamese had invaded their neighbor. Surprisingly, instead of saying they wanted to stop the mass kill-ings, which would have put their actions in a more favorable light, he in-formed me that the Khmer Rouge's human rights abuses had nothing to do with it. He referred to the continued killings of hundreds of thousands of Cambodians as a "purely internal matter" and matter-of-factly explained that his country had invaded Cambodia because the Khmer Rouge had

been attacking Vietnamese soldiers and villagers across the border in Vietnam. In what was clearly a manifestation of his xenophobia and megalo-
mania, Pol Pot had gone too far. This fatal miscalculation resulted in the
downfall of his hateful regime.

On one occasion, because I had been identified as someone in Congress who championed the cause of the Cambodian people, I had a visit
from Lon Nol. As the Khmer Rouge marched into Phnom Penh he had
escaped to Hawaii, where he was now living in exile. He asked me to help
get arms and other forms of military assistance from the administration
so he could go back to Cambodia and fight the Khmer Rouge. I asked him
what assurance he could give me that he would be more successful this
time than he had been previously, when the corruption and incompetence
of his own government paved the way for the triumph of Pol Pot. To this
sad but pointed question he had no response. I neither saw nor heard from
him after he left my office that day.

On one trip to Thailand I met Prince Ranariddh, one of Sihanouk's
sons and the leader of the Armée Nationale Sihanoukiste (ANS), the military arm of the Sihanoukist movement, whose political component was
the National United Front for an Independent, Neutral, Peaceful, and Cooperative Cambodia (FUNCINPEC). I also met the former Prime Minister Son Sann, whose Khmer People's National Liberation Front (KPNLF)
opposed both the Vietnamese-dominated puppet regime and the Khmer
Rouge. They too wanted me to help them get arms from the US government. However, it was only a few years after the Vietnamese invasion of
Cambodia, and memories of the Vietnam War were still vivid in Congress
and the country. Any effort to arm the non-Communist resistance forces
(collectively known as the NCR) would have generated a tidal wave of opposition on the grounds that it would inevitably lead to another war with
Vietnam and the potential reintroduction of American troops into Indochina. In the late 1970s, George McGovern, the 1972 Democratic presidential candidate, had called for the use of force to remove the Khmer Rouge
from power. I thought at the time that McGovern's proposal was greatly
to his credit, because it recognized the moral imperative of doing something to stop the killing. But it was totally ignored, which only underscored the extent to which such action was beyond the realm of political
possibility.

Then, in the mid-1980s, two things happened. The first was an op-ed piece in the *Washington Post* by Elizabeth Becker, a highly respected journalist who had covered Cambodia for the *Post* in the 1970s before the Khmer Rouge came to power and certainly was not known as a hawk on Indochina. She argued that the United States should begin providing assistance to the NCR. At about the same time, at a closed session of my subcommittee with representatives of the intelligence community, Robert Torricelli, a New Jersey Democrat and subcommittee member, also said he thought we should help them. These two expressions of support for the PRK's non-Communist opponents gave me a sense that sentiment had changed, so that what a few years earlier would have been unthinkable was now possible. I decided to introduce an amendment to provide $5 million in assistance, including military assistance, to the NCR. I discussed this legislation with Dante Fascell, the chairman of the House Foreign Affairs Committee, who wanted to minimize controversy over the foreign aid bill in which my amendment, if approved by my subcommittee, would appear. "I hope you know what you're doing," Chairman Fascell told me, as he reluctantly agreed to support the amendment. It was adopted in my subcommittee and then accepted by the full committee.

When the legislation reached the floor of the House, Jim Leach of Iowa, who had just become the ranking Republican on the subcommittee, and who agreed with virtually all of my legislative initiatives, offered an amendment striking the provision authorizing military assistance to the non-Communist resistance forces. But I managed to persuade a majority to reject Leach's effort, and the administration was given the option of using the money for military or nonmilitary assistance. In the end, the administration was concerned that military aid to the NCR would generate too much political heat at home, so the aid was limited to nonlethal assistance. Even with that restriction, the assistance we provided was a big morale booster for the NCR and helped strengthen it as a viable alternative to both the Khmer Rouge and the PRK.

Both before and after the Vietnamese invasion of Cambodia, in an effort to help Cambodians who had managed to escape the prison and torture chamber that their country had become, I visited some of the refugee camps in Thailand. This was always a moving experience. Once I was asked to address several thousand people at a location known as Site 2, a

With Congressman Joel Pritchard at the Tuol Sleng Genocide Museum
in Phnom Penh, at a site formerly used as a secret prison by the Khmer Rouge.
On the wall is a map of Cambodia made of skulls.

camp for Cambodians who were part of Son Sann's KPNLF. I asked everyone who had had a member of their family killed by the Khmer Rouge to raise their hands. About 95 percent of those present did so. It brought home to me the magnitude of the Cambodian holocaust.

Given the presence of tens of thousands of refugees confined to these camps, whom other countries were unwilling to accept, I felt strongly that the United States should take in those who had a legitimate claim to refugee status. Many who did have such a claim were being rejected. One good example was Lon Nol's cook, who was denied refugee status on the grounds that he didn't meet the test of having "a well-founded fear of persecution" if he returned to Cambodia. I saw this as a classic example of bureaucratic insensitivity. The notion that Lon Nol's cook wouldn't have a "well-founded fear" of being cooked himself if he went back to Cambodia was ludicrous. Ultimately, by arguing his case with the relevant officials at the State Department, my staff got him admitted to the United States.

I was also concerned about two groups who at that time were suffering the effects of the aftermath of the Vietnam War: prisoners in reeducation camps and "boat people" trying to escape Vietnam by sea. Throughout the 1980s, I met often with Nguyen Co Thach at the Foreign Ministry in Hanoi and at the UN in New York and pleaded the cause of the thousands of Vietnamese that his government had consigned to so-called re-education camps, where they wasted away under a very harsh regimen. Since most of the prisoners had been associated with the United States as civilian or military officials of South Vietnam, I urged the foreign minister to let them leave Vietnam for the United States, where they could do no harm to his government. Unfortunately, my pleas had no effect. He claimed that if his government permitted the prisoners to go to the United States, it would be only a matter of time before they went to Central America to join forces with the Contras waging a guerrilla war against the Sandinista regime in Nicaragua. I retorted that unlike Vietnam, our country left people free to go wherever they wanted, but that it was inconceivable to me that the reeducation camp prisoners, most of whom had been broken in body if not in spirit, would leave the comforts of life in the United States to fight in the jungles of Nicaragua. It took several more years, and the departure of Nguyen Co Thach as foreign minister, before most of these prisoners were released.

During one of his rare visits to Washington, Thach met with the members of the Foreign Affairs Committee. As chairman of the Subcommittee on Asia, I was asked to introduce him. He began by proudly informing us that his government had translated Paul Samuelson's textbook on economics into Vietnamese. It was his way of indicating that Vietnam was prepared to embark on a number of market reforms. I congratulated Thach on this initiative but expressed the hope that his government would translate John Stuart Mill's classic tract *On Liberty* into Vietnamese as well.

But perhaps my most vivid memory of this turbulent period is a conference at Princeton University that I attended in the 1980s on the boat people, who were fleeing Vietnam on flimsy vessels across the Gulf of Thailand, hoping to achieve a better life in other lands. The conference was organized by Tiffany Ho, a freshman at Princeton, who told the conferees the story of her escape from Vietnam five years earlier, at the age of thirteen. At two o'clock one morning, someone knocked on the door of her home and told the family it was time to go. She traveled by bike with her parents for a few hours to rendezvous with a boat that was to take her away. Her parents did not accompany her because they couldn't afford the cost.

Tiffany described how she begged her parents not to make her leave alone. "If you really love me, as you say you do, why are you sending me away?" she cried. Her mother could only respond, "One day you will understand that it's because we do love you that we're sending you away." Tiffany survived the long journey, and because she had an aunt living in the United States, she was allowed to come to America. It is a testament to her fortitude and intelligence that although she arrived in the United States speaking not a word of English, she was admitted five years later to Princeton.

I was deeply moved by the plight of the boat people. Even as they managed to escape, they were murdered, raped, and tortured by Thai pirates on the high seas. Determined to do something about this humanitarian outrage, I held hearings on the issue and got $10 million into the foreign aid bill to establish an antipiracy program in Thailand. Some of the money was used to purchase spotter planes intended to protect the people who were fleeing. To take a closer look at the program, I went to Songkhla, a town on the east coast of Thailand where the antipiracy program was based. I arranged to go up in one of the spotter planes. Peering down at the vastness of the Gulf of Thailand, I quickly realized that the whole thing was a feckless charade. It was obvious that from the plane there was no way to detect people being raped and murdered at sea.

Clearly the antipiracy program wasn't accomplishing anything. But I had what I thought was a really creative idea, which I explained to Squadron Leader Prasong, the Thai official responsible for the program. It involved giving the local fishermen the means and incentive to fish for people as well as for fish. All the Thai fishing boats would receive two-way ship-to-shore radios, so that whenever the fishermen saw a group of boat people, they could radio the location and stay with the boat until one of Prasong's coast guard cutters arrived. The fishermen would then be paid a bounty for every person they saved. Such a program, I argued, would give them an incentive to save people instead of robbing and raping them, as many were doing.

I was taken aback when Prasong said my idea was terrible. "If we adopt such an approach," he explained, "we'll have more refugees than we can deal with." For once in my life, I was speechless. He was responsible for protecting the boat people, yet he was obviously more interested in preventing them from coming to Thailand than in saving them from the pirates.

Meanwhile, I was still trying to find a way to bring the Cambodian conflict to an end in a manner that would facilitate genuine self-determination. Efforts at a diplomatic settlement were stymied because Vietnam and the Hanoi-supported PRK, now led by Hun Sen, took the position that a political settlement had to require the resistance forces to lay down their arms and agree to participate in elections run by the PRK. Hun Sen was willing to permit foreign observers to monitor the election but insisted that the election itself had to be under the authority of his regime.

The Cambodian resistance movements, supported by ASEAN, China, and the United States, agreed that there had to be an election, but refused to recognize the legitimacy of the PRK and maintained that any election it ran couldn't possibly be fair. Instead they demanded the dissolution of the PRK and its replacement by a so-called quadripartite government, in which power would be divided equally among the PRK, the two non-Communist resistance factions, and the Khmer Rouge. All factions could participate in the election, to be held under the auspices of the quadripartite government. This proposal was rejected by the PRK and Vietnam, which asserted that dissolving the PRK and permitting the Khmer Rouge to return to Phnom Penh as part of an interim government would create a power vacuum and risk a return to power by Pol Pot and the Khmer Rouge.

One day during spring 1989, sitting at lunch under the shelter of a *shamiyana* (a tentlike structure) in Site B, an ANS camp controlled by Prince Ranariddh, I came up with an idea that provided the basis for the eventual settlement of the conflict. My idea was to permit the existing bureaucracy to remain in place, while putting it under direct UN supervision. The UN could then supervise the elections without the resistance having to recognize the PRK and without the PRK having to fear a possible return of the Khmer Rouge. I thought my plan addressed many of the concerns that were blocking progress and asked Prince Ranariddh what he thought. He responded that if everyone else accepted it, he would too. I asked Lee Kuan Yew, whom I saw a few days later in Singapore, for his opinion. He thought it would be an ideal solution but doubted that Vietnam would go along. Somewhat to my surprise, I received positive responses from some other regional leaders as well.

The Bush administration, however, was less than enthusiastic. I tried to get the relevant officials on board, but they were locked into the quadri-partite government proposal. Since the PRK, Vietnam, and the Soviet Union (which supported Hanoi and Phnom Penh) had already rejected that proposal, it was not surprising that a conference held in Paris to resolve the Cambodian conflict in summer 1989 failed to reach an agreement.

A short time later, I met with Gareth Evans, the foreign minister of Australia, at the residence of his country's UN ambassador in New York. Evans indicated that he was increasingly uncomfortable with his country's support for the ASEAN-Chinese position, because he was getting criti-cized in Australia for supporting a policy that would let the Khmer Rouge participate in the Cambodian government. Sensing that he might be re-sponsive, I described my idea and urged him to adopt it. I thought that having a major country in the region on board would give the idea of a UN-supervised election a credibility it wouldn't have if it came just from a member of Congress. Seeing in my proposal both a solution to his politi-cal problem in Australia and a possible way to break the Cambodia log-jam, Evans embraced it. Two weeks later, in a speech on the floor of the Australian Senate, he put it forward as an Australian initiative. He then dispatched Mike Costello, the top career officer in the foreign ministry, to try out the idea on other countries in the region. After Costello's trip the Australian Foreign Ministry published a "Red Book" describing the plan and other countries' responses to it.

The Red Book indicated that the plan was widely regarded as viable. Other nations responded favorably, and the plan was picked up by the five permanent members of the UN Security Council, who all concluded that it offered the best chance for a resolution. Over the next year and a half the "Perm Five" hammered out a formula that ultimately did end the con-flict. Perhaps fittingly, Charlie Twining, who was now the director of the State Department office handling Cambodian affairs, played a useful role in bringing the negotiations at the UN to a successful conclusion. So, too, did Richard Solomon, the assistant secretary of state for Asia, who pro-vided strong support for a UN-based resolution. But there was opposition to the plan in the US Congress. In the Senate especially there was a be-lief that Washington's main objective should be to stop the Khmer Rouge from returning to power and that the Hun Sen regime was the most for-midable obstacle to that possibility.

I felt we had two objectives: preventing the Khmer Rouge from returning to power and facilitating the establishment of a truly independent
Cambodia that would not be a puppet of Hanoi. The best way to achieve
both was to shift the struggle from the battlefield to the ballot box. Recognizing the PRK, as some members of Congress proposed, would preclude
NCR participation in an election, prolong the war, and deprive the Cambodian people of genuine independence. Moreover, once embraced diplomatically by the United States, Hun Sen would have no incentive to agree
to a political settlement, as he eventually did.

Those who favored US recognition of the PRK also criticized our aid
to the NCR on the ground that they were in a coalition with the Khmer
Rouge and cooperated with them on the battlefield. It is true that a diplomatic alliance existed, known as the Coalition Government of Democratic Kampuchea. But this coalition had been forced on the NCR by
their ASEAN supporters as a way of preventing the PRK from securing
the Cambodian seat at the UN and had no other operational significance.
As for the charge that the NCR were cooperating with the Khmer Rouge
militarily, it was completely untrue. The NCR were just as opposed to the
Khmer Rouge as they were to the PRK.

I argued that if the Vietnamese ever did withdraw and the Khmer
Rouge tried to return to power, the non-Communist forces would have
to play an important role in preventing that from happening. And in retrospect, my position was completely vindicated by events. Under the umbrella of the largest UN peacekeeping mission in history, a free and fair
election was held in 1993, in which the non-Communist parties, particularly the Sihanoukists, actually received the most votes, leading to the establishment of a coalition government headed by Hun Sen and Prince
Ranariddh. By requiring that China sever its military tie with the Khmer
Rouge, the UN settlement effectively pulled the rug out from under Pol
Pot and induced him to accept the peace agreement, resulting in the mar-
ginalization and collapse of his murderous movement. It also facilitated
the return of 300,000 Cambodian refugees and the verifiable withdrawal
of all Vietnamese forces. Instead of remaining a Vietnamese dependency,
Cambodia became a truly independent nation once again. After more
than half a century of almost continuous warfare, Indochina was finally at
peace and free to get on with the job of economic development.

Why did the four fractious and conflicting Cambodian factions agree to accept this settlement? The answer is that they either had no choice or believed they would benefit. The Khmer Rouge would probably have lost Chinese aid and Thai sanctuary if they rejected the UN plan, so they felt they had no alternative. The two non-Communist factions realized that their best and probably only chance of taking power was through a free and fair election, along with the withdrawal of Vietnamese forces. In addition, since ASEAN and the United States strongly supported the proposal, the NCR would have alienated their key supporters if they rejected it. The PRK liked the cut-off of Chinese aid to the Khmer Rouge and also believed they would win the election. Vietnam's support for the UN proposal undoubtedly carried weight with the Phnom Penh regime as well. As for myself, conceiving the idea on which the UN plan was based was probably the most creative initiative of my years in Congress; it remains a source of enduring satisfaction.

Beyond the details of policymaking, one bright light stands out, illuminating all my efforts in this area. At one point in the 1990s, the Indochinese communities of the Washington, D.C., area held a big dinner to thank America for letting them come here, and I was asked to speak. I told the inspirational story of Tiffany Ho and her escape from Vietnam. A few minutes after I finished my speech and sat down, a woman came up to me and said, "I'm Tiffany Ho." She told me how she had graduated from Princeton, gone to medical school, and become a psychiatrist. It turned out that my staff had helped her parents come to America. That story, at least, had a happy ending.

6

THE PHILIPPINES

The Impossible Dream

〜

There are moments in life one never forgets. For me such a moment came in summer 1983, in the midst of a congressional trip to Asia. On a hot, humid Sunday afternoon, I was relaxing at the guest house of the American ambassador in Bangkok when I received a call from the US embassy in Manila. It brought tragic news: Benigno "Ninoy" Aquino Jr., returning from a three-year exile in the United States, had been assassinated by a gunman as he stepped off a plane at Manila's international airport.

To me this was a personal as well as a political tragedy. Having met Ninoy on several occasions, I admired him as a political leader and liked him as a man. Our first encounter was at a coffee shop in Newton, Massachusetts, where he lived. We talked for several hours. He was charming and charismatic, and spoke eloquently about the need to restore democracy in the Philippines.

Born into a prosperous Philippine family of landowners, Ninoy had become the preeminent leader of the political opposition to the dictatorship of Ferdinand Marcos. Charged with murder and other trumped-up crimes, he was found guilty by a military court and sentenced to death. He then languished in prison for over seven years while Marcos hesitated to execute him, fearing it would turn him into a martyr. When Ninoy suffered a heart attack, Marcos resolved this dilemma by allowing him to go for surgery to the United States, where he would presumably remain in exile. By 1983, however, Ninoy had concluded that the struggle for democracy against the dictatorship required that he return to the Philippines. There were reports that Marcos was in failing health, and Ninoy felt he had to go back if he was going to play a role in shaping his country's future.

So it was that on June 23, 1983, in a great act of courage, he announced this intention before my Subcommittee on Asian and Pacific Affairs. Ninoy was determined to return despite the real possibility that he might be killed or imprisoned. At the hearing he made an eerie prediction: "I was sentenced to death in 1977. That sentence is now with Mr. Marcos. If I go back to the Philippines and he decides to have me shot, he can have it done the moment I arrive." In response, I stated that his decision "constitutes a tremendous tribute not only to your courage but to the depths of your commitment" to the restoration of democracy in the Philippines. I was planning to go to the Philippines that August and asked Ninoy if he wanted me to meet him in Manila. Such an action would demonstrate to Marcos that Aquino's fate was important to the US Congress and the American people, so Ninoy responded that he very much hoped to see me there.

Originally, Ninoy had planned to return to the Philippines in July, before my arrival. As fate would have it, Imelda Marcos, the dictator's wife, asked him to postpone his return for a few weeks (for reasons that remain unclear), and Ninoy agreed. Thus when I arrived in August, Ninoy was not yet there, and I had to leave the day before his return.

On that day, August 20, I met with Marcos in Manila's Malacanang Palace, the traditional seat of power ever since the Philippines became a Spanish colony three centuries earlier. He had been incommunicado for the previous couple of weeks. The official cover story was that he was writing several books. In reality, as I later discovered, he was having a kidney operation. Certainly—especially compared to the energetic Aquino—the dictator looked frail. He had a yellowish pallor and walked haltingly, although he displayed his customary intellectual vigor. Whatever else might be said about Marcos, no one could deny that he was very intelligent and politically shrewd. Our conversation covered the full range of issues concerning the Philippines, but since Ninoy had not yet returned, and I wasn't planning to come back, I refrained from asking Marcos to meet with Ninoy.

I left Manila for Bangkok that night, only to learn the terrible news of Ninoy's death the next day. As I discussed it with Nina, who was with me on that trip, the first question in my mind was whether to cancel the rest of my itinerary and return to Manila to pay my respects to Ninoy's family and supporters. Nina thought this was the right thing to do, reminding me that in the Jewish religion, when tragedies like this happen you drop everything and go to the people affected. But I didn't in any way want to make it appear that I was grandstanding. So I asked the official in the US

*Meeting with Ferdinand Marcos (second from right) on
August 20, 1983, the day before Ninoy Aquino was assassinated.*

embassy in Manila who had alerted me to Aquino's death to ask his family
and friends if they would like me to return. An hour or two later he called
back to say that they would. On that assurance, I canceled my trip and set
off for the Philippines.

As it happened, the fastest route to Manila was via Singapore, where
I was able to arrange a meeting with Lee Kuan Yew. He strongly urged
me not to return to the Philippines, arguing that doing so would constitute an implicit indication that Marcos was behind the assassination
and that if the Filipino people thought the United States held Marcos responsible, there could be destabilizing political consequences. The Philippine government had already put out the story that Ninoy was killed by
a rogue Communist who had shot him as he was disembarking from the
plane. Conveniently, this "assassin" had been killed immediately by soldiers
on the tarmac. Reluctant to reject Lee's view out of hand, I called David
Steinberg, a good friend and leading Philippine scholar, for his opinion.
Failing to take into account the time difference between Singapore and
Boston, where David lived, I awakened him at 4 a.m. David agreed with
Nina that the right thing to do was to pay my last respects to Ninoy. This
convinced me to continue on to the Philippines.

It was probably the best decision I ever made as a member of Congress. At a time when our government publicly supported the Marcos regime, my presence showed the Filipino people that there were Americans who shared their anguish over the brutal murder of this widely admired opposition leader. I went to Manila primarily as a gesture of sympathy and support; it never occurred to me that this act would link me to the fate of the Philippines, and that Ninoy's assassination would set in motion a democratic transformation whose ripples would be felt far beyond the country's shores.

Arriving in Manila, I went immediately to the US embassy, where I was briefed about the assassination and its implications. Of all the people I spoke to at the embassy and elsewhere, the only one who thought the Marcos government wasn't responsible was the CIA station chief, who seemed to agree with Marcos that the Communists had done it. Nina and I were then driven to Ninoy's home by Salvador "Doy" Laurel, the most prominent opposition leader still in the Philippines, to view the bloodied body. Outside Ninoy's house, thousands of Filipinos from every walk of life formed a line snaking through the surrounding streets, waiting to pay their respects to the latest martyr in the long history of the Filipino struggle for freedom. Ninoy's mother, Doña Aurora Aquino, had insisted that the coffin remain open and that his wounds not be cleaned. She wanted the Filipino people to see what had been done to him. Deeply saddened by this last glimpse of my youthful, energetic friend, I decided at that moment to rededicate myself to the cause of restoring democracy in the Philippines.

After viewing Ninoy's body, we were escorted into another room in the house that was crowded with guests. There was no electricity or air conditioning, and many people were fanning themselves. Adding to the gloomy mood, the sun was setting, and the only light in the room filtered in through a high window. Here we were introduced to Doña Aurora, an elegant, beautiful woman, who poured her heart out to us. She said she had pleaded with Ninoy not to return. But he had told her that "if Marcos wanted to kill him he could just as easily have done it on the streets of Boston as the streets of Manila" and that "he would rather die on the soil of his own country than on that of a foreign land." I assured her I would do everything I could to make sure Ninoy had not died in vain.

Later that evening we had dinner by candlelight in the home of Doy

Laurel, together with other opposition leaders and two of Ninoy's sisters. The conversation was very subdued until, toward the end of the evening, the Filipinos started singing "The Impossible Dream" from the Broadway musical *Man of La Mancha*. As the moving melody unfolded, there wasn't a dry eye in the room. At that moment, the dream of democracy in the Philippines did seem like an impossibility. But less than three years later, in one of the great political miracles of our time, the dream came true — without a single shot being fired.

Inspired by Ninoy's heroism, I determined to use whatever influence I had to align US foreign policy with those who were leading the struggle for democracy in the Philippines. During the year after the assassination, the Philippines underwent its most severe economic and political crisis in decades, and the credibility of the Marcos regime diminished daily. At the same time, the growing popularity of a Communist-oriented insurgency led by the New People's Army (NPA) added a third pressure point. Few Americans would have been sorry to see Marcos go, but in those days of the Cold War, no one seriously involved in US foreign policy wanted to see the Philippines spin out of control and end up in the hands of a Communist regime.

I returned to Asia in July 1984, in part to assess recent developments in the Philippines. Once again I went to Singapore to meet Lee Kuan Yew. He told me he believed that the Marcos regime's hold on power was tenuous, but that the United States had no choice other than to stick with him lest the country fall to the NPA. Lee had seen Marcos recently at a regional meeting of Asian leaders in Brunei. He observed that although Marcos had taken the trouble to be there to show the other leaders that all was well in the Philippines, he actually gave the opposite impression. Two thinly disguised ambulances followed him around, and three aides with "medical looking bags" attended him at the dinner.

Economically and politically, the Philippines wasn't in much better health than Marcos. Real wages had fallen more than a third over the previous decade, and the country's foreign debt had mushroomed to $25 billion. Marcos and his inner circle had siphoned off the nation's wealth on a vast scale in what came to be known in the Philippines as "crony capitalism." It was a form of government best described as kleptocracy — government of the thieves, by the thieves, and for the thieves.

Beginning in December 1985 and continuing into the next year, I held a number of hearings on the Philippines that raised the curtain on the widespread corruption of the Marcos regime, and in particular on assets that he and Imelda had allegedly acquired in the United States. I hoped that proving these allegations to be valid would help the democratic opposition by further delegitimizing the regime. The story of these hearings resembles the plot of a dime-store novel more than a standard legislative procedure.

I was first alerted to the possibility that the Marcoses might be funneling their wealth into the United States by articles in the *New York Times*, *San Jose Mercury News*, *Wall Street Journal*, and *Village Voice*. The stories alleged that Marcos had acquired about $350 million worth of prime properties in New York—not bad for someone whose only legitimate source of income was his salary of $7,500 a year as president of the Philippines. If Marcos was corruptly acquiring that kind of money, much of which could have been stolen from the foreign aid we were providing, my subcommittee clearly had a right to investigate. And so on December 3, 1985, I commenced a series of hearings to investigate Marcos's "hidden wealth" in the United States.

Ferreting out the truth was not easy. We were plodding along, not making much progress, when I got a telephone call from someone named Victor Politis. I had never met him, but I was soon referring to him as my "Deep Throat." Politis, who had read about our hearings, told me he had gotten to know Mrs. Marcos very well, and that he had information about Marcos's investments in Manhattan.

Politis was a Greek Jew who had lived in Israel, England, and the United States. In the summer of 1982, he had met two brothers, Joseph and Ralph Bernstein, who were trying to market a commercial property in Manhattan known as the Herald Center. He said he had direct knowledge that Marcos and his wife had bought that and other properties in New York, and that the purchases were made through the Bernstein brothers. This was blockbuster information that could directly link Marcos to the corrupt acquisition of hundreds of millions of dollars worth of Manhattan real estate.

Clearly, I had to meet Politis so I could determine the veracity of his claims. He suggested we get together at his apartment on the Upper West

Side of Manhattan. That was fine with me, but Nina was nervous that the whole thing might be a setup. She called Jules Kroll, a good friend who had established a global private investigation agency, to ask his opinion on how to proceed. Jules agreed that I shouldn't go to see Politis by myself and sent some security guards to accompany me.

As it turned out, I found Politis to be credible and reliable. As a result of what he told me, I subpoenaed the Bernstein brothers to testify before my subcommittee. They refused to answer most of our questions on the grounds that this would require them to violate the attorney-client privilege. When I asked if they had ever conducted business with the Marcoses, their typical response went like this: "We never actually conducted business with President Marcos. Our relationship with him had more of a legal nature. We never really discussed real estate with him." The problem for the Bernstein brothers, however, was that one of them wasn't an attorney, and, in any case, the purchase of real estate—which in fact they had discussed with Marcos—isn't covered by the attorney-client privilege. Therefore my subcommittee, and then the full House of Representatives, voted to hold them in contempt.

Even without their cooperation, by late January 1986 our subcommittee was developing significant information about the Marcoses' secret New York real estate holdings. The next month, Marcos was forced to flee the Philippines, and on April 6 I announced at a subcommittee hearing that if the Bernsteins would tell us in open session what they had by then told us in private, they would remove any lingering doubts that the Marcoses owned some of the most prestigious properties in Manhattan, and we would not need to prosecute them for contempt of Congress. Now that their golden goose had fled the coop, the Bernsteins agreed to cooperate, and we dropped the contempt citation. In this way they managed to avoid the jail time that being held in contempt of Congress would probably have entailed. Meanwhile the revelations before my subcommittee, which were big news in the Philippines, undoubtedly undermined Marcos's position.

I had always viewed events in the Philippines in a broader context. By 1984, the Philippines was beginning to look like South Vietnam in the late 1950s. The Marcos dictatorship faced an increasing challenge from the NPA. Furthermore, no one seemed to buy the government's version of the Aquino assassination: most Filipinos believed that Marcos himself,

Imelda, and/or the military chief of staff, Fabian Ver were responsible. I couldn't help but wonder whether, like Vietnam, Cambodia, and Laos, the Philippines too might fall under Communist control. Once again, the United States appeared tied to a corrupt, repressive government that had lost the confidence of its people. After America's disastrous experiences in Vietnam and Cambodia, and with the Cold War still a strategic and geopolitical reality, the threat posed by the NPA couldn't be dismissed as irrelevant.

In addition, by alienating the Filipino people, our support of Marcos was jeopardizing our long-term use of two strategically important military facilities in the Philippines, the naval base at Subic Bay and an air base at Clark Field. Both were deemed essential to America's long reach to Asia and the Pacific, which helped us preserve the peace and protect our allies in the region from the threat of Communist aggression. Our challenge was to find a way to pressure Marcos to make needed political and economic reforms—thereby showing the Philippine people that the United States was on the side of democracy—without jeopardizing our access to the bases.

Since we were obligated under the terms of the base agreement to provide $180 million a year to the Philippine government, eliminating the aid or even cutting it could give Marcos an excuse to deny us access to Clark Field and Subic Bay. The solution I came up with—which Congress accepted—was to maintain the overall level of aid but to change the mix by increasing economic assistance while decreasing military assistance. The purpose was to send a signal to the Filipino people that we were more interested in helping them deal with their economic and humanitarian challenges than in propping up a military which was increasingly seen as an instrument of domestic repression rather than of national defense.

In order to learn more about the NPA guerrilla movement, which operated mostly in the countryside, I held a clandestine meeting with the leaders of its political arm, the National Democratic Front (NDF), somewhere in Manila. I say "somewhere" because I never knew where the meeting took place. It had been set up before my arrival and had some of the trappings of a James Bond adventure. I was accompanied by Nina, Bernie Nussbaum (an old friend who subsequently became President Clinton's first White House counsel), and Stanley Roth, the director of my subcommittee staff. The Filipinos who picked us up at our hotel brought us to a car and blindfolded us. We then drove in circles around Manila for about half an hour. For all I knew, we might have ended up around the corner from the hotel. The driver finally brought us to a nondescript safe house where the NDF leaders were waiting.

The State Department would never have sanctioned this meeting. But I felt, as a member of Congress, that I had an obligation to better understand those we were opposing and that there was no better way than to meet with them myself. My objective was to get a sense of whether they were hard-core Communists or just nationalists who opposed the kleptocracy in the Philippines and its close ties with the United States. We were soon involved in a lengthy discussion about Marxism. Having just arrived after a long flight from Washington, we were jet-lagged, and Nina, Bernie, and Stanley soon fell asleep. Later, I kidded Bernie that the Communist threat in the Philippines began to decline from the moment of that meeting. When the NDF leaders saw the Americans falling asleep, they concluded that they had no hope of getting American support! My own conclusion was that they were a muddle-headed bunch of anti-American nationalists whose commitment to Communism was more a rhetorical flourish than a deeply rooted ideological conviction. But even if they weren't hard-core Communists, I had no doubt that their victory would be a strategic set-back for the United States and a political and humanitarian tragedy for the Filipino people. Whatever their propaganda suggested, they weren't simply a group of agrarian reformers determined to restore democracy and honest government.

Corazon "Cory" Aquino, Ninoy's widow, now back in the Philippines, took part in many of the anti-Marcos demonstrations during the two years after her husband's assassination. It was the first time in her life that she had stepped out of her role as a housewife into the public arena. Many underestimated her. But she had a sharp intelligence and a deep commitment to the restoration of democracy. Despite her somewhat fragile and soft-spoken appearance, it soon become clear, as Nina put it, that she had a fist of steel inside a velvet glove. She was no pushover and was fully prepared to put her life on the line to bring Marcos down.

By 1985, Marcos faced a rapidly deteriorating political and economic situation combined with increasing American pressure for fundamental reforms. Hoping to improve the former and deflect the latter, he surprised both his domestic opponents and foreign supporters by calling for a "snap" election in February 1986. Many people, including me, worried that a palpably dishonest election would lead the democratic opposition and the Filipino people to conclude that the path to peaceful change was blocked, that democracy could not be restored, and that the only viable alternative to Marcos was the New People's Army. But Marcos had miscalculated. A top Filipino businessman, Joaquin Roces, organized a movement supporting Cory Aquino for president. She was reluctant to run, and Doy Laurel, who had led the internal opposition to Marcos, wanted to run for president himself. However, after a ten-hour retreat in a Catholic convent, Cory and Doy agreed that she would be the opposition candidate for president and he would be her running mate for vice president.

In an effort to maximize the prospects for an honest election, President Reagan asked Senator Richard Lugar and Congressman Jack Murtha to co-chair a delegation of American election observers. I was asked to join it. As much as I wanted to witness the election, I thought it best to decline. I felt that, as a vehement critic of Marcos and a strong supporter of Aquino, my credibility as an impartial observer would be open to challenge. I did, however, suggest to Congressman Murtha that the delegation include my staff director, Stanley Roth. Stanley was more knowledgeable about the situation in the Philippines than any other congressional staffer, and I told Murtha that he would benefit greatly by having Stanley with him. As it turned out, Stanley's advice was very helpful in persuading the delegation not to prematurely give the US seal of approval to the election.

Given the long history of electoral fraud in the Philippines, especially under Marcos, it was to be expected that the kleptocrat in chief would try to steal the election. The real question was how he would do it. In the early hours of voting, when the observers failed to detect any blatant examples of ballot stuffing, some of them made statements to the press suggesting that the election would be free and fair. Yet even as the ballots were being counted at the main election center, a dozen computer operators assigned to tally the vote claimed they were being forced to enter false results and staged a dramatic walkout, taking refuge in a nearby church. Their actions unfolded live on international television, convincing the observers that the election was in the process of being stolen. A few days later, one

of Marcos's top aides, Defense Minister Juan Ponce (Johnny) Enrile, publicly acknowledged fraudulently adding 350,000 votes to Marcos's total in
his home province of Cagayan.

Undaunted, Marcos declared victory, but the country's Catholic bish-
ops, along with American and international observers, condemned the
election as fraudulent. There was, however, one dissenting voice. In a statement issued by the White House, President Reagan took a more benign
view, asserting that "there was cheating on both sides." Informed of Reagan's comment, I told the *New York Times* that it constituted "proof positive that they are smoking marijuana in the White House."

To send a strong signal to the Filipino people that the United States
had lost confidence in Marcos and was on the side of democracy, I convened a meeting of my subcommittee to adopt legislation eliminating our
military assistance to the Philippines. Two top Reagan administration officials, Paul Wolfowitz and Richard Armitage, came to my office to plead
with me not to do this. Cutting off military aid, they contended, could
lead to a collapse in the morale of the Philippine military and a Communist victory, which would be a strategic disaster for the United States. I
agreed that a Communist victory would be a humanitarian and political
disaster for the Philippines and a strategic setback for us. But I maintained
that Marcos had now become the recruiting sergeant for the NPA and that
his removal from power was essential if a Communist triumph was to
be avoided. With revelations of massive electoral fraud being reported on
American television, my subcommittee voted unanimously to terminate
military assistance. Even stalwart defenders of Marcos like Congressman
Gerry Solomon, who had previously opposed efforts to reduce military assistance, were now prepared to support a total cutoff. It was an indication
of how sentiment in Washington had turned against Marcos. Before the
legislation could be brought before the full committee, however, he had
fled. But he and the Filipino people had gotten the message that Congress
was ready to withhold support from his corrupt, repressive regime.

The political end for Marcos came quickly. On February 22, 1986, two
of his key allies, Defense Minister Enrile and Fidel "Eddie" Ramos, chief
of the Philippine national police force, abandoned him. With a small
group of supporters, they took refuge in a military encampment in the
heart of Manila. Almost immediately, Jaime Cardinal Sin, the ranking

With Cardinal Sin at his home in Manila, 1980s.

Catholic prelate in the Philippines, went on Radio Veritas, the church's broadcasting station, and urged people to come to the defense of Enrile and Ramos.

I had met often with Cardinal Sin, who was both privately and publicly critical of Marcos. He was a warm, wise man known for his sense of humor. Whenever I visited him in his rectory, he would open the door and say, "Welcome to the house of Sin." In a 1984 speech to the Rotary Club of Manila, he remarked: "Forty years ago, President Quezon of the Philippines said he would rather live in a Philippines governed by the Filipinos like hell than in a Philippines run by the Americans like heaven. Today, forty years later, President Quezon's wish has come true." Because of his wit and wisdom, his quiet charisma, and his stature as the leader of the Catholic Church in this overwhelmingly Catholic country, his call to action carried great weight.

Within hours of his radio appeal, over a million Filipinos took to the streets in support of Ramos and Enrile. Marcos called out his troops and sent tanks to break up the demonstration. But with nothing more than their prayers and their presence, nuns, priests, and ordinary people stopped the tanks in their tracks. Soldiers who had been sent to capture or kill Enrile and Ramos refused to fire on their own people. "How could I fire on my own grandmother?" said a tank commander. Three days later, after learning from Senator Paul Laxalt, President Reagan's best friend in the Senate, that Reagan thought the time had come for him to bow to the inevitable and step down, Marcos fled the Philippines. That same day, Cory Aquino was sworn in as president.

One lesson I learned from this experience is that if you're a dictator and want US support, you shouldn't steal an election on American television. Previously, many congressmen and senators who disapproved of the Marcos regime's corruption nevertheless felt we should continue to support it for strategic reasons and also because Marcos was considered a friend of the United States. They had seen what had happened in Iran and Nicaragua after other "friends" of the United States, the shah and Anastasio Somoza, had been overthrown, and they feared the worst in the Philippines if Marcos was deposed. But blatantly stealing an election was more than they could stomach, and with a million Filipinos in the streets demonstrating against Marcos, they finally turned against him.

A week after Cory Aquino became president, I once again visited the Philippines, this time to pay tribute to her and to the Filipino people. The State Department had urged me not to go, arguing that the situation was still unstable. But I told them wild horses couldn't keep me away and went anyway. It was wonderful to be in a free Philippines, with people proudly proclaiming their commitment to freedom and peacefully reclaiming their birthright. Two and a half years after that dinner at Doy Laurel's house, the "impossible dream" had come true.

Moreover, a bigger picture was emerging from the victory of the People Power movement, as the nonviolent demonstrations were called. The Philippines — as impoverished and imperfect as it was — had become a model for the aspirations of people suffering from repression elsewhere around the world. Although it was difficult to draw a direct connection, democracy soon spread in the previously arid political soil of South Korea, Taiwan, Chile, South Africa, and ultimately, after the collapse of Communism, in Eastern Europe and the former Soviet Union.

I was the first foreigner taken on a tour of the Malacanang Palace after Marcos's flight. It was still in a shambles, reflecting his hasty departure. His bedroom had a sign reading "The King's room"; in his wife's bedroom, the sign said "The Queen's room." Her huge bed—the size of a volley-ball court—was, as my colleague Gary Ackerman put it, "big enough for Imelda and the Seventh Fleet." The Marcoses certainly lived like royalty. In the palace basement, which consisted of one enormous room the size of a department store, Imelda Marcos kept her clothes and the 3,000 pairs of shoes that became an infamous marker of her embarrassing extravagance. The amazing thing was that she had multiple pairs of the same styles, and you could see that a number of them had never been worn.

For me, the greatest treasures were in Marcos's office, which was sur-prisingly small—although his desk was on an elevated platform, so visi-tors had to look up at him. Papers were scattered all over the floor. Always curious, I got down on my hands and knees, looked through the trove, and discovered a letter from Marcos to the Bernstein brothers, in which he authorized them to purchase properties on his behalf. There now was no doubt that this connection had existed.

When I came out of the palace, dozens of journalists were waiting to interview me. Asked for my impressions, I commented that, given what I had seen, it was fair to say that "compared to Imelda Marcos, Marie Antoi-nette was a bag lady." That quote got picked up all over the world. About a month later, I received a letter from a Texan who said he was a direct descendant of Marie Antoinette and resented my allegations against his ancestor. Marie Antoinette, he claimed, had absolutely nothing in com-mon with Imelda Marcos. Shortly after that, I got another letter from a disgruntled Texan. "Until I saw you on the McNeil-Lehrer show last eve-ning," he wrote, "I always thought my own congressman, Henry B. Gonza-les, was the most stupid member of the House of Representatives. I now realize how wrong I was. Congressman Gonzales is clearly only the second most stupid member of Congress. You are the first."

Not all the letters I received were so critical. One of the nicer ones came from Senator Pat Moynihan, who wrote to say: "You have simply been magnificent throughout this whole Philippines episode. You first ex-plained to us a year and more ago which way events were heading. You steadily predicted what would be next, and at the end you were instru-mental in bringing off one of the genuine triumphs of democracy we have seen in our lifetime.... This constituent writes to express his profound ad-miration and respect."

Above all, my efforts on behalf of Philippine democracy offered the enormously satisfying opportunity to put my commitment to democracy into action in a very meaningful way. My work was appreciated in Manila as well. I remember in particular one unusual honor bestowed on me in the days after the triumph of People Power. Doy Laurel, now vice president, inducted me as an honorary son of Batangas, the province he came from. At the ceremony, I was given a knife with a very sharp edge, which I had to plunge into a metal coin in order to pick it up. According to the rules of this esoteric initiation rite, if you can't pick up the coin, you have to take a swig of a very potent rice wine. I think it took me three tries, but I finally did it. I immediately took out a scroll I had brought with me and proclaimed my good friend Doy Laurel an honorary son of Brooklyn. Getting into the spirit of the induction — or perhaps fueled by too much rice wine — I told him we were both now honorary SOBs!

Equally gratifying, the Filipino opposition's ability to triumph without resorting to violence gave heart to people struggling for democracy elsewhere. On a trip I took to Poland in 1987, Adam Michnik, a legendary Polish dissident and one of the founders of Solidarity, said to me, "The Polish people want you to do for us what you did for the Philippines."

Although the Philippines was now a democracy, I was painfully aware that economically the country was in very bad shape. Unless Cory Aquino's government could transform the promise of democracy into a better life for the Filipino people, the Communists still might be able to overthrow the new government. So I began putting together an ambitious aid package to help the country get back on its feet. To make this package politically acceptable, I needed bipartisan support, so I went to an influential Republican, Congressman Jack Kemp of New York, who served on the Foreign Operations Subcommittee of the House Appropriations Committee, which had jurisdiction over our foreign aid program. He immediately agreed to support a major increase in aid. So did Senator Richard Lugar, the highly respected Republican from Indiana, and Senator Alan Cranston, a senior Democrat from California, both of whom served on the Foreign Relations Committee. The four of us — two Democrats and two Republicans — signed a letter to Secretary of State George Shultz urging the administration to embrace our proposal.

Shortly afterward, we four were invited to meet with Secretary Shultz in his ornate office on the seventh floor of the State Department. Shultz, an economist by training, was receptive to our proposal. But he was also a hard-nosed realist. In a letter to me while the package was being considered, Shultz wrote, "As you and your colleagues explore ways to provide additional assistance to the Philippines, keep in mind the very severe restraints" imposed by the federal budget. The plan that emerged was referred to as a mini-Marshall plan, a reference to the post–World War II anti-Communist economic initiative that rebuilt a starving and shattered Western Europe. On September 18, 1986, President Aquino helped generate support for our plan when she addressed the US Congress in a rare joint session. It was a stirring moment. As she walked down the aisle, wearing a simple yellow jacket and skirt, she received a sustained standing ovation. Yellow symbolized People Power in the Philippines; on the day of her husband's assassination, many of the people waiting to greet him had worn yellow T-shirts, and yellow streamers had rippled in the breeze.

Now, less than four years later, his widow entranced the congressmen and senators, many wearing yellow carnations in their lapels. In a stirring peroration, she said: "Three years ago, I said thank you, America, for the haven from oppression and the home you gave Ninoy, myself, and our children, and for the three happiest years of our lives together. Today I say, join us, America, as we build a new home for democracy, another haven for the oppressed, so it may stand as a shining testament of our two nations' commitment to freedom."

Observing the response to this deeply moving address, I decided to strike while the iron was hot and get a bill providing additional aid approved that same day. I spent the next several hours scurrying around the House chamber and congressional office buildings, getting the support of the leadership on both sides of the aisle, as well as the chairmen and ranking members of the relevant authorizing and appropriations committees, for an immediate increase in aid to the Philippines. With their support, it was possible to bring up a bill later in the day to provide an additional $200 million in aid, above and beyond what we were currently providing, and separate from the plan created by the four of us, on the basis of a unanimous consent request that enabled us to avoid the process of committee hearings and markups that ordinarily takes weeks. After the bill passed but before the House adjourned for the day, Senator Bob Dole of

Kansas was heard to comment, "It was the biggest honorarium in American history." If so, it was a well deserved one.

When I had first floated the idea of a mini-Marshall plan for the Philippines, most people thought it was a quixotic initiative doomed to founder on the rocks of our own fiscal difficulties. But after almost two years of hard work and personal lobbying, the dream not only became a reality but exceeded my wildest expectations. With America taking the lead, other countries were willing to join us. An international conference held in Tokyo in July 1989 on the plan, now known as the Multilateral Assistance Initiative (MAI), produced pledges of $3.5 billion in additional aid by twenty countries.

Yet just a week before the conference, its prospects had been jeopardized by a legislative maneuver in Congress. Congressman Toby Roth, a Wisconsin Republican, offered an amendment to cut by 60 percent the additional $1 billion in funding for the Philippines that was to constitute our share of the MAI, to $400 million. I took the lead on the House floor opposing the amendment, pleading with my colleagues to reject it. I argued that if passed, it would guarantee the failure of the international pledging conference in Tokyo, since other donors would have scant incentive to increase their own aid to the Philippines. Additionally, I said, Secretary of State Shultz, who would be representing the United States in Tokyo, would be humiliated before all the other countries there. Foreign aid has never been particularly popular, and amendments to cut it are difficult for many members to oppose. Fortunately, Roth's effort failed by a 233–185 vote. On July 7, 1988, I received a letter from Cory Aquino, which read in part: "You have been such a good friend to us, to our government and to our country, showing great concern, exerting so much effort and mustering support in our behalf. We cannot thank you enough for this."

The MAI was an encouraging expression of support for the restoration of democracy and helped stabilize the Philippine economy. For me personally, however, the most rewarding moment of my involvement in the Philippines came in July 1987, when I returned to Manila as the head of an American delegation to the opening of the newly elected Philippine Parliament. My purpose was to pay tribute to my friend Cory Aquino and her parliamentary colleagues for their accomplishment in restoring democracy to the Philippines. My relationship with Cory was always warm and friendly, but never more so than when she offered a toast at a luncheon in honor of the foreign delegations in attendance. I was deeply honored when she referred to me as "the Lafayette of the Philippine revolution," and went on to describe how I had been "a lonely voice in the desert of official indifference to the fate of the Filipino people. . . . I think I can say," she continued, "for those whose bodies were broken in the safe houses of the dictatorship, for those whose shame brought them near to despair, that the name of Steve Solarz was the last hope, if not of effective rescue, then at least of a loud and eloquent testimony to the pain and universal rightness of their cause. Steve," she concluded, "you can have no idea how dear a place you have in all our hearts, how deeply and permanently you are inscribed in the grateful memory of our race. The great event that will take place tomorrow we owe in no small measure to you."

I was very moved by these generous comments. But I also couldn't escape the feeling that it was a classic example of how rhetorical embellishment by political leaders was not limited to the campaign trail. In truth, the real credit for the peaceful and almost miraculous transition from dictatorship to democracy belonged to Cory, Doy Laurel, Monching Mitra, Sonny Alvarez, Serge Osmena, Steve Psinakis, and the other opposition leaders who were prepared to risk their lives, their fortunes, and their sacred honor to oppose the Marcos dictatorship; to Eddie Ramos and Johnny Enrile, whose courageous break with Marcos precipitated the events that led to his downfall; to Cardinal Sin, who called on the people to defend Ramos and Enrile; and to the hundreds of thousands of Filipinos who put their lives on the line by standing up to Marcos's tanks and troopers. In the final analysis, the triumph of People Power reflected the commitment to democracy of the Filipinos themselves. The Philippine revolution was neither made in America nor the work of a particular American.

But I would also not be telling the truth if I didn't say that I will cherish Cory's remarks to the end of my days. Like most people in public life, I've received my share of commendations (and criticisms too). But this topped them all. For a kid from Brooklyn, it was heady stuff indeed.

· 7 ·

KOREA AND TAIWAN
The Struggle for Democracy and Human Rights

⌒

The first time I traveled to Seoul, it was a far cry from the bustling, pros-perous city it would become. In the summer of 1975, South Korea was still under martial law. A curfew required people to be off the streets by 10 p.m. The tallest building, six stories high, was the Chosun Hotel, where I stayed. Soon the city would look like New York or Chicago, with one high-rise after another lining broad avenues choked with cars, as if to taunt the impoverished Communist neighbor to the north. The contrast between South and North Korea, like that between West and East Germany, made the case that democracy and free-market economies were far more able to satisfy the human aspiration for freedom and prosperity than one-party dictatorships and state-controlled economies.

South Korea's economic success, facilitated by wise economic policies, is also a tribute to the Korean people's work ethic and commitment to ed-ucation. A higher percentage of their students receive a college education than in any other country in the world. But in 1975, South Korea wasn't yet a democracy. I met with President Park Chung-hee, a military dictator who was a bit like a bantam cock: very short, but strong and always ready for a fight. His emphasis on export-led growth created the basis for Ko-rea's economic leap forward. But I was never one of Park's cheerleaders. His economic policies were commendable but his political inclinations were deplorable. Under his leadership, opposition parties were banned and his critics were imprisoned and tortured.

In fact, I spent much of my time during visits in the late 1970s and early 1980s trying to help Kim Dae-jung, whom the Park government had tried to assassinate. Kim was a human rights activist who had been defeated in a disputed presidential election in 1971. In August 1973, during a trip to Japan, he was kidnapped from his Tokyo hotel by agents of the South Korean government. They brought him to a boat which put out to sea, where he was strapped to a board and weighted down. Before he could be

*With Kim Dae
Jung in South Korea,
January 1988.*

thrown overboard, however, a plane obtained by Don Gregg, the CIA station chief in Tokyo, who had found out about Kim's abduction, buzzed
the ship. Realizing that their plot to eliminate Kim had been discovered,
his abductors decided not to consign him to the deep.

Back in Korea, Kim continued to participate in antigovernment protests and in 1980 was put on trial and sentenced to death on trumped-up
charges of treason. The sentence was eventually commuted because of a
creative deal worked out by Richard Allen, President Reagan's national security advisor. Chun Doo-hwan had succeeded Park Chung-hee as president after Park was assassinated in 1979 by his chief of intelligence. Reagan
agreed to receive Chun as his first official visitor in exchange for sparing
Kim's life. But even though Kim was not executed he remained imprisoned, becoming the Korean counterpart of Nelson Mandela: a symbol of
the people's desire for democracy.

Kim Dae-jung had a number of medical problems, and during several
visits to South Korea, I was able to have him transferred from prison to a
hospital so he could get better healthcare. Eventually, as a result of American pressure, Kim was put under house arrest at his home in Seoul, where

I visited him whenever I was in South Korea. He later went into exile for a couple of years in the United States. During this period, he visited me several times at my home in McLean, where we had long talks about how to promote the cause of democracy and human rights in South Korea. I also met several times in Seoul with Kim Young-sam, another opposition leader under house arrest; we discussed what the United States could do to facilitate a transition to democracy in his country. Both Kims, "DJ" and "YS" as they were called in Korea, made it clear that they didn't want the US troops deployed in South Korea to be withdrawn lest that tempt North Korea to launch another war on the Korean peninsula. Though they wanted us to apply political pressure on the South Korean government to permit free and fair elections, they didn't want us to do anything that could undermine their country's security.

By 1987, agitation for democracy had generated a mass movement in favor of political reform. The economic miracle in South Korea had produced a substantial middle class whose members wanted to determine their own destiny. The triumph of People Power in the Philippines the year before inspired Koreans, who felt that if the Filipinos could peacefully bring about the end of a dictatorship, they could too. As Chun Doo-hwan's term as president came to an end, he designated another military man, Roh Tae-woo, as his successor. Since presidents were chosen by an electoral college controlled by the government, Roh's election seemed assured. But Chun's decision to turn the reins of power over to Roh precipitated prodemocracy rallies in Seoul and other cities across the country. Tens of thousands of demonstrators called for a direct presidential election in which all South Koreans could vote. I endeavored to lend the moral and political support of the United States to this movement by introducing and securing passage of a resolution urging the Korean government to hold a direct election for president. At a hearing of my Subcommittee on Asia, Gaston Sigur, the assistant secretary of state for Asia, expressed the administration's support for a direct election as well.

In response to these developments, Roh promised widespread reforms, including a more democratic constitution, and agreed to a popular election for president. Holding a direct election meant that Roh could no longer be sure of becoming president. It was clearly a major political risk on his part. But with the stability of the nation hanging in the balance, he wisely decided to yield to the demands of the demonstrators for genuine democracy. In the election, the two major opposition figures, Kim Young-sam and Kim Dae-jung (both of whom later became president) were unable to overcome their differences and consequently split the opposition vote. Roh thus won a narrow victory and became South Korea's first democratically elected president.

My concerns about South Korea's political future did not diminish my interest in preserving peace on the Korean peninsula. I wanted to find ways to reduce tensions between the two Koreas and between the United States and North Korea. The division of the Korean peninsula into two hostile countries created a major challenge for American foreign policy. North Korea had more than a million men in arms and was determined to reunify the peninsula under Communist control. With North Korean forces deployed in an offensive configuration just north of the thirty-eighth parallel, another Korean war remained a real possibility. Since 42,000 American troops were deployed just south of the demilitarized zone, such a conflict would inevitably involve the United States. We had no diplomatic relations or even contacts with North Korea, and I thought that visiting the country as a member of the Foreign Affairs Committee and meeting with the North Korean leaders would enable me to explore the prospects for a more stable and secure peace on the peninsula. I therefore arranged to go to North Korea in the summer of 1980 — something no American official had done since the end of the Korean War in 1953.

In this I had the help of Prince Sihanouk, whom I had gotten to know when he came to New York after the Vietnamese invasion of Cambodia in 1978. In the 1970s, after being overthrown by Lon Nol, Sihanouk had lived for a time in exile in Pyongyang, where Kim Il Sung, the leader of North Korea, built him an eighty-room palace with a private lake and an indoor movie theater on the outskirts of the city. When I found out that Sihanouk was still spending much of his time in Pyongyang, and that he had gotten to know the "Great Leader," as Kim Il Sung was called, I asked if he could possibly arrange a visit for me. After a while, I received a message from Sihanouk saying I was welcome to visit North Korea as his guest. I accepted this invitation, but to actually go there in my official capacity, I needed the approval of the Foreign Affairs Committee chairman, Clem Zablocki, a cold warrior from Wisconsin who had a dim view of North

*With Kim Il Sung
in North Korea,
summer 1980.*

Korea and was reluctant to give me permission. But after Richard Hol-
brooke, then assistant secretary of state for Asia, told him the administration had no objection, Chairman Zablocki withdrew his, and I made plans
to go after a trip to South Africa in July.

I think I may be the only person in history who ever flew from Pretoria to Pyongyang. After all that flying, I spent only four days in North
Korea, where I stayed at the prince's palace. I had many hours of conversations with Sihanouk about all the famous people he had known, including Dwight Eisenhower, Nikita Khrushchev, and Charles de Gaulle — not
to mention such third-world leaders as Chou En-lai, Jawaharlal Nehru,
Gamel Abdel Nasser, Josip Broz Tito, and Sukarno. But the highlight of
the trip was my encounter with Kim Il Sung, who led North Korea from
its founding in 1948 until his death in 1994. During his reign, he established a cult of personality that made the personality cults of Stalin and
Mao look like exercises in modesty.

I met with the Great Leader for four hours in one of his guest houses in Hamhung, on the northeast coast of the country. What struck me most was the contrast between the harsh reality of his rule and his engaging private persona. One of the world's must brutal dictators, he was amiable and avuncular in person. He smiled continuously and spoke softly. Still, I found it very difficult to conduct a normal conversation. I was able to ask a few questions, but he clearly wasn't used to being queried by his inter-locutors. He knew what he wanted to say and said it at great — sometimes interminable — length.

When Kim entered the room, he repeated to me a Korean proverb, "Beginning is half done." "You are the first American politician to visit our country," he said, "and we feel that you will break the ice." I took that to mean we would get down to business right away. So after telling him that I looked forward to our talks and hoped they would help facilitate the eventual re-unification of Korea, I began to ask a series of questions. I inquired whether he would be willing to follow through with South Korea on prior political and humanitarian agreements to make possible the reunification of families that had been separated by the Korean War. I wanted to know if he would agree to athletic and cultural exchanges with the United States as a way of improving relations and reducing tensions between our two countries. Since I hadn't been empowered by Washington to negotiate with North Korea, I kept these and other exploratory questions broad and general.

He reiterated his welcome and pronounced my precedent-setting visit to be "brave conduct, a wonderful thing." He acknowledged that "a single visit couldn't solve all our problems because we have been estranged for such a long time. You may have prejudices against us and we may have some against you. So we both view everything from a subjective point of view. Of course, differences cannot be solved all at once, but more frequent contacts will overcome such differences."

Now Kim got into the diplomatic thickets. The attitude that the us government and South Korean authorities took toward solving the Ko-rean question was very important, he maintained. The main question was whether they wanted to divide the Korean peninsula permanently, creat-ing two Koreas, or whether they wanted to take steps toward unification of the Korean people, who were a homogeneous nation. "If our country is to be divided into two Koreas forever, what is the use of exchanges?" he asked, and continued: "We think it is possible to hold tripartite talks, but what matters is the attitude or position one takes — whether one takes the position for reunification of two Koreas. That is why, so far, we are against tripartite talks on military matters or to solve the military armistice question. Our two sides are in a state of neither war nor peace." Reading between the lines, what Kim was telling me was that there was one Korea and it was North Korea.

He then went out of his way to emphasize that he would not meddle in South Korean affairs. He cited an incident in the city of Kwangju, where there had been a popular uprising two months earlier against South Korea's military dictatorship. His government, he claimed, had said at the time that it had no intention of getting involved. "This shows," he contended, "that the threat of a North Korean invasion talked about by the South Korean authorities is nonexistent."

I conceded that North Korea had not taken advantage of the troubles in Kwangju and that this was a constructive attitude on its part. Kim then returned to my opening comment about family reunification and an exchange of letters between separated families. "We have made proposals in the past," he said. "If they are willing to agree, we are always ready to do things. This is our demand. Therefore, we are not against it."

This was a very important point, I told him. I asked: "Are you saying that if the South were willing to agree on family reunions and the exchange of mail, you would also be ready to agree, even in the absence of a political agreement on resolving the differences between the two Koreas?" "Yes," he responded, "this is what the people demand. There is no mistrust among the people. In principle we agree to family reunions and the exchange of letters. It would be a good thing." He added that he would also agree to trade with the South without political conditions.

All this sounded encouraging at the time, but it soon became clear that the Great Leader was speaking with a forked tongue. It took more than a decade before arrangements could be made for even limited family reunifications, and no exchange of letters is possible even today. The North Korean government remains far more intent on preventing its people from having contact with South Koreans than in ameliorating the humanitarian consequences of a divided peninsula.

We were now nearing the end of our formal meeting, and I wanted to make sure that Kim had no illusions. So I stated that, speaking as someone who strongly supported improving us-North Korea relations, it would be unrealistic to expect the withdrawal of us forces from South Korea without a significant reduction of tension on the peninsula. "When I tell my friends in Washington that I don't believe North Korea intends to go to war against South Korea," I explained, "they respond that North Korea is infiltrating agents into the South, digging tunnels under the Demilitarized Zone, spreading belligerent propaganda, and engaging in a very substantial buildup of its armed forces, all of which contributes to a continuing danger of war in Korea."

"No matter how much we try to convince you," Kim responded, "you would never believe us. Even if I said here that we would not invade the South, not send spies, and had not dug tunnels, you would never believe us. Therefore, I won't deny it." Then he turned philosophical. "No man is without his faults — only Buddha," he concluded. This verbal maneuver was his artful way of implicitly acknowledging the truth of allegations he appeared to be denying. But his unwillingness to abjure such provocations in the future underscored the continued threat his country posed to the security of South Korea.

At lunch, I asked Kim about what in North Korea was called his "on-the-spot guidance" of the people. He visited each of the ten provinces once a year, he explained, staying ten to fifteen days in each, as well as in the three cities that were directly administered by the central government. He said he learned much from talking to the people. For example, "the people say that rice should be transplanted around May 30. But a government agency sent an order to the people to transplant the rice much earlier, and they complained. Now, after countermanding the previous order, the people tell me they have a bumper crop this year."

As a reality check, I then inquired whether the North Korean press had the right to criticize the government. "Yes," he assured me, "the press criticizes and the Supreme People's Assembly also criticizes." The trouble with this picture of a benign ruler being guided by his people and by the rule of law was that it clashed with the reality of a brutal dictatorship that ruled over a nation where there was no personal freedom, and the media was government owned and controlled. Kim Il Sung clearly did not agree with the often-expressed view that the job of the press is to comfort the afflicted and afflict the comfortable.

I was also taken for some sightseeing. Pyongyang was a beautiful city, with very broad boulevards and thousands of weeping willows. I toured the subway system, which was modeled on Moscow's metro. I must acknowledge that the stations were rather splendid, much more so than those in my Brooklyn district. In one, seeing a group of school kids in uniforms standing on the platform, I immediately walked up to them and introduced myself as a congressman from America. I asked a young girl who looked about twelve what she thought of the United States. "You should stop supporting the fascist clique of Chun Doo-hwan," she replied. To me this response reflected a level of political precocity unknown in most other countries — or, more likely, the politicalization of the educational system.

At a maternity hospital in Pyongyang, I noticed that every room but one had a portrait of Kim Il Sung on the wall. The exception was the ward for premature babies, who they probably figured could not properly appreciate the Great Leader's visage. I also visited the Opera House, which made the Palace of Versailles look like an Appalachian hovel. I saw a performance of an opera called *The Song of Paradise*, which recounted how Kim Il Sung had created a paradise on earth in North Korea. It could be billed as a musical comedy if it was ever performed in the United States as part of a cultural exchange program.

My escort — or minder — was a Mr. Joo, who spoke good English. When it came time for me to leave, he escorted me to the station where I was to board a train for the twenty-three-hour ride to Beijing. I said goodbye to Mr. Joo and told him that when I returned to my congressional district in Brooklyn, the first thing my constituents would ask was whether there are any Jews in North Korea. "I'm going to tell them that there certainly are," I said, "since I spent four days here with a Joo." The fact that he laughed reflected his mastery of English as much as his sense of humor.

While I hadn't expected this trip to win me the Nobel Peace Prize, I did hope it might lead to a reduction of tensions on the Korean peninsula and some progress in ameliorating the humanitarian consequences of the Korean War, such as the separation of families across the thirty-eighth parallel. On both counts, my trip was a total failure. The two Koreas remained locked in a bitter struggle for political and ideological supremacy, and it was another two decades before some limited progress was made in facilitating family reunifications. I did, however, get some useful insights into the realities of life in North Korea. It was truly the most repressive regime in the world, bar none. Not everyone at home appreciated my efforts, however. After my visit, a newspaper in New York owned by the Reverend Moon, a South Korean evangelist, ran an editorial noting, "A short while ago the leader of North Korea, Kim Il Sung, opened the door to his communist Kingdom and in slithered New York Congressman Stephen Solarz."

After several days in what is perhaps best described as a combination of a Hollywood movie set and a Potemkin village, I had little interest in returning to North Korea. But by the early 1990s, our intelligence community was picking up indications that North Korea had embarked on an effort to create nuclear weapons. If true, this would clearly constitute a serious threat to the security of South Korea and to the cause of nuclear nonproliferation around the world. So I decided in December 1991 to go to North Korea for another meeting with Kim Il Sung. We met at what appeared to be a restaurant or country club in Pyongyang. Kim came in and shook my hand. We hadn't seen each other in over ten years, and he said it was good to see me again. At lunch, Kim, who had put on a lot of weight, had to be helped by several aides into his chair. Huge amounts of food were brought in; he had a hearty appetite. He also had a large goiter, the size of an apple, on the back of his neck, which I had noticed during my 1980 trip.

Everyone in his retinue paid total deference to him. At one point I asked a question about something he had said earlier. Kim Il Sung pointed to Kim Yong Nam to answer it. The other Kim, a senior government official — he was then foreign minister and later became prime minister — literally jumped to attention and stared at the ceiling as he recited his answer. In fact, whenever Kim looked at one of his minions that person rose to his feet, then sat down when the Great Leader's eyes moved elsewhere, so the general impression was of a bunch of Korean jumping jacks. This display of obeisance made normal manifestations of sycophancy by subordinates, especially in dictatorships, look like indifference.

When I asked Kim about reports that he was in the process of building a nuclear reactor that could produce weapons-grade fissile material, he blithely denied it, contending that the project was nothing more than a "radio-chemical" laboratory. This assertion — much like Hitler's protestations at Munich of his desire for a lasting peace — was a bald-faced lie that was soon exposed by the actions of his own regime. It underscored for me the sad truth that national leaders, especially those who preside over repressive regimes, cannot be taken at their word.

Unfortunately, such regimes were not limited to the Communist world. The so-called free world also had its share. During the 1970s, as a member of the Subcommittee on Asian and Pacific Affairs, I had visited Taiwan, which was then under martial law and had no organized political opposition. While the ruling Kuomintang (KMT) government wasn't as bad as the Communist dictatorship in China, it was still a very repressive regime that did not hesitate to jail its critics, stifle the press, and prevent the establishment of opposition political parties. Shortly after I became chairman of the subcommittee in 1981, I was approached for help by Trong Chai, a Taiwanese American professor at Medgar Evers College of the City University of New York. Chai, a skilled political organizer, was president of the Formosan Association for Public Affairs (FAPA), sort of an Asian equivalent of the American Israel Public Affairs Committee (AIPAC), the legendary Israel lobby. FAPA's members were Taiwanese Americans committed to the creation of real democracy and the eventual establishment of an independent Taiwan.

There was always a little tension in my relations with Chai and FAPA. While I strongly supported ending martial law and establishing real democracy in Taiwan, I was not prepared to unequivocally endorse their goal of formal independence. I believed that if the US came out in favor of an independent Taiwan, it would result in a rupture in our relations with China. From a geopolitical and strategic point of view, that would have been counterproductive. I tried to square the circle by working with Jim Leach to secure adoption of a congressional resolution in 1991, stating that the future of Taiwan should be determined peacefully and in a manner acceptable to the Taiwanese people. This has, in fact, become official US policy and has been affirmed by every administration since. For us to abandon Taiwan to its fate should Beijing try to resolve the issue by military force would be unjust and unforgivable. As a vibrant democracy with which we've had a close relationship for more than a quarter of a century, Taiwan is entitled not only to our sympathy but to our support. Once martial law was repealed and a multiparty democracy established, I was determined to make sure that Taiwan received that support.

At the time I met Chai, the United States had normalized relations with China and severed ties with Taiwan. One of FAPA's biggest complaints was that, in the process of establishing diplomatic relations with Beijing, we had eliminated the separate quota for Taiwan of 20,000 immigrant visas a year. As a result, Taiwanese who wanted to come to the United States had to compete for these visas with one billion Chinese on the mainland. Shortly after Chai brought this problem to my attention, an immigration bill happened to be making its way through Congress. When it came to the floor, I proposed an amendment to restore a separate Taiwanese quota of 20,000 visas, which the House adopted. With Ted Kennedy carrying the ball for my amendment in the Senate, it was accepted by the conferees and became law. Since then, over 100,000 Taiwanese have emigrated to the United States and have greatly enriched our economic, social, and scientific life.

The next problem FAPA brought to my attention involved Chen Wen-chen, a Taiwanese American professor at Carnegie Mellon University, in Pittsburgh. Chen had attended a FAPA meeting at the university. When he returned to Taiwan during the summer, he was picked up by the garrison command, a state paramilitary agency, and brutally interrogated. A few days later, he allegedly committed suicide by jumping out of a window on the top floor of a university library in Taipei. No one who knew Chen believed this cock-and-bull story for a moment. It was obvious that the garrison command had murdered him.

I convened a hearing on the circumstances of Chen's death that led to the discovery of a surreptitious surveillance program of Taiwanese students in the United States by the KMT regime. Even members of the subcommittee who supported Taiwan as an anti-Communist ally felt this was an outrageous interference in our internal affairs and an utterly unacceptable effort to prevent Taiwanese students in the United States from criticizing their own government. I was able to get legislation adopted prohibiting arms sales to countries that intimidated their nationals in our country. The action worked. Badly needing military assistance from us, the Taiwanese government quickly terminated its intimidation project in the United States.

During a 1984 trip to Taiwan, I arranged to give a talk at a Taipei luncheon to the Tangwai, the nonparty political opposition. Since opposition political parties were prohibited, the only way KMT opponents could run for office in Taiwan's one-party elections was as independents. It was one of the most important speeches I ever gave. I knew that while I spoke to the few dozen independently elected officials at the luncheon, my address would be broadcast to a much larger audience on television. My objective was to encourage progress toward democracy, in a way that might also have some influence on the KMT.

I started by assuring the audience that I was a friend of Taiwan who cared about their future. I said there was no doubt that Taiwan enjoyed a good international reputation as a showplace for economic growth, with one of the highest per capita incomes in the world. But equally important, I continued, Taiwan now needed to respond to the challenge of political development. "Can the economic miracle, which has given you the benefit of prosperity, be matched by a political miracle that will give you the fruits of freedom?" I asked. It was not enough for Taiwan to be merely better than its Communist adversaries. What democratic politics offered, I explained, was a creative balance between authority and individualism, between conflict and harmony. The balance point would be different for each society, and here culture might play a role. But I was confident that Taiwan could accelerate the trend toward democracy and that a democratic system suited to Taiwan's conditions would enhance Taiwan's security and stability. At a time when Taiwan was still very much concerned about the military threat posed by China, I pointed out that one reason Israel enjoyed so much support from the United States was that it shared our democratic values. And I suggested that the best way for Taiwan to ensure continued US support as a deterrent against any act of aggression by China would be to become a genuine democracy as well.

As I spoke I noticed something remarkable. In order to appeal to the KMT as well as the Tangwai, I alternated between paragraphs praising the economic miracle on Taiwan and paragraphs calling for a political miracle. Whenever I talked about the economic miracle, the TV lights went on and the cameras rolled. But as soon as I mentioned the need for a comparable political miracle, the lights went out and the cameras stopped. It was a not so subtle reminder that the cause of democracy still had a long way to go in Taiwan.

In the following years, Taiwan made considerable progress on the political front. Martial law ended in 1987, although it was replaced by a similar, but less strict, national security law in 1991. Opposition political parties were permitted. The aging KMT legislators, known in Taiwan as the "old thieves," who had been elected on the mainland in 1947 and never had to run for office again, retired. And in 1991, the ruling party gave up its claim to all of China. Many Taiwanese political activists in the United States returned to Taiwan and some, such as Trong Chai, were elected to Parliament. In 2000, Chen Shui-bian, an opposition leader in Taiwan who had visited me in my office during the years of martial law, was elected president of Taiwan as the candidate of the Democratic Progressive Party, which had become the main alternative to the KMT.

During several trips, I met with every Taiwanese president since the death of Chiang Kai-shek. The first was Chiang Ching-kuo, Chiang Kai-shek's son. Short and heavyset, he was the opposite of his charismatic father. But he deserves credit for realizing that the one-party system wasn't in the country's best interests and had to be opened up. He was succeeded by Lee Teng-hui, a Taiwan native and KMT member with a Ph.D. from Cornell University who spoke fluent English. I have to confess I was partial to Lee, who awarded me Taiwan's highest civilian medal, the Order of Brilliant Pebbles, for my efforts to facilitate the establishment of democracy there. The third president I met was Chen, who started out as a reformer pledging to clean up Taiwanese politics but ended up being convicted for corruption himself.

Victory, the Chinese like to say, has a thousand fathers, while defeat is an orphan. In promoting the cause of democracy and human rights in Taiwan, some very good colleagues worked with me, including Congressman Jim Leach, the ranking Republican on my subcommittee, and Claiborne Pell and Ted Kennedy in the Senate. In Taiwan we became known as the Gang of Four, and I was proud to be in such commendable company.

· 8 ·

SOUTH ASIA

The "Voice of India in Congress" and "the Lafayette of Pakistani Democracy"

I made my first trip to South Asia in 1976, as part of a fact-finding mission looking at economic development in the Third World. The Foreign
Affairs Committee was responsible for authorizing our annual foreign aid
program, and I wanted to get a better sense of what worked and what
didn't. That trip took me from Taiwan, a real development success story,
to Bangladesh, among the poorest of the poor, as well as to India, which
had more people living in poverty than any other country, except possibly
China. One lesson that trip taught me was that even among the poor there
are degrees of poverty. In Bangladesh, for example, most people didn't have
shoes or sandals and walked around barefoot. They slept on the floors of
their homes with nothing between them and the ground but a straw mat.
In India, by comparison, even the poorest seemed to have footwear and
slept on rope cots.

On this trip I met for the first time with Indira Gandhi, then prime
minister of India. I was escorted to her home by David Korn, the us
chargé d'affaires, who told me not to be surprised or put off if the prime
minister just sat there and said nothing, because she often lapsed into long
silences. I later discovered in a biography of her father, Jawaharlal Nehru,
India's first prime minister, that he often used this technique when he was
asked questions he didn't want to answer. He just stared silently into the
distance until his interlocutor gave up and went on to another question. In
this respect at least, Mrs. Gandhi was apparently a chip off the old block.

It was the height of the "Emergency," a form of martial law declared by
Mrs. Gandhi after the High Court of Allahabad found her guilty of using
illegal practices during the previous election campaign. The court ordered
her to vacate her seat in Parliament, which would have required her to step
down as prime minister. In response she declared the state of emergency,
under which her political foes were imprisoned, constitutional rights ab-

Meeting with Indira Gandhi in Washington, 1970s.
Congressman Bill Broomfield is at left.

rogated, and the press placed under strict censorship. During this same period, she launched a birth control project designed to reduce the population growth rate. The whole country was divided into sections and subsections, and the administrators put in charge were given quotas of men to sterilize. In theory the sterilizations were supposed to be voluntary. In practice they were often compulsory. The birth control program produced a political backlash that contributed to her defeat in the next election, in 1977. As an example of the fears this program had generated, Mrs. Gandhi told me during our meeting about a rumor that had swept through Calcutta. Apparently, all the rickshaw wallahs, the people who pulled these rickety conveyances, believed they were going to be sterilized. All of them fled the city, and for two weeks it was impossible to find a rickshaw. It was only after the authorities managed to persuade them that this wasn't the intention that they returned to their jobs.

Prime Minister Gandhi also said that Indian women favored control-
ling family size, but that men did not because they thought it would encourage immorality. She contended that India had made a dent in the
overpopulation problem largely due to economic development, since when
people have a better standard of living, they want fewer children. Next, she
described how her government had launched a major campaign against
tuberculosis and leprosy by starting inoculations in the schools. However,
thousands of parents dragged their children out of school, fearing they
would be sterilized. There had even been stories of teachers warning children not to go to school. Mrs. Gandhi went on to assert that India was
too large and populated to have a social security system, adding that such
a system dehumanizes families. She thought it was much better for families to remain together and take care of their elderly themselves. Possibly
the state, sometime in the future, could help lessen the burden, but the responsibility should ultimately be on the family.

Responding to her disquisition about the population problem, I asked
Mrs. Gandhi whether she thought there was a relationship between development and democracy. Far from lapsing into silence in response to
what she might have considered a provocative question, she responded at
length. I felt I had turned on a faucet. For the next half-hour she talked
without interruption about the importance of democracy for development. Her basic point was that democracy provided feedback to the leaders of a country through a free press and the rough and tumble of political
activity, giving them a much better sense about what was happening at the
grass roots and what problems needed to be addressed.

I asked why she couldn't accomplish everything she had done during
the Emergency without having declared the Emergency in the first place.
She replied that if India had been able to function before the Emergency,
it wouldn't have needed the equivalent of martial law. In 1971, she noted,
her party got over two-thirds of the seats in both houses of Parliament.
The opposition parties thought they would never win another election. So
they adopted "a program of hatred against me," with the extreme left and
the extreme right joining forces in an unusual combination. "We should
have taken a firm stand, but we didn't," she said. "The students didn't study,
the workers didn't work, they struck and they sabotaged. In 1973, there
was a national railroad strike. In a big country like India it isn't possible to

tolerate such instability. There was a lot of sabotage. People came to see me and said, 'You must stop this!' But I didn't want to arrest the politicians." Eventually, however, she declared the Emergency and threw many of her political opponents into jail. I suspected, however, that this decision had more to do with the High Court's ruling her election invalid than with this catalogue of more substantive justifications.

I emerged from her house to face a swarm of reporters who wanted to know what we had discussed. Based on our conversation, I said I wouldn't be surprised if Mrs. Gandhi called an election in the near future. Most of the journalists looked at me as if I were a naive foreigner who had been sold a bill of goods by this wily woman. But sure enough, a couple of months later she did call an election. Much to her surprise, I'm sure, she was repudiated by the voters and forced out of office. Ironically enough, she had been under the impression that she would win—precisely because she had been denied the feedback democracy provides. Surrounded by those who told her only what she wanted to hear, she didn't appreciate the extent to which she had alienated the country, through imposing both the Emergency and her population control program.

With all its faults, including the chaos inherent in such a large and varied population, I found India the most fascinating country I had ever visited. Its culture and civilization were so different from those of the West. Yet in spite of its poverty and its linguistic, religious, and cultural diversity, it had maintained a commitment to democracy and preserved its territorial integrity. When India became independent in 1947, most experts thought it had little prospect of remaining either democratic or united. The fact that it was able to do both was truly impressive. I had been interested in India from the time I was a young boy growing up in Brooklyn. I was fascinated by the life of Mahatma Gandhi and considered the Indian struggle for independence one of the great political dramas of the twentieth century. The Indian people's enduring commitment to freedom has vindicated my firm belief that even illiterates and people who are desperately poor are capable of participating in and enjoying the benefits of democracy.

During another trip, I decided that in addition to meeting the leaders of the government in New Delhi and the captains of industry in Mumbai, I should go to the villages where the great majority of Indians lived, and together with Nina, I visited a number of villages in the countryside. When we arrived, the village men would assemble before us, while the women watched from the rooftops. I asked a lot of questions of the villagers, but Nina suggested I ask them if they had any questions for me. This give-and-take turned out to be very useful and productive. I often learned more about what people were thinking by the questions they asked me than from their answers to my questions.

The villagers I met invariably asked two questions. The first was, "What are your [agricultural] yields in the United States?" As the representative of an urban district with only eight full-time farmers (whose farms I never discovered, but whose crop I suspected was an illicit substance used to get high), I was at a loss. Taking an educated guess, I responded that the yields in the United States were as good as the yields in Punjab, considered the breadbasket of India. The other question was, "Do you practice birth control?" I said I did, hoping it might encourage them to voluntarily do so as well.

I met a number of impressive politicians in India, including Manmohan Singh, who was the chief civil servant in the Finance Ministry when I met him in 1976 and subsequently the first Sikh to become prime minister. In the 1970s, he was an articulate defender of the Indian economic system, which featured a high degree of protectionism with considerable state control over both industry and agriculture. By the early 1990s, however, recognizing that India's economic policies were stunting its economic growth, Singh became an equally eloquent champion of reduced tariffs and less regulation.

I also became friendly with Rajiv Gandhi, Mrs. Gandhi's oldest son, whom she was grooming to succeed her, after her youngest son Sanjay had been killed in an airplane accident. I met Rajiv for the first time during one of his mother's trips to Washington. He had been a commercial airplane pilot before his brother's untimely death and appeared to have little interest in either politics or policy. After encountering him at a reception at the Indian embassy, I told Nina that we had better hope his mother had a long life. This hope was futile; Mrs. Gandhi was assassinated in 1984 by her Sikh bodyguards in retaliation for the assault she had authorized against the Golden Temple, the holiest shrine in Sikhdom, to flush out a Sikh terrorist who had taken refuge there.

Meeting with Rajiv Gandhi (left) in his office in New Delhi, 1980s.

My initial impression of Rajiv turned out to be badly mistaken. While he might not have wanted or been prepared for the job of prime minister, he quickly grew into it and embarked on an ambitious effort to modern-ize India. But his work was tragically cut short when he was assassinated by a female suicide bomber in the midst of an election campaign. This hit job had been ordered by Velupillai Prabhakaran, the leader of the Tamil Tigers, a notorious terrorist organization that pioneered the technique of suicide bombing long before it was embraced by Osama bin Laden. Prab-hakaran, whom I had met several years earlier in India while trying to get a better understanding of the conflict between the Tamil minority and the Sinhalese majority in Sri Lanka, was nondescript looking, more like the owner of a noodle shop than the leader of a major terrorist organization. The killing was revenge for Rajiv's earlier decision to send Indian troops to Sri Lanka to help the government there prevent the establishment of a separate Tamil state, which Rajiv feared might generate separatist senti-ments in Tamil Nadu, a Tamil majority state in southern India.

The House of Representatives was in session when the news of Ra-jiv's assassination reached me. Like the Kennedy family, the Gandhi family had now experienced two deaths by assassination and one in a plane crash. With the support of Dante Fascell, the chairman of the Foreign Affairs

Committee; Bill Broomfield, the ranking Republican on the committee; and Jim Leach, the ranking Republican on my subcommittee, I secured unanimous consent to bring up a resolution expressing the profound regret of the House over the assassination of yet another Indian prime minister. I paid tribute to this courageous man who had given up a life of luxury to serve his people and went on to say: "The bomb that went off in India today was a bomb intended to explode democracy in India itself. It is entirely possible that this dastardly deed may have brought the leading political dynasty in South Asia to an end, but I have every confidence it will not bring the cause of democracy in India to an end." My prediction about the Gandhi dynasty turned out to be mistaken—Rajiv's Italian-born wife Sonia eventually became leader of the ruling Congress Party—but my confidence in Indian democracy was amply justified.

Because of the insight these trips gave me into Indian politics and policy, I played a leading role in persuading Congress to lift the ban on foreign aid to India. The ban had been imposed in 1974, when India exploded a nuclear device. Under existing legislation, we were obligated to cut off aid to any country that took such an action. In 1977, however, I was able to convince my colleagues in the House to adopt an amendment to the foreign aid bill lifting the ban on the ground that, if we were serious about economic development in the Third World, we could not maintain a prohibition on aid to India—where there were more poor people than anywhere else—that contradicted our policy goals.

During this period, there was a widespread suspicion of India on the part of the administration and many members of Congress, who were uncomfortable with India's relatively close relationship with the Soviet Union. This connection was reflected by, among other things, India's refusal to vote for a resolution in the UN General Assembly criticizing the Soviet Union for its invasion of Afghanistan. What these American critics didn't appreciate was the extent to which US support for Pakistan, particularly in the form of military assistance, made India feel it had no alternative but to look to the Soviet Union for military supplies and political support—which it certainly did not do out of any ideological affinity for Communism. American policymakers were also unhappy with India's role as a leader of the nonaligned movement, which tended to be far more critical of the United States than of the Soviet Union. From my perspective, however, these considerations were more than outweighed by India's commitment to democracy, and I felt strongly that we should strive for a more cooperative relationship between the world's most powerful and populous democracies. The fact that India was also the dominant power in South Asia and a potential counterweight to China also figured significantly in my desire to find ways to bring our countries closer together.

As my involvement in building a more cooperative Indo-American relationship developed, I was barely aware that there was an Asian Indian community in our country. In my own district there were no more than a handful of Asian Indians, if there were any at all. My interest was solely in doing what I thought was necessary to improve the relationship between these two great democracies. Whereas today the Indian caucus in the House of Representatives has over 150 members, when I was in Congress the Indian caucus could have met in a phone booth, where I (as its only member) wouldn't have suffered from claustrophobia. As time went by, thanks largely to *India Abroad*, a weekly newspaper for the US Asian Indian community that featured frequent stories about my often lonely efforts to support India, I became widely known to Asian Indians throughout the country. I also got to know the leaders of many of their communal organizations.

They were a truly impressive community that had become a great American success story. Composed mostly of professionals and businessmen who had come to the United States in the 1950s and 1960s, they had a far higher per capita income than the American people as a whole. Having established themselves socially and economically, they were starting to become politically active, and I was the vehicle through which many chose to do so. The best example was the response to a fundraising mailing I sent out to the 50,000 *India Abroad* subscribers. Usually, such solicitations result in a response rate of 1 or 2 percent, and 3 percent is considered a great success. The response rate to my letter asking for contributions to my 1984 reelection campaign was 29 percent. Realizing that this community could be a source of significant financial support, I began to hold fundraisers at the homes of Asian Indian community leaders around the country. It was a source of personal and political satisfaction to receive such substantial benefits from doing what I thought was in the best interests of the United States, especially since I had no idea this would happen when I first embarked on the effort to improve Indo-American relations. To keep my friends and supporters in the Asian Indian community apprised of my efforts, I began sending them newsletters, dealing mostly with my efforts to thwart various anti-India measures in Congress. In August 1989, for example, I sent out a mailing describing efforts by Representative Wally Herger, a California Republican, to cut off U S aid to India. The letter said, "I was deeply distressed that no one other than me rose on the floor of the House to explain India's position and to rebut the misrepresentations spread by the supporters of the Herger amendment," which I was pleased to report had been defeated.

A couple of years later, when my Subcommittee on Asian and Pacific Affairs recommended over $1 billion in development assistance and food aid for India, some of my colleagues wanted to cut the funds and take other anti-India measures that would have chilled the climate for further improvements in our bilateral relationship. Before this legislation came up for consideration on the House floor, I learned that Dan Burton, a conservative Republican from Indiana, might offer an amendment to cut development assistance to India on the ground that Indian security forces were mistreating Kashmiris, violating their human rights.

The issue of Kashmir had long bedeviled India and Pakistan. When both countries became independent in 1947, Jammu and Kashmir was one of several hundred princely states given the right to decide whether they wanted to be affiliated with India or Pakistan. The maharajah of Kashmir, Hari Singh, a Hindu who ruled over a majority Muslim population, hoped he might somehow remain independent and couldn't make up his mind which way to go. The Pakistanis, believing that Kashmir as a contiguous Muslim majority state rightly belonged to them, dispatched thousands of tribal invaders to take control of it. As the tribals raped and plundered on their way to Srinagar, Kashmir's capital, the maharajah called on Prime Minister Nehru of India to dispatch Indian troops to repel the invasion. Nehru said he would only do so if the maharajah formally acceded to India, and Singh agreed. Nehru's forces managed to push the tribal invaders back but could not completely force them out of Kashmir, which now found itself divided into two states — Azad Kashmir, occupied by Pakistan, and Jammu and Kashmir, controlled by India.

The U N Security Council called for a referendum in which the Kashmiris would opt either for India or for Pakistan. The relevant resolution called for the withdrawal of all Pakistani troops from Kashmir before the referendum was held. But because the Pakistanis never withdrew their forces, India refused to permit the referendum to go forward, and Kashmir remained divided. Over the following years, Pakistan went to war at least three times to wrest control of Jammu and Kashmir from India. When these attempts failed, it resorted, beginning in the late 1980s, to supporting terrorist groups resisting what it considered the Indian occupation of Kashmir. In response, the Indians deployed up to 500,000 security forces in Kashmir, in an effort to snuff out the insurgency. It was the actions of these forces that Burton was pointing to.

Working with other friends of India in Congress, I devised a strategy to derail Burton's effort. I was frankly concerned that some of my colleagues, while they supported development assistance to India, might feel compelled to support Burton's amendment because of their general desire to promote human rights. While I certainly shared their concerns, I didn't think cutting aid to India would improve the situation, while it would set back the effort to lift the poorest of the poor out of poverty. What was needed was an alternative legislative vehicle, which I drafted in conjunction with Ed Feighan, Democrat of Ohio. Our amendment expressed concern about human rights issues in India (and also condemned abuse by terrorists in Kashmir and Punjab) but didn't wipe out our assistance program. By enabling members to register their concern over the human rights situation in Kashmir while leaving our aid program intact, the Feighan-Solarz amendment passed the House as a substitute for the Burton amendment.

The Indians were certainly grateful to me. On one of my trips, Murli Deora, a member of Parliament from Mumbai, invited me to speak at a gathering in his district. When I arrived, several hundred people were waiting. The event was held outside on a street in what appeared to be one of the poorer neighborhoods of the city. A huge banner hung above the street said, "Welcome His Lordship Congressman Stephen Solarz." When the rally was over they gave me the banner, and I brought it back to Brooklyn and put it in my congressional office. Shortly afterward, a constituent came in with a problem she wanted help solving. I couldn't resist taking her to the room where the banner hung. She looked at it and said,

"Well, you can be sure I'll never refer to you as your lordship." Of course that wasn't my intention, but I thought her response reflected the healthy cynicism many of my constituents had toward their elected officials.

On one other issue regarding India, my involvement attracted consider-able attention in that country. In 1984, on a sunny day, the Union Carbide chemical plant in the city of Bhopal sprang a leak, sending out a cloud of poison gas that enveloped the city. Thousands of Indians lost their lives and many were permanently disabled. Since Union Carbide was an Amer-ican company, this tragic incident had potentially explosive consequences for Indo-American relations. To make matters worse, a horde of inter-national ambulance-chasing American attorneys descended on Bhopal to sign up litigants for lawsuits against the company. A few days after the ac-cident, I flew to Bhopal with Dr. Ross Brechner, a New Orleans ophthal-mologist whom I had grown up with. When we arrived in Bhopal, we were met by several dozen Indian journalists who wanted to know why we were there. I told them we had come to demonstrate that you didn't have to be a negligence attorney to be concerned about the tragedy in Bhopal, and that I wanted to determine how the United States could help ameliorate the consequences of the accident.

Over the next several months, I held hearings and tried to encourage a responsible resolution of the claims against Union Carbide. A settlement was eventually achieved in which Union Carbide paid $470 million to the Indian government for compensation to the victims of the disaster. It ex-ceeded by far any previous damage award in India, and the Indian Su-preme Court described it as "just, equitable, and reasonable."

My engagement with South Asia necessarily involved several trips to Pakistan. Almost all the Pakistanis I met with were quite engaging, even though I frequently found their politics troublesome. For most of the 1980s, Pakistan was a military dictatorship, unlike India, which remained a democracy. Thus I naturally felt more at home with my Indian interlocu-tors than with their Pakistani counterparts.

My first involvement with Pakistan concerned an effort to prevent the sale of F-16 fighter planes to that country. The Reagan administration was seeking congressional approval for the sale as part of our effort to help Pakistan in the aftermath of the Soviet invasion of Afghanistan in De-cember 1979. Not only did that invasion pose a direct threat to Pakistan, but we needed Pakistan's assistance if we were going to provide aid to the mujahedin, the Afghan insurgents, who were resisting the invasion. Still, I felt very strongly that the F-16s would do very little to help Pakistan defend itself against the Soviet Union, which could easily overwhelm the Pakistanis if it decided to cross the border, and had much more to do with Pakistan's desire to arm itself against India. I thought any military assistance to the Pakistanis should be limited to support that would be useful in helping them deal with Afghan contingencies. In addition, I was concerned that providing sophisticated weaponry to Pakistan would create real strains in our relationship with India, which was sure to resent our equipping the Pakistani air force with planes much more likely to be used against that country than against the Soviet Union. Though I vigorously opposed the aircraft sale, I couldn't stop it from going forward. But my effort won me a lot of friends in India and in the US Asian Indian community, which viewed the sale with equal concern. To make matters worse, even though the administration witnesses before our committee had testified that the F-16s could not carry nuclear weapons, I found out many years later that in fact, they could. Had I known at the time that these witnesses were playing fast and loose with the truth, I would have urged the Justice Department to consider indicting them for perjuring themselves before a congressional committee.

Even as the administration pushed for the sale of the F-16s, it and Congress were seriously concerned about Pakistan's effort to produce nuclear weapons. The fear, which I shared, was that a Pakistani nuclear arsenal would likely fuel a nuclear arms race with India and constitute a major blow to the global antiproliferation regime. There was also concern that Pakistan would either transfer its nuclear weapons to other Islamic countries or help them produce such devices themselves. I did not share this concern, because I found it hard to believe that Pakistan would actually share its nuclear weapons or technology with other countries. Here I was wrong. After obtaining these weapons, Pakistan proceeded to set itself up as a global nuclear supermarket, providing equipment and technology to a number of other countries that wanted to join the nuclear club.

Around this time, Pakistan was caught secretly trying to obtain devices and materials in the United States for its clandestine nuclear weapons program, in violation of our export control regulations. Since the last thing anyone wanted was for Pakistan to acquire nuclear weapons, I managed to get legislation adopted prohibiting aid to any country that attempted to advance a nuclear-weapons program by acquiring materials for it in the United States. Unfortunately the Pakistanis were not deterred so easily. On Capitol Hill there was a flickering suspicion that they were continuing their surreptitious acquisitions, but whenever I inquired about this I was fobbed off by the administration. When incontrovertible evidence emerged that Pakistan had violated the Solarz amendment restrictions on the acquisition of nuclear weapon components in the United States—which required cutting off our economic and military assistance programs—President Reagan used the presidential waiver contained in the legislation to continue them.

Admittedly, the administration confronted a difficult problem. Our ability to arm the Afghan resistance to the Soviet invasion depended on Pakistan's allowing all our military assistance to move through its territory. The administration feared that if we cut off aid, the Pakistanis might end this cooperation. For both the Reagan and Bush administrations, making the Soviet Union pay a heavy price for the invasion in order to discourage Moscow from invading other countries was apparently a higher priority than stopping Pakistan's effort to obtain nuclear weapons. In fairness, it is doubtful that Pakistan would have abandoned its nuclear weapons project even if we had terminated our aid program. Zulfikar Ali Bhutto, who had launched Pakistan's nuclear weapons program after India exploded a "peaceful" nuclear device in 1974, had famously said that "Pakistanis would eat grass" if necessary to obtain nuclear weapons. When President George H. W. Bush finally felt he had no choice but to terminate our aid program—which he was legally obligated to do once Pakistan had actually assembled an atom bomb—the Pakistanis continued on their merry way producing even more nuclear weapons.

On August 2, 1989, I conducted a classified hearing on Pakistan's nuclear weapons program under elaborate security precautions (this hearing is described in Deception, by Adrian Levy and Catherine Scott-Clark, a deeply disturbing account of the Reagan administration's earlier refusal to enforce the antiproliferation laws). The room was swept for electronic bugs moments before the hearing began. An armed guard stood outside the door. Presumably these precautions were intended to prevent the leakage of highly classified intelligence on Pakistan's nuclear weapons program. In view of what happened at the hearing, however, these precautions were hardly necessary. To put it bluntly, the administration witnesses lied about what they knew of the Pakistani nuclear program. Instead of revealing the full scope of the Pakistani procurement effort in the United States, which was quite extensive, they indicated that the violations of US law involved were limited to rogue businessmen acting on their own initiative. As with the earlier hearing on the F-16s, I was unaware of this until years later — and again, if I had known, I would have attempted to secure indictments against these witnesses for perjury. As is now known, Pakistan's effort went far beyond obtaining nuclear weapons itself. Under the direction of A. Q. Khan, the father of the Pakistani bomb, it was engaged in a systematic effort to facilitate the acquisition of nuclear weapons by several other rogue regimes, including Libya, North Korea, and Iran.

Throughout most of the 1980s, Pakistan was a military dictatorship under the rule of Muhammad Zia-ul-Haq, who became president after seizing power in a military coup. He died in 1988 in a mysterious plane crash that also took the life of Arnie Raphel, the highly regarded US ambassador to Pakistan. During the years I spent dealing with Pakistan as chairman of the Subcommittee on Asia, I made various efforts to encourage the establishment of democracy there, which led me to become friendly with Benazir Bhutto, daughter of Zulfikar Ali Bhutto, the Pakistani prime minister whom Zia overthrew in 1977 and eventually executed. Impressed by her commitment to democracy, I visited her several times at her home in Karachi and also met with her in the United States and London. A graduate of Harvard and Oxford, she spoke flawless English, and I found her a most attractive, engaging, determined, and courageous young woman.

After Zia's death, the Pakistani military decided to hold elections and return to their barracks. Knowing how much the Pakistanis revered her martyred father, I wasn't surprised when the Pakistan Peoples Party, led by Benazir, won the election and she became prime minister. In a speech she subsequently gave in Washington before the National Democratic Institute, she referred to me as "the Lafayette of Pakistani democracy" — the first time in history that the leader of a Muslim country compared an American Jew to a French Catholic. However not all Pakistani leaders

With Benazir Bhutto in Washington, 1980s.

were so complimentary. Zia-ul-Haq denounced me as the "voice of India in Congress," and Nawaz Sharif, who succeeded Benazir as prime minster, called me "the leader of the Hindu-Zionist conspiracy against Pakistan." I was never sure which branch of the conspiracy I was responsible for.

A call from the FBI one day during the 1980s alerted me to a more ominous expression of Pakistani hostility. According to the agent I spoke to, the intelligence community had intercepted a telephone call from Pakistan to a Pakistani in New York in which the expatriate was instructed to assassinate me. The FBI wanted me to be aware that this threat existed so I could take whatever precautions I thought necessary. When I asked whether the FBI knew who had been on the receiving end of the call, he said they didn't know his identity but they did know he owned or worked at a gas station in New York City. Since there were a finite number of gas stations in the city, I suggested they systematically canvass them to identify my putative assassin. But this seemed too daunting for the FBI, which declined to take my suggestion. Fortunately, the individual who was

told to kill me was apparently no more interested in carrying out his instructions than the FBI was in detecting and detaining him. Since nothing
happened, I dismissed the instruction as the idle threat of a disgruntled
Pakistani rather than an official order of the Pakistani government.

Despite this threat, I continued to visit Pakistan because I wanted to
get as good an understanding as I could of its problems and politics. On a
later trip, for example, I arranged to be taken to the FATA, formally known
as the Federally Administered Tribal Areas, where the writ of the Pakistani government had not run since the day of independence. To learn
more about an antinarcotics program there, I went to what was known as
the Malakand Agency, an area that would make Dodge City look tame.
Every man I saw carried a Kalashnikov rifle, and no Pakistani military or
police were anywhere to be seen. I flew by helicopter deep into the Malakand Agency, where I received a briefing about the antinarcotics program
from the colonel in charge of the Tribal Levees, the local militia responsible for law and order. At the end of his presentation I said: "Colonel,
this has been a very impressive briefing. You obviously have accomplished
a great deal. I want you to know that when I return to New York, I am
going to recommend to my very good friend Mayor Koch that he appoint
you police commissioner of New York City." The colonel, who apparently
didn't realize I was kidding, replied: "Oh, I couldn't possibly do that. It's
much too dangerous in New York."

On still another trip to India and Pakistan, I met both with Benazir,
who had just become prime minister, and with Rajiv Gandhi, who was
then prime minister of India. In separate meetings with these youthful
leaders, who I felt represented the future of their countries, I said: "Prime
ministers of India and Pakistan, unite. You have nothing to lose but your
bureaucracies." Unfortunately, they were not prepared to lose their bureaucracies, and the rapprochement between India and Pakistan that I
thought this new generation of political leaders might make possible never
occurred.

My overall impression of the potential for negotiating with the Pakistanis is summarized by one illuminating incident during a 1978 trip. I had
traveled to Azad Kashmir, the Pakistani part of Kashmir, whose name
means Free Kashmir (the Indians call it Pakistani Occupied Kashmir). In
the capital of the province, Muzaffarabad, the territorial prime minister

held a luncheon in my honor. During our conversation, I asked who he thought was responsible for President Zia's death. His plane had taken off on a clear, sunny day from a military airfield and a few minutes later plummeted to earth, killing everyone on board. The prime minister said it was the CIA. I tried to reason with him, suggesting that someone asked to investigate the incident would begin by drawing up a list of possible suspects. The list would certainly include the KGB and the Soviet Union, because of the help Zia was giving the mujahedin; KHAD, the Afghan KGB, which also would have good reason to resent Zia and want him out of the way; dissident elements within the Pakistani military who, for one reason or another, might have wanted to eliminate their commander in chief; the political opposition to Zia in Pakistan itself; and RAW, the Indian intelligence agency, which resented Zia's support for the anti-Indian insurgency in Kashmir. But the notion that the United States was responsible via the CIA was ludicrous, I asserted. For one thing, we had a very good relationship with Zia, who was cooperating with the United States in facilitating aid to the mujahedin in Afghanistan — a major US foreign policy priority. For another, I asked whether the prime minister really thought that even if we wanted to kill Zia, we would do it in a way that would also cause the death of our ambassador and the general in charge of our military mission (who was also on the plane). The prime minister's response: "This is proof positive that the CIA was behind it, because it diverted suspicion from them" as the architects of the crime.

This conversation underscored for me the extent to which conspiracy theories were an integral part of the worldview of Pakistanis, who appeared to live in a different political universe than we did. Anyone who thought the CIA responsible for Zia's death obviously had a very tenuous grip on political reality. But the people of Pakistan, much like many Arabs, are entrapped in their conspiratorial view of the world, in which the most logical explanation of events is invariably trumped by theories of the "hidden hand."

One conclusion I drew from my dealings with Pakistan and its dealings with other governments was that for Pakistani officials, perpetual prevarication was a routine way of conducting diplomacy. Their penchant for dissimulation gave renewed meaning to the observation that the job of a diplomat is to lie for his country. They told the Soviet Union that they weren't providing arms to the mujahedin, when they obviously were. They told India and the United States that they weren't providing assistance to terrorist groups that wanted to destabilize India by fomenting rebellion in Kashmir, when they clearly were. They denied that they were trying to obtain nuclear weapons right up to the point when they exploded several of them in the late 1990s.

Over time it became clear to me that Pakistani officials had virtually no credibility. Even now, decades later, they provide assistance and sanctuary to the Afghan Taliban while denying that they do so. Taking Pakistani protestations at face value is a formula for self-deception that cannot and will not serve our national interests. With the Soviets, President Reagan used to say, we should "trust but verify." In the case of Pakistan, we should verify but remain wary. Truth is not a word in their diplomatic vocabulary.

For much of the 1980s, whenever I held a hearing on the situation in the subcontinent, the highest-level administration official I could get to testify was the deputy assistant secretary in the Bureau of Near Eastern Affairs. NEA, as it was called, was responsible for formulating and implementing our policy toward the Middle East and North Africa as well as South Asia. Given the high priority attached to resolving the conflict between Israel and its Arab neighbors, as well as the strategic significance of the Persian Gulf and its oil, NEA seemed to have little high-level time left for South Asian issues.

Considering that a billion people lived in South Asia, that it was the site of an incipient nuclear arms race between India and Pakistan, and that we were engaged in a covert war in Afghanistan, I began to think it would make bureaucratic sense to remove South Asia from NEA and place it in a newly created bureau with its own assistant secretary of state and supporting staff. I believed that such a bureau would not only make it possible for the subcontinent to receive a higher level of attention in the State Department but also facilitate a more sympathetic policy toward India, the dominant power in the region. I wrote to all the living former secretaries of state, asking what they thought of this idea. Interestingly, the Republican secretaries — William Rogers, Henry Kissinger, and Al Haig — all thought it was a bad idea, while their Democratic counterparts — Dean Rusk, Cyrus Vance, and Edmund Muskie — all thought it was a good one. So I drafted a bill to create a new bureau.

It was a reflection of both the administration's lack of attention to South Asia and the enduring truth that nothing galvanizes a bureaucrat like a threat to reduce the scope of his responsibilities that the only time I got the assistant secretary for NEA to testify before my subcommittee was when I convened a hearing on this legislation. By that time it was too late for him to protect his turf, and, with the help of Senator Pat Moynihan, who had been our ambassador to India, I was able to persuade the House and Senate to approve legislation creating this new bureau. Since then, the former Asian republics of the Soviet Union, now independent Central Asian states, have been added to the bureau's jurisdiction. How it will function and how much influence it will have in shaping our policy toward that part of the world remains to be seen.

9

CENTRAL AMERICA AND CUBA

Revolutions Closer to Home

⤳

I must confess that I paid little attention to Central America before 1981, when the Reagan administration came into office. During the 1970s, Central America was eclipsed by the main event of the Cold War, the US-Soviet struggle for global preeminence, as manifested during that decade by the Red Army's invasion of Afghanistan and Moscow's efforts, backed by Cuban troops, to extend its influence in Angola and Ethiopia. In comparison to the turmoil in the Middle East, Africa, and Asia, Central America seemed relatively conflict free. But it soon became evident that leftist rebel movements — particularly in El Salvador, Guatemala, and Nicaragua — presented an increasingly serious challenge and threatened to produce instability close to home.

The Reagan administration, which regarded Central America as a new front in the Cold War, concluded that the United States needed to shore up the Salvadoran government's ability to beat back the challenge from the Farabundo Marti National Liberation Front (FMLN), a rebel group with a significant Communist component. The Salvadoran government reacted to the growing danger by deploying death squads; each week, hundreds of Salvadorans were killed both by leftist guerrillas and by government death squads. There was a historic precedent for such brutal suppression of an indigenous leftist uprising. In the 1930s, in response to a similar threat, the government had launched *la matanza* (the slaughter), in which tens of thousands of Salvadoran peasants were massacred. Now history seemed to be repeating itself. By torturing and murdering thousands of men and women, many innocent of any involvement in the armed struggle, the government was alienating its own people.

As often happens, a pivotal event brought this conflict into sharp focus for the United States. On the afternoon of December 2, 1980, an American nun and a lay missionary, who did aid work among the poor, picked up two other nuns who had just arrived at the airport and began the long ride through the countryside to San Salvador, the capital. The right wing in El Salvador regarded religious activists, including those from the United States, as dangerous leftist enemies. Five Salvadoran National Guard members, out of uniform, stopped the vehicle. They took the four women to an isolated spot, then brutally raped and murdered them.

News of the attack caused widespread anger in the United States and, indeed, throughout the world. A quick investigation in El Salvador was sharply criticized as a coverup, provoking more anger. Eventually, the United Nations appointed a truth commission. In the end, several low-level soldiers were convicted and two generals were sued by the women's families in US courts. The incident exposed the shallowness of justice in El Salvador and the shadowy, but dominant, role of the military.

In January 1981, I decided to go there, as well as to other countries in Central America, to get a better understanding of the situation and see for myself what could be done about this dangerous, deteriorating state of affairs close to home. I went to the headquarters of the Christian Democratic Party to meet Ray Prendes, the mayor of San Salvador. When the meeting ended, we stood together for several minutes at the entrance of the headquarters, which the day before had been the target of a drive-by shooting by the guerrillas. This time, happily, nothing happened. I also met with Minister of Defense Vides Casanova, who was in charge of the security forces. When I asked him about allegations of death squad activities by units under his command, he responded, "Why did you drop the atom bomb on Hiroshima?" It was an oblique acknowledgment that the Salvadoran military was guilty of the human rights abuses it was accused of.

On my return to Washington, I wrestled with how to resolve the contradiction between the strategic importance of denying the Communists another toe-hold in the hemisphere and the need to rely on the Salvadoran government to achieve this. Cuba was already in the Communists' grasp, the leftist Sandinistas had taken power in Nicaragua, and it would be disturbing at best, and destabilizing at worst, if the FMLN prevailed in El Salvador. The only way to stop the guerrillas' advance — short of introducing American troops, which even the Reagan administration wasn't asking for — was to provide military assistance to a government engaged in terrible human rights abuses. Entire villages were being wiped out. Peasants were found on the side of the road with their thumbs tied together, shot and killed.

I turned to legislation in the form of an amendment to the foreign aid authorization bill, which made our military assistance contingent on an annual certification by our president that the government of El Salvador was making substantial progress toward eliminating human rights abuses. It was an effort to resolve the differences between those (mostly Republicans) who wanted to continue providing assistance to El Salvador, regardless of its human rights record, in order to prevent the guerrillas from taking power, and those (mostly Democrats) who wanted to cut off assistance precisely because of those abuses, even if the result was a guerrilla victory. With the support of mainstream Democrats and moderate Republicans, the legislation passed.

Most of my Brooklyn constituents were not greatly concerned with the controversies in Congress over El Salvador. But this issue was a focus for peace activists in my district who vehemently opposed our military assistance. At one town hall meeting in Brooklyn Heights, to which I invited Les Aspin, chairman of the Armed Services Committee, we had to run the gantlet of a group of demonstrators dressed in skeleton outfits denouncing us as "death squad Democrats." Aspin later commented that it was quite a contrast to the town hall meetings he held in his rural district in Wisconsin, where he was lucky if eight men in bib overalls showed up.

Over the next couple of years, whenever it came time to decide whether to continue our aid program, the president would submit a certification that the government of El Salvador was making substantial progress in diminishing human rights violations. These certifications became the subject of congressional hearings and considerable political controversy because, for the most part, the abuses continued unabated and the progress—to put it charitably—was minimal. The one bright spot on the political landscape was José Napoléon Duarte, the leader of the Christian Democratic Party, who in 1984 became president. I had met him during my first trip there and was convinced that he was a genuine democrat, clearly committed to protecting his people's human rights. But he didn't control the military and seemed unable to prevent its horrendous abuses.

The administration became more and more uneasy over the issuance of presidential certifications increasingly unrelated to reality, and President

Reagan eventually dispatched Vice President George H. W. Bush to read the riot act to the Salvadoran military leadership. Bush warned that — given Congress's concerns and the content of American law — unless the Salvadorans stopped the abuses, the Reagan administration would be unable to continue its political support. This démarche helped bring about a significant improvement in the human rights situation. The abuses continued, most notably the murder of several Jesuit priests by the security forces in 1989. But American pressure and an overall decline in abuses led in January 1992 to a negotiated settlement that ended the conflict and made free and fair elections possible.

Meanwhile, in 1987, President Oscar Arias of Costa Rica had presented what became known as the Arias Plan, calling for negotiated settlements of the conflicts in El Salvador, Nicaragua, and Guatemala. I strongly supported his efforts and secured adoption of a congressional resolution supporting his plan. While Arias was not directly involved in negotiating the El Salvador peace agreement, his plan created the context that made this possible. I met with Arias several times and got to know him well. In fact, we became so friendly that we took a rafting trip together down two rivers in Costa Rica, the Pacuare and the Reventazon, where Arias proved as capable of running the rapids as of negotiating political conflicts.

I traveled as well to Guatemala, which also had a violent, repressive military, and met with President Efraín Ríos Montt, a born-again Christian who was Guatemala's military dictator. I told him I had heard reports that he had been able to eliminate death squad activity in the cities, and I was curious how he had done it. He looked at me and said, "I didn't do it." I asked who had. "God did it," he said. However, Ríos Montt neglected to mention that at the same time that his government had stopped the death squads in the cities, it had intensified the repression in the countryside.

Guatemalan officials took me by helicopter to a village in the highlands where I hoped to get the views of ordinary people about the conflict between the guerrillas and the government. But this foray into the countryside turned out to be a bad joke. When the helicopter landed, a dozen soldiers with rifles jumped out and formed a protective cordon around me. Surrounded by the very same soldiers who were presumably repressing the villagers, it was impossible to talk candidly with them about government repression.

*Rafting trip with Oscar Arias (second from right, in sunglasses).
I am second from left, and Nina is next to me.*

This somewhat bizarre visit was reminiscent of a trip I had made in October 1991 to Peru, then experiencing the vicious insurgency of the Shining Path, or Sendero Luminoso, the Andean equivalent of the Khmer Rouge. I was taken to a Pueblo Joven, or New Town, on the outskirts of Lima. Having received reports that the Sendero Luminoso were coming down from the highlands and establishing a presence in the cities, I asked the young Peruvian social worker who escorted me how people there felt about the Sendero Luminoso. She responded cautiously, observing that in her Pueblo Joven they preferred not to have an opinion. It was her way of saying that if people told someone from the military they supported the Sendero Luminoso, they would be killed. But if they told someone from the Sendero Luminoso that they supported the government, they would also be killed. One way or the other, people were intimidated, and the truth about their feelings was an elusive commodity.

Nicaragua too was going through a revolutionary period, but the Sandinistas were never as violent or fanatical as the Sendero Luminoso or the

Khmer Rouge. Perhaps this reflects the gentler nature of the Nicaraguan people. The Sandinistas took their name from Augusto César Sandino, who had led the Nicaraguan resistance against the US occupation of Nicaragua in the 1930s. In 1979, the Sandinistas overthrew the corrupt dictatorship of Anastasio Somoza, whose downfall occurred after he stole international aid donated in the aftermath of a severe 1972 earthquake. The theft helped swell the Sandinistas' ranks and persuaded the populace that Somoza had to go.

The Reagan administration, however, objected to the Sandinistas' leftwing politics and secretly funded a counterrevolutionary force known as the Contras. I was very much opposed to this funding because, based on my discussions with the Sandinista leadership, I believed it was possible to negotiate an arrangement in which the Nicaraguan people could determine their own destiny through a free and fair election. Ultimately, this is what happened, and it resulted, much to the amazement of many, in the Sandinistas' defeat. I also met with the Contra leadership at one of their training camps along the Honduran-Nicaraguan border. To get there, I flew in a puddle jumper hired by the CIA, escorted by an agency operative who wore a baseball hat bearing the slogan "Admit nothing. Deny everything. Make counteraccusations."

By the mid-1980s, although there were almost no US casualties in Central America, our policy toward the region in general, and Nicaragua in particular, was becoming a hot button issue in Washington. At one point, a few of us in the House of Representatives, including Majority Leader Jim Wright of Texas, sent a letter to Daniel Ortega, the Sandinista leader and president of Nicaragua, urging him to hold a truly democratic election. For some reason, the person who actually put the letter together addressed him as "Dear Comandante." The Republicans jumped all over us, asserting that this greeting suggested that Democrats were somehow soft on the Sandinistas. In the midst of this brouhaha, I was invited to appear on the CNN show Crossfire — the TV version of a mosh pit.

The other guest was Newt Gingrich, one of the Republican leaders in the House. The moderator, Tom Braden, asked Gingrich why he objected to the "Dear Comandante" letter. Gingrich launched into a tirade for several minutes, denouncing me and the other signatories of the letter for usurping the president's constitutional prerogatives by communicating with a Communist tyrant. Such a communication, he said, legitimized the Sandinista regime and was harmful to American national interests. When Gingrich finished his diatribe, Tom Braden turned to me.

I was ready. Reaching into my breast pocket, milking the moment for all it was worth, I said: "Tom, I have a letter here. It's addressed to Mr. Yuri Andropov, Chairman, Supreme Soviet, the Kremlin, Moscow, USSR. And, lo and behold, one of the signatories of the letter is none other than Newt Gingrich. Here he is accusing me of writing to a little Communist tyrant, when he is corresponding with the biggest Communist tyrant of them all!" Gingrich was stuck. The best he could do was protest, "There's a big difference."

"What's the difference?" Braden asked.

"Well, we have no covert operations against the Soviet Union," Gingrich replied. To which Braden — who had served in the OSS during World War II and knew something about clandestine government activities — responded, "I certainly hope we do."

Gingrich was apparently too flustered to ask what the letter to Andropov was about. If he had, I would have said: "Congressman, to your credit you signed a letter urging Andropov to permit a Soviet Jew who simply wanted the right to leave his country to do so. We sent a letter to Daniel Ortega urging him to hold a free and fair election. What's wrong with that?" After this exchange, whenever I crossed paths with Gingrich on the House floor, the reaction I got from him was exactly what you would expect when you stand up to the schoolyard bully — a degree of respect and deference not previously noticeable.

How did I know he had signed that letter? When I got the invitation to debate Gingrich, I asked someone on my staff to contact the National Conference on Soviet Jewry. At that time, congressmen frequently sent letters to the Soviet leaders imploring them to let Soviet Jews emigrate. Sure enough, Gingrich had signed one.

Meanwhile, our efforts to convince the Sandinistas to hold honest elections — plus the pressure we applied — bore fruit. In retrospect, I suppose the Sandinistas took the gamble on holding elections in 1990 because they controlled all the levers of power and didn't think they could lose. But

they did lose — to Violeta Chamorro, a member of a prominent, aristo-
cratic Nicaraguan family and the widow of a courageous publisher who
had been critical of the Somoza regime and was assassinated in 1978.

I went to Nicaragua the week of the election to get a sense of whether it
would be free and fair. Virtually everybody was predicting an Ortega victory. But the economy was a mess, and one had to assume that dissatisfac-
tion with the regime was rampant — rather like Herbert Hoover running
for reelection in 1932. The turnout at opposition rallies was unexpect-
edly huge, and that didn't augur well for the Sandinistas. After a few days,
based on what I had heard and seen, I concluded that Mrs. Chamorro was
going to score an upset. I called Nina from the US ambassador's residence
and told her to get out a pencil and paper. "Write this down," I said, "59/41."
Nina asked if I thought Ortega was going to win by that much. "No," I
said, "that's what Chamorro is going to win by."

While I was in Nicaragua, I ran into Robert Novak, the conservative
columnist, at a Chamorro rally I was observing. I couldn't help thinking
it was lucky I hadn't met him at an Ortega rally; if I had, Novak would
undoubtedly have written, "Not content to cheer the Sandinistas on from
afar, left-leaning New York Congressman Stephen Solarz was seen cheer-
ing Daniel Ortega at a rally in Managua." I found out from various infor-
mants that the Ortega rallies were mostly attended by people who had
been bused in and, in fact, had been pressured to go. Polls indicated that
Ortega would win by a comfortable margin. But polls are useless in repressive regimes where people are afraid to tell the truth about what they
think. One night during the campaign, I was having dinner at the home of
our ambassador, Tony Quainton, along with Virgilio Godoy, Chamorro's
running mate for vice president. Toward the end of the evening, I asked
the two women Godoy had brought as his interpreters whom they were
planning to vote for. Even though it was abundantly clear by now that my
sympathies were with Chamorro and Godoy, it took about fifteen minutes
to extract from them the fact that they were going to vote for Chamorro.

I flew back to Washington and went to a cocktail party at the George-
town home of Pamela Harriman, where Jim Lehrer, co-host of *The Mac-
Neil/Lehrer Report*, was chatting with Nina. She told him I had just
returned from Nicaragua and was predicting a Chamorro victory. He
came over and asked about the situation there. I said I thought Ortega

would lose and Mrs. Chamorro would win. That surprised him. "Everybody thinks Ortega is going to win," he said. "Would you be willing to state your view on television?"

"Why not? That's what I think," I told him.

I appeared on his show the following evening with Stanley Greenberg, who later became the pollster for Bill Clinton's first presidential campaign. He told me my prediction was wrong, saying that he had done polling all over Latin America and had never been more than 1 or 2 percentage points off. "We show Ortega winning by a substantial margin," Greenberg asserted.

"With all due respect, Stanley," I countered, "if you sent one of your interviewers out to the countryside and he asked some poor *campesino* if Ortega was doing a good job, what kind of answer can you expect in a country where, if you're identified as a critic of the government, you can face serious consequences?" When the election was held a couple of days later, my prediction came closer to the truth than Greenberg's. Chamorro won by one point less than I had predicted in my call to Nina.

On a lighter note, my experiences with government and opposition forces in Central America led me to a counterintuitive principle regarding food. On the last day of a visit to Guatemala, I was given a dinner by an organization called Los Amigos del País, or Friends of the Country, a chamber of commerce for the economic elite. The dinner consisted of some parsley sandwiches and a few carrots — skimpy fare, to say the least. The next day, I went to Costa Rica, where I had dinner with Edén Pastora, better known as Comandante Zero. Originally a Sandinista commander, Pastora was turned off by the leftward drift of the revolution and became a leader of the Contras. He treated me to a sumptuous ten-course dinner with all the fixings. These two culinary experiences led me to formulate Solarz's Law of Central American Dining: If you want to eat like a revolutionary, dine with the capitalists; if you want to eat like a capitalist, dine with the revolutionaries!

Speaking of revolutionaries, in the late 1970s and early 1980s I had several long meetings with the voluble granddaddy of them all, Fidel Castro. Our first encounter, in 1978, lasted from 5 p.m. to 2 a.m., and he did most of the talking. Afterward he had enough energy to drive me in his Soviet-made limousine to the guesthouse where I was staying. During those long

First encounter with Fidel Castro, in his office, 1978.

nine hours, our conversation ranged from Che to Carter and from Cuba to
Katanga. His interpreter, a very attractive woman who was rumored to be
more than just his interpreter, provided a simultaneous translation, gear-
ing the pitch and pace of her voice to his, matching him when he spoke
faster and louder or slower and softer. Though to most Americans, including me, Castro's philosophy and politics are highly objectionable, his
personality is unquestionably captivating. Highly articulate, perpetually
passionate, very intelligent, and seemingly inexhaustible, he is the embodiment of charisma.

Much of our conversation dealt with President Jimmy Carter's contention that Cuba had provided arms and assistance to the Katangan rebels in
Angola, who had just invaded Shaba Province in Zaire for the second time
in two years. Castro vehemently denied that Cuba had anything whatsoever to do with the Katangans. Such a contention, he insisted, was "not a
half lie, not a partial lie, but an important lie." Indeed, not only did Cuba
have nothing to do with the Katangans, Castro claimed, but he had actu-

ally tried to stop them when he heard rumors of an impending invasion a few months earlier.

Back in Washington, many people asked if I thought Castro was telling the truth about this. He is clearly capable of saying one thing and doing another. But having heard CIA chief Stansfield Turner brief our committee for three hours in executive session on the extent to which the Cubans were responsible for the invasion of Zaire, I can only say that, while the possibility of Cuban involvement could not be ruled out, the evidence on which the administration based its conclusion was highly circumstantial and far from conclusive. It was impossible to determine definitively whether the Cubans really were involved.

After several hours of listening to Castro's repeated denials, I managed to move into a discussion of the Cuban presence throughout Africa. When I asked about Ethiopia, in contrast to his determined denials of an association with the Katangans, Castro openly acknowledged that there were thousands of Cuban troops in that country. Why, I asked, did he feel obligated to send troops to Ethiopia? Because if not for Cuba, Castro responded, "one of the great crimes of the epoch" would have been perpetuated against Ethiopia. He claimed he had tried to prevent the outbreak of war between Somalia and Ethiopia and had even traveled to the Horn of Africa in a futile effort to end their dispute. But when Somalia invaded the Ogaden, in southeastern Ethiopia, and was on the verge of victory, he felt the only way to prevent the dismemberment of Ethiopia and the collapse of the "Ethiopian revolution" was to repel the Somali invaders.

Although the rulers of Ethiopia were among the worst human rights abusers in Africa, Castro clearly had a strong ideological identification with the Ethiopian revolution and a high personal regard for its leader, Colonel Mengistu, the most prominent member of the Derg, the military junta that ruled the country. Castro used a rather incongruous comparison to indicate that he had no intention of withdrawing his forces from the Ogaden: "Like Lincoln, I am absolutely opposed to secession." He also told me he favored a political solution in Eritrea but did not believe one was possible in Angola, because the political and ideological differences between Angola's leader and Jonas Savimbi, the rebel leader and Cold War figure embraced by US conservatives, were too great to overcome.

All this time, Castro was smoking one cigar after another. Eventually,

I took a cigar from his humidor and began smoking myself. After a while, because the cigar didn't have a band around it, I inquired what brand it was. He asked why I wanted to know. I told him that I liked the cigar and might want to buy some before I returned home. He asked if I could accept a gift. I told him I could, but only if it was worth less than $35, the prescribed limit on the value of gifts congressmen could accept. When our meeting ended several hours later, Castro asked me to excuse him for a minute and left the room. He returned with his arms full of Cohiba cigar boxes. In those days these cigars, the top-of-the-line Cuban brand, were made just for him, and he used to give them as gifts. He handed me a few boxes and said, "It's only $35." I did some quick calculations and figured that if I brought them back, and somebody raised a question with the Ethics Committee about accepting something that was arguably worth more than $35, I could say that Cuba had a command economy in which the state set the price. And if the "Maximum Leader of the Revolution" said the gift was worth $35, that's what it was worth. But for better or worse, the matter never came up.

My next visit to Cuba, the last stop on a five-week trip to Argentina, Peru, Brazil, Colombia, and El Salvador, was in January 1984. Anticipating another long meeting with Castro, I thought it would be interesting to get his views on the political situation in the countries I had just visited. So I decided to start at the bottom — geographically — and work my way up. I began with Argentina, which had just experienced its first honest election in decades, restoring democracy to the country, which had suffered from decades of military rule and economic misrule. Forty-five minutes later Castro was still holding forth on Argentina. That meeting lasted six hours. Another meeting two years later lasted three hours. He was clearly prepared to let each meeting go on as long as I wanted.

I don't want to suggest that I had any fondness for Castro. But I must confess that while I was certainly aware that he was a dictator, I didn't fully appreciate the magnitude of his tyranny until later, after reading two books that had a profound impact on my thinking about the Maximum Leader. I regret that I didn't read them before my meetings with El Jefe.

Family Portrait with Fidel, by Carlos Franqui, recounts the experiences of the author, who fought alongside Castro in the Sierra Maestra. Franqui became the first minister of culture in the revolutionary government and the editor of *Granma*, the official Cuban newspaper. His book makes it clear that Fidel was a Communist from the very beginning of the revolution. The romantic notion of many American liberals and European leftists that Fidel was driven into the arms of the Soviets because of US-imposed sanctions, Franqui argues persuasively, is just false. It was a destination to which he was heading from the outset.

In contrast, Armando Valladares's *Against All Hope* is the memoir of a Cuban who was arrested and thrown in jail at the age of nineteen or twenty after being overheard at the water cooler in his office making a joke about the regime. The harder they pushed him in jail, the more he resisted. Valladares wound up spending twenty years in prison, where he was repeatedly tortured for telling that joke and for resisting the demands of his interrogators. Over time he became an international cause célèbre. He was finally released from prison only because of international pressure, particularly from French President François Mitterrand. In his book, Valladares describes in detail the tortures inflicted on him and other political prisoners in Cuba. Given this systematic abuse, and the nature of the Cuban government, it was obvious that the institutionalized mistreatment of the regime's political opponents had to have been condoned by Castro.

Two exhibits I saw in Miami also strongly influenced my thinking about Cuba. The first was set up by the Cuban community in a Miami park. It displayed the various devices people had used to make the ninety-mile journey across the open sea from Cuba to the United States, including rubber tires and pieces of wood. They were a moving commentary on the risks Cubans were prepared to take to escape from tyranny and live in freedom. The other exhibit, also in a Miami park, which I saw a couple of years later, displayed a variety of torture devices used by Cuban authorities. The one I remember most vividly was a cell without windows, about six feet long and three feet wide, that was meant to hold four adults. Prisoners were kept there for months at a time, and the only way to sleep would be for one person to stretch out on the concrete floor for several hours while the others straddled him with their legs apart. These too were systemic cruelties that Fidel had to have known about.

As the years passed, Soviet subsidies kept Castro's Cuba on life support. For most of that time, although increasingly skeptical about the value of the sanctions we had imposed on Cuba, I nevertheless supported them as a gesture of solidarity with the Cuban community in the United States. But when the Soviet Union collapsed, the subsidies ended, and it was no longer certain that the Cuban regime could stay in power. I felt there was now a case to be made that maintaining the sanctions might force the Cuban government to open up, even possibly help bring it down. But as more time passed and a variety of factors — including foreign tourism and European investment — enabled the regime to hang on, I concluded that sanctions were no longer serving a useful purpose, and that lifting them might actually be a better way to facilitate change.

There was one issue on which I did achieve some progress during my marathon sessions with Castro. I brought up the several hundred dual nationals — citizens of both Cuba and the United States. — who lived in Cuba but wanted to be reunited with their families in the United States. Denied the right to leave Cuba, they had been separated from their loved ones for many years. I asked if Castro would be willing on humanitarian grounds to let them go. Somewhat to my surprise, he agreed, as a gesture of good will. A short while later, a charter flight was arranged to bring them out. I went down to Cuba and had the privilege of escorting 480 of these dual nationals back to the United States where, amid scenes of joy and jubilation, they were finally reunited with their families.

10

ENCOUNTERS IN EUROPE

Turkey, Cyprus, and Poland

While I spent much of my time and effort as a member of the Foreign
Affairs Committee dealing with challenges confronting us in the Middle
East, Africa, Asia, and Central America, I also dealt at times with European issues. One such case involved the conflict between Turkey and Cyprus; another, the struggle against Communism in Poland.

Some foreign policy issues were political losers for me. Others were winners. The first is exemplified by my work to lift the arms embargo against
Turkey; the second, by my efforts to facilitate a transition to democracy
in Poland. But in both cases what motivated me was the determination
to advance important national interests regardless of the political consequences. My work on Turkey lost me the support of the Greek American
community in my district. My efforts on behalf of Poland gained me the
support of the district's Polish American community. But I can honestly
say that even if I had known these outcomes in advance, I would still have
acted exactly the same in both cases.

My Turkish involvement began in spring 1975. The previous July, while
I was in the midst of my first campaign for Congress, Turkey had invaded
Cyprus. I paid little attention, since I was focused entirely on my campaign, and none of my future constituents ever raised this issue. It was
only after I took office in January 1975 that I began to get lots of letters
from the Greek Americans in my district urging me to support the arms
embargo against Turkey that Congress had enacted in December. They
were a small minority in the district, but they were extremely well organized. I also had a close relationship with a number of Greek American political activists who had supported my campaign. The little I knew
about this issue gave me the impression that the Turks were the bad guys
and the Greek Cypriots were the good guys. Since the only people in my
district who seemed to care were the Greeks, and because I didn't want to
disappoint my Greek American friends, I responded to the flood of mail

by saying that I shared their outrage over the Turkish intervention and that they could count on me to continue supporting the embargo. It was an easy commitment to make; I assumed that since the embargo had just been enacted, the issue was unlikely to come up for a vote in Congress.

Shortly afterward, however, Secretary of State Henry Kissinger announced that the Ford administration planned to make a major effort to persuade Congress to repeal the embargo. Because this question would come first before the House Foreign Affairs Committee, on which I now served, I thought it would make sense to go to the eastern Mediterranean, where I had never been before, to see the situation for myself. So it was that, during the 1975 spring recess, I went on a fact-finding mission to Greece, Turkey, and Cyprus.

In Cyprus, I met with Archbishop Makarios, who was the secular and religious leader of the Greek Cypriot community as well as president of the internationally recognized Republic of Cyprus, and with Rauf Denktash, the political leader of the Turkish Cypriot community. I also met with Glafklos Klerides, another Greek Cypriot leader. He was an impressive man who had the rare capacity to understand how his adversaries viewed the situation. In Greece, I met with Prime Minister Kostas Karamanlis and other political leaders. In Turkey, I met with Prime Minister Bulent Ecevit, who had ordered the military intervention, and Suleyman Demirel, the opposition leader and Ecevit's successor as prime minister. In each country, I also met with the American ambassador and other foreign diplomats.

By the end of the trip, several factors had led me to conclude that the embargo was a big mistake and that prohibiting the sale of American arms to Turkey contradicted vital American interests. First, I became aware of the London-Zurich Agreement, a 1959 accord among Turkey, Greece, and the United Kingdom, which gave the signatory powers the right to intervene in Cyprus if there was a serious threat to the constitutional order established when it became independent from Britain in 1960. The constitution was designed to protect the rights of the Turkish minority within the framework of a democracy in which the Greeks constituted the great majority of the population.

Prior to the Turkish intervention in July, a coup on Cyprus led by Nikos Sampson, a psychopathic Greek Cypriot committed to *enosis*, or the unification of Cyprus with Greece, had overthrown Makarios and the existing constitutional order. This coup posed an extremely serious threat to the security and possibly the survival of the Turkish Cypriot community. Sampson, who emerged as the new leader of Cyprus, had been responsible for the murder of a number of Turkish Cypriots in the past. Turkey was understandably fearful that the Turkish Cypriots might be slaughtered by the new regime. Given these circumstances, and the terms of the London-Zurich Agreement, Turkey was clearly within its rights to intervene militarily.

Second, I learned the important role that Turkey played in protecting the southern flank of NATO. Not only did it tie down twenty-two Warsaw Pact divisions that might otherwise have been shifted to the German border; it also enabled the US Sixth Fleet to preserve its naval supremacy in the eastern Mediterranean. Third, it became clear to me, from a political perspective, that the Turks would not respond well to pressure, and that continuing the embargo would actually make a negotiated resolution of the conflict — and the withdrawal of Turkish forces that the embargo was ostensibly designed to bring about — more difficult. Since the United States had a substantial interest in resolving the conflict and avoiding further tensions between Greece and Turkey, two important NATO allies, it seemed to me that the embargo was only making things worse.

I returned to Washington having jettisoned my previous position. A fashionable theory of that political moment held that the American people were looking for leaders who had the courage of their convictions. Under its influence, I promptly wrote to all the Greek Americans in my district who had urged me to support the embargo to let them know why I now believed it would be in the best interests of the United States to lift it. Before long it became obvious that the theory was incorrect. After a flood of letters denouncing me for changing my position, I realized that people admire political leaders who have the courage of their convictions when those convictions coincide with their own. Consequently I lost the support of the Greek Americans in my district. To be sure, they made up only a small part of the district, but there were two significant Greek Orthodox churches whose political influence was not inconsiderable. It was a painful experience, personally and politically.

I figured I could compensate for the lost support of the Greek Americans by winning the support of my Turkish American constituents. So I started looking for them. After several years, I finally found one: Albert Cohen, a Sephardic Jew from Istanbul, who did become a supporter. Still, though I had the satisfaction of knowing I had acted according to what I believed were the best interests of the country, from a purely political perspective I was a net loser. The episode taught me another lesson about life in Congress: how even a handful of letters from constituents could strike fear into most congressmen's hearts, particularly on an issue about which the rest of their constituents were mostly indifferent or unaware.

As a result of my trip to the eastern Mediterranean, I became very active in the congressional effort to lift the arms embargo on Turkey, returning to Cyprus several times to get a better sense of how to achieve a political resolution of the conflict. On one occasion Rauf Denktash, the Turkish Cypriot leader, took me on a three-hour drive around the Turkish sector of the island. Every ten minutes he stopped and pointed to a place where, he claimed, Turkish Cypriots had been massacred by Greek Cypriots. At one point, to illustrate how bad it was to grow up in Cyprus as a Turkish Cypriot, he informed me that the Greek whores wouldn't even sleep with Turkish johns.

On another trip, I met with Makarios's successor as archbishop, a hefty divine named Chrysostomos. Greek Orthodox archbishops are addressed as "your beatitude," just as a cardinal in the Catholic Church is addressed as "your eminence." At the end of our meeting, His Beatitude said he wanted to give me a little gift. An aide quickly left the room and returned a few minutes later with a book filled with pictures of Greek Orthodox icons that had been found in Cyprus. The archbishop said he wanted to inscribe it for me, which I thought was a nice gesture. Several minutes later he handed me the book. Eager to see what he had written, I opened it and read: "To Congressman Stephen Solarz, a representative of the United States of America, which in July of 1974 unleashed its vicious Turkish dogs against the innocent men, women and children of Cyprus, who then proceeded to murder, rape and plunder our people. With affection and regards, Chrysostomos."

In Congress, where there was still strong support for the embargo, it took a couple of years to finally get it lifted. We had to keep introducing new bills, until finally one passed. On one early vote, the yeas and nays were almost evenly balanced, and the outcome was in doubt, so a roll call vote was demanded. Members now had fifteen minutes to cast their votes. After this period expired, members who hadn't yet voted were given a little bit of extra time. Late arrivals went to the well of the House, where there was a box of red cards for a no vote and a box of green cards for a yes vote.

Tom Harkin, then a Democratic congressman from Iowa, had come in late. Unsure how to vote, he held a red card in his left hand and a green card in his right. John Brademas, Democrat of Indiana, who was leading the effort to preserve the embargo, urged him in one ear to vote no, while I urged him in the other to vote yes. In the midst of this rhetorical tug of war Millicent Fenwick, a distinguished New Jersey Republican who had once been a model, began to scold us like a schoolteacher admonishing two recalcitrant boys. "Why don't you leave him alone and just let him vote?" she said. Chastened, we backed off and left Harkin to his own devices.

During debate on still another of the bills to lift the embargo, I received a phone call from Meade Esposito, the legendary leader of the Democratic Party in Brooklyn. I went to the cloak room, which was just off the House floor, and picked up the phone. "Stevie," I heard Esposito say, "I understand you have some vote on Turkey today." I couldn't understand why Esposito, whose interests didn't usually encompass abstruse foreign policy issues, would care about the arms embargo on Turkey. In fact, I was surprised he was aware of it at all. "Stevie, I want you to vote against it," Esposito said.

"Meade, if only you had called me earlier," I replied. "I just spoke on the floor of the House an hour ago in favor of the bill. If I vote against it now, I'll look like a fool. I'd love to help you, but I really can't do it."

He grumbled, but what could he say? I subsequently discovered that he had called because Lee Alexander, the Democratic mayor of Syracuse and a Greek American, had been asked by the Greek American lobby to call Esposito and induce him to pressure me into voting against the bill. I didn't relish telling the boss of my local party that I wasn't going to do his bidding, but I felt I had no alternative.

Two days later, just as the Foreign Affairs Committee was about to go into session, I got another phone call from Esposito. "Stevie," he said. "I heard Kissinger and Mansfield over the weekend on the radio talking about this Turkey bill. You know something, I'm glad you didn't take my advice. You're a gutsy guy. You did the right thing." I almost fell off my chair listening to him compliment me for defying his instructions.

Years later, in the mid-1980s, another issue involving Turkey surfaced in Congress. In 1915, hundreds of thousands of Armenians were killed or died during an enforced evacuation over several hundred miles from eastern Anatolia to the Syrian desert. The Ottoman leadership had decided to relocate the Armenians after armed Armenian bands, hoping to win independence, rose up behind Ottoman lines as the Russian army advanced into the Anatolian heartland. A resolution was brought to the House floor expressing the sense of Congress that Turkey had inflicted genocide on the Armenian people.

This left me with an extremely difficult dilemma. As a Jew, I was particularly sensitive to the meaning of the Holocaust, which was a major factor in shaping my view that nations had a responsibility to prevent such a horror from occurring ever again. At the same time, I believed that adopting the resolution would have extremely negative consequences for Turkish-American relations. This was hard for many of my colleagues to understand. If the Turkish parliament had adopted a resolution accusing the United States of committing genocide against Native Americans, no one would have paid much attention. But the Turks attached great importance to the resolution, and our adopting it would have had a chilling effect on the two countries' relationship that could have prejudiced vital American interests dependent on Turkish cooperation. Nevertheless, I would have felt obligated to support the resolution if I were convinced that what had happened to the Armenians could fairly and indisputably be characterized as genocide.

As I attempted to grapple intellectually and morally with this issue, I was greatly influenced by a few dozen American scholars of the Ottoman Empire and the Turkish Republic who in March 1985 took out an ad in the *Washington Post*. It was an open letter to the US Congress arguing that the Armenian tragedy was more akin to a civil war than to genocide, and appealing to us to reject the resolution. The signatories included such luminaries as Bernard Lewis of Princeton, probably the preeminent American scholar of modern Turkey, and J. C. Hurwitz of Columbia, a noted specialist on the Middle East. It was one thing, I thought, to risk rupturing our relationship with a strategically important ally in the service of historical truth. It was quite another to take such a risk on the basis of a version of history that was disputed among serious scholars. These professors were not the equivalent of the fringe characters and anti-Semites who denied the existence of the Holocaust. They were serious and, in some cases, renowned historians whose views could not be dismissed out of hand.

Having decided to oppose the resolution, I spoke against it on the floor of the House. Somewhat to my surprise, despite the political clout of the Armenian community and the feeling on the part of most members that a genocide had taken place, the resolution was defeated. Right after the vote, I went over to Tony Coelho, a California Democrat who represented the district with the largest number of Armenians in the country. Coelho had led the fight for the resolution. A firm believer in the proposition that it was possible to disagree without being disagreeable, I extended my hand in a gesture of friendship and reconciliation. But he turned on his heel and walked away. He was so angry he wouldn't even shake my hand.

The defeat of the resolution did not, however, mean that it was destined to remain buried forever in the parliamentary graveyard. Determined to secure recognition of their suffering by having it labeled genocide, the Armenians and their supporters in Congress brought it back several times more. I continued to play a leading role in the effort to defeat it, which didn't exactly endear me to the Armenian community in New York. During their annual parade down Fifth Avenue one year, a separate float was devoted just to me, in which I hung in effigy, twisting slowly in the wind as the float rolled down the street.

Over the years I devoted considerable time to understanding what had happened to the Armenians during World War I. I read several books, from both Armenian and Turkish perspectives, and spoke to scholars and diplomats in both the United States and Europe. I came to the conclusion that the events were terrible indeed. There is no question that hundreds of thousands of Armenians lost their lives, and that what the Ottomans did to them could fairly be described as a war crime and a crime against humanity. But it was by no means clear that it could also be defined as genocide, which, according to the UN Genocide Convention, requires an intent to eliminate in whole or in part an ethnic, racial, or religious community. Whether the Ottomans intended to kill as many Armenians as possible, as opposed to removing them from the zone of conflict so they could no longer provide support to the invading Russian army, hasn't been clearly established, in my judgment.

If the Ottomans really did intend to eliminate the Armenians in whole or in part, why did they refrain from exterminating the Armenian communities in Istanbul and Smyrna? Why did they court-martial over a thousand Ottoman officers and soldiers for mistreating Armenians? Why did they divert scarce supplies from their own forces in order to provide food and shelter to those Armenians who survived the long march to the Syrian desert? Those who make the claim of genocide argue that the mere fact that the Armenians in eastern Anatolia were sent on a forced march for several hundred miles to Syria without any preparation is proof that the Ottomans wanted to eliminate them. Yet there were no rail links from that part of the empire to Syria, and once the decision was made to remove them from the conflict zone, that was the only way to do it. By comparison, the Armenians in Cilicia, on Turkey's Mediterranean coast, were sent to Syria by rail because there it was possible to do so. If the Ottomans had intended that these Armenians be killed, why weren't they forced to go on foot as well? While the answers to these questions don't necessarily prove that the event was not genocide, they certainly raise serious, legitimate questions about whether it was.

Sympathetic to the anguish and concerns of the Armenians, but also determined to prevent a serious breach in our relationship with Turkey, I spent a lot of time talking to both Armenians and Turks in an effort to forge a compromise. But it eventually became clear that if the resolution contained the word "genocide," it would be unacceptable to the Turks. And if it didn't contain that word — even if it referred to the massacre of hundreds of thousands of Armenians and characterized what had happened as war crimes or crimes against humanity — it wouldn't be acceptable to the Armenians. So it was impossible to satisfy both sides. The issue remains a continuing source of frustration for the Armenians and a bone in the throats of the Turks.

The organized Jewish community was not involved in either the embargo issue or the genocide issue (though in the late 1990s, following a significant improvement in relations between Turkey and Israel, several major Jewish organizations urged Congress not to pass the genocide resolution). Israel, however, wanted to prevent a rupture in Turkish-American relations that could have opened the way to an extension of Soviet influence in the Middle East. I remember one occasion before the embargo was lifted, in the mid-1970s, when I met with Prime Minister Demirel of Turkey during a trip to the eastern Mediterranean. At the end of the meeting, after others had left the room, I pulled the prime minister aside and told him that I understood there was a feeling on the part of his government that Israel had been urging its friends in Congress to vote to keep the embargo, and I wanted to let him know that this wasn't the case. Indeed, to the extent that Israel had a position on the issue, it was quietly letting its congressional supporters know that it favored lifting the embargo, because it saw Turkey as a barrier to Soviet military intervention in the Middle East. I pointed out that some of Israel's best friends in Congress — like me, Jack Bingham, and Millicent Fenwick — were among the strongest supporters of the effort to lift the embargo. He responded that this was very interesting information and that nobody had ever told him that before. "But if what you say is true," he added, "how do you explain the role being played by Congressman Rosenberg?" He was referring to Ben Rosenthal, a leader of the effort to maintain the embargo. I explained that although Rosenthal was Jewish, on this particular issue he didn't reflect the views of Israel. When I got back to Washington, I told Rosenthal, who was a good friend and fellow member of the New York delegation, what Demirel had said. I jokingly added that from now on I was going to call him Congressman Rosenberg!

My position on the embargo certainly enhanced my reputation with the Turks. Sometime in the mid-1980s, I attended the annual dinner of the Assembly of Turkish American Associations in Washington. The main speaker was Defense Secretary Caspar Weinberger. As the program started, the master of ceremonies took note of some of the dignitaries in attendance. Most whose names were mentioned received polite applause, but I got a two-minute standing ovation. I was told subsequently that Weinberger, whom I had never met before that evening, asked one of his people: "Who is this Congressman Solarz, and why is he getting such a reception? What's going on here?"

What was going on was that, while I was not the only member of Congress sympathetic to Turkey, I certainly was the most active and prominent in the effort to lift the embargo. And if the public at large and even some leading administration officials were unaware of this fact, the US Turkish community certainly knew it. In fact, when the embargo was finally lifted in October 1978, we had a party at my house in McLean. Congressmen, staffers, and key people in the administration who had played a part in the effort all came to celebrate this milestone in Turkish-American relations.

Poland was far removed from the turmoil in the eastern Mediterranean, but it was headed for some turmoil of its own. By the late 1970s, the Communist regime in Warsaw was losing its grip on the Polish people, and events were about to unfold that would shake the Communist world to its roots. No one knew it at the time, but Poland's troubles were the harbinger of the historic, largely peaceful revolutions of 1989, which swept Communism out of Eastern Europe with startling speed.

Although this struggle included many heroes, the man who came to embody this counterrevolution against Communist rule was Lech Walesa. A devoutly Catholic electrical technician at the Lenin Shipyard in Gdansk with a limited formal education, Walesa surprised Poland and the world with his courage and charisma. On August 14, 1980, he became the leader of a strike (illegal in the Communist "workers' paradise") that was the inspiration for other strikes and civil disobedience that erupted across Poland. He also played a key role in organizing Solidarity, the first truly independent trade union in Poland since the establishment of Communist rule after World War II. Solidarity soon had millions of members, and for a while it looked like the first real proletarian revolution in history might be taking place in the dictatorship of the proletariat.

My first trip to Poland was in fall 1980, when Solidarity had already been formed. It was an exciting time to be there. Cracks in the Communist monolith were appearing and there were high hopes, which I shared, for a better and freer future for Poland. In Warsaw, I met some of the leaders of Solidarity, three of whom in particular were very impressive. Adam Michnik had spent many years in prison but played a key role in devising the tactics Solidarity used to carve out a measure of autonomy amid the repressive reality of a Communist government backed up by Soviet power. Bronislaw Geremek, a medieval historian, was one of the wisest and most impressive political figures I ever met. Judicious in his judgments, with an incisive intellect, he was a classic example of an intellectual who speaks truth to power. In the late 1990s, he became foreign minister. Jacek Kuron, a working-class intellectual, was a Polish version of Eric Hoffer, an American longshoreman who wrote books on philosophy and politics as easily as he unloaded ships in San Francisco harbor. I came away from this and other trips to Poland believing that the most creative political thinking in the world was going on there, as the Solidarity leaders struggled to reconcile their people's overwhelming desire for freedom and independence with the geopolitical reality of Communist rule and Soviet power.

Walesa and his advisors knew very well what had happened in Hungary in 1956 and Czechoslovakia in 1968, when the people of those countries rose up against their Communist overlords and were crushed by Russian troops and tanks determined to prevent the emergence of governments not controlled by Moscow. They understood that if they went too far they would probably face a similar crackdown, ending in much bloodshed and the reassertion of Soviet domination. And in fact, a crackdown took place in Poland in December 1981, when General Wojciech Jaruzelski, the prime minister, declared martial law and outlawed Solidarity, justifying the move by saying it was needed to prevent a Soviet invasion. He then arrested virtually the entire Solidarity leadership.

By the mid-1980s, most of the Solidarity leaders had been released from prison, although Solidarity itself was still outlawed. I met with Walesa in the rectory of Saint Bridget's, his church in Gdansk. Sig Rolat, a good friend and staunch supporter, accompanied me; he was a Holocaust survivor and spoke fluent Polish. Walesa was accompanied by his priest, Father Jankovsky, who struck me as very decent and, given his relationship with Walesa and his support for Solidarity, commendable. Only years later did I learn that he was a confirmed anti-Semite. In any case, I spent several hours with Walesa in Saint Bridget's, discussing the situation in Poland and what could be done. I had never met Walesa before, but on the basis of what I had read about him, plus my impressions at this meeting, it was clear to me that he was an extraordinary man, endowed with tremendous charisma and an intuitive feel for the politics of the possible. At that moment, however, the thought that a few years later he would become president of Poland was scarcely imaginable.

The church, nearly destroyed in World War II, had been rebuilt, and its interior walls memorialized some of Poland's heartbreaking history,

Meeting with Lech Walesa in Saint Bridget's, 1980s.

including the infamous Soviet massacre in the Katyn Forest—where, on Stalin's orders, his secret police killed thousands of Polish officers taken prisoner when the Soviet Union invaded Poland in September 1939. There was also a shrine to Father Jerzy Popieluszko, Solidarity's chaplain, who had been beaten to death by the Polish secret police in 1984. In the chapel, I saw a young couple getting married.

We then drove to the train station for the trip back to Warsaw. On the way, we passed the Lenin Shipyard, where Solidarity was born. There is a huge monument to the workers who were killed there during an earlier anti-regime demonstration in 1956, and I asked the driver to stop the car so I could see it up close. When I reached it, I saw the same young couple who an hour before had been married in the church. They were laying a wreath at the base of the monument. This remarkable tableau spoke volumes about the immediacy of Polish history for the Polish people and their passion to be free from the chains of Communism. Could anyone, I thought to myself, imagine an American couple, after their wedding ceremony in Washington, going to lay a wreath at the Lincoln Memorial in their first act as a married couple? This incident left a lasting impression and deepened my resolve to find ways of being helpful to the people of Poland.

I had come to believe that the best way to determine how the United States could assist people struggling for self-determination and human rights under repressive regimes was to consult the brave leaders of these struggles. In Poland, Walesa, Michnik, Geremek, and the other leaders of Solidarity felt that the time had come to lift the sanctions the United States had imposed after martial law was established in 1981. So it was that I undertook a successful effort to convince my colleagues in Congress to repeal these sanctions, which were lifted in early 1987. In 1989, in a historic roundtable agreement negotiated by the Polish government leaders and Solidarity, the Polish authorities agreed to permit the first free and fair election since the end of World War II. Solidarity, which by then had been legalized, won in a landslide, and Communism in Poland came to a sputtering and inglorious end. A year later, I saw perhaps the most convincing evidence of the change that had taken place after a talk I gave to the association of foreign correspondents in Washington. At the end of my speech, I was approached by Zygmunt Broniarek, the Washington bureau chief of *Trybuna Ludu*, which had been the official organ of the Communist Party of Poland. He gave me his card on which, under *Trybuna Ludu*, he had stenciled in "the leading opposition paper in Poland."

It seemed to me, however, that taking the survival of democracy in Poland for granted would be a mistake. A lot depended, Walesa and his associates advised me, on whether the new democratically elected government could satisfy the Polish people's pent-up aspirations for a better life. So I undertook, again successfully, to convince my colleagues in Congress to increase by $200 million the economic assistance package the administration had proposed for Poland after the election.

Another profound satisfaction resulting from my involvement with Poland was getting to know Jan Nowak, one of the most remarkable and commendable men I ever met. Jan had been the head of black propaganda for the Polish Home Army during World War II. It was his job to recruit and organize a Polish underground in Nazi Germany to distribute anti-Nazi propaganda in the Third Reich. He made over thirty trips into Germany, which required great heroism, since if the Gestapo had caught him, he would undoubtedly have been tortured and executed as a spy.

Jan was also an emissary from the Polish underground to the United Kingdom and the United States, reporting to Churchill, Roosevelt, and other leaders of the Allies about what was happening in Poland, and about the Holocaust in particular. After the war, he became head of the Polish section of Radio-Free Europe and through that job became an iconic figure in Poland. He once described to me his first meeting, in the mid-1970s, with Karol Wojtyla, then cardinal of Krakow and later Pope John Paul II. They met at a conference in Munich where Jan introduced himself. "Mr. Nowak," Cardinal Wojtyla replied, "you don't have to introduce yourself. I knew who you were the minute you spoke to me because every morning when I wake up and get ready for the day, your voice is the first voice I hear on Radio-Free Europe."

By the time I became involved in Polish issues, Jan had left Radio-Free Europe and was living in Washington, where Zbigniew Brzezinski, then President Carter's national security advisor, had hired him as a consultant to the National Security Council on Polish affairs. After Carter left the White House, Jan became the head of the Washington office of the Polish American Congress, which tried to shape US policy toward Poland just as AIPAC tried to influence American policy toward Israel. Before and after my trips to Poland, I would meet with Jan. I always came away from those meetings thinking that there really wasn't any need to go to Warsaw because, in one hour with Jan, I invariably learned more about what was going on in Poland than I did after spending a few days there myself.

In the 1990s, I worked with Brzezinski and Dan Fried, who had been the American ambassador to Poland, to persuade President Clinton to award Jan the Presidential Medal of Freedom. In our letter to the president, we mentioned Cardinal Wojtyla's remark as a way of illustrating Jan's importance to the Polish people. I was gratified, but not surprised, when Jan received the Medal of Freedom from Clinton shortly afterward.

My district included a very large Polish American community in Greenpoint, a neighborhood in northern Brooklyn. Once Poland had achieved genuine independence and began to hold democratic elections, Poles living abroad were allowed to vote in them, and Lech Walesa got more votes in Greenpoint running for president of Poland than I got there running for Congress. Of course it was also true that many Poles in that neighborhood were not American citizens and couldn't vote in our elections.

Zbig Brzezinski had been my professor at graduate school at Columbia in the early 1960s, and I had become friendly with him after he came to Washington. I once got him to come to a town hall meeting I organized in Greenpoint. It was by far the most successful town hall meeting I ever held. Usually only a few dozen people showed up at these events, but Brzezinski was something of a celebrity among Polish Americans, and several hundred people packed the hall. The fire marshals closed the room when it was filled to capacity, and we had to rig up a microphone so people outside could hear. My introduction of Zbig was followed by what the Soviets used to call "stormy and prolonged applause," and women in the audience threw flowers at him. The next day he called me and somewhat jocularly said he was so impressed by this reception that he was thinking about running for Congress in my district. I couldn't resist retorting that it was a free country and, if he wanted to, he could run against me. But, I added, he should know that Greenpoint was only 5 percent of my district. Of course, he wasn't serious. With the support of my Polish American constituents and signs that read, in the distinctive Solidarity script, "Solarz for Congress: From Greenpoint to Gdansk, He Fights for us," I was reelected.

II

THE GULF WAR

When Evil Is on the March, It Must Be Confronted

In the summer of 1990, Saddam Hussein invaded neighboring Kuwait, imperiously proclaiming it the nineteenth province of Iraq. This action set off alarm bells in Washington and other Western and Arab capitals, which feared the political and economic consequences. No one could be sure that Saddam wouldn't attempt to take over the other oil-producing Persian Gulf states, which were clearly unable to ward off an advancing Iraqi juggernaut. In an effort to deter any further Iraqi aggression, President George H. W. Bush induced Saudi King Fahd to accept the deployment of 250,000 American troops in Saudi Arabia. This was politically difficult for the Saudis to accept but, with the very real possibility of an Iraqi invasion staring him in the face, King Fahd obviously felt it would be the better part of wisdom to invite the American infidels to defend his kingdom than to depend on the forbearance of the Iraqi dictator.

Early in December 1990, after the midterm elections, the House Democrats held their organizing caucus for the next session. A special meeting was devoted to Kuwait. Usually, caucus meetings were sparsely attended; a couple of dozen members were considered a crowd. But this meeting drew over 200. President Bush had recently announced a doubling of the American troops in Saudi Arabia to 500,000. It didn't take much imagination to realize that the drums of war were beating. The question for the Democrats was what to do about it.

Over the next few hours, about two dozen members rose to speak. Every one of them opposed a war against Iraq. One member reported that at a town hall meeting in his district, with a thousand people present, everyone was against going to war. Others said that a war to liberate Kuwait would be another Vietnam, and that thousands of Americans would be killed in the desert sands. Instead of using military force to liberate Kuwait, my colleagues argued, we should maintain the sanctions that had been imposed by the UN in hopes of pressuring Saddam to withdraw his forces from Kuwait.

I was the only one who contended that if we were really opposed to Iraq's annexation of Kuwait, as everybody claimed to be, we had to recognize that sanctions alone wouldn't do the job. Even with the sanctions in place, Iraq had a substantially higher standard of living than some Arab countries that had joined the coalition against it, and Saddam, unlike President Bush and British Prime Minister Thatcher, did not have to worry about the wrath of voters in the next election. If Kuwait was going to be liberated, I argued, we had to use military force or, at the very least, credibly threaten it. Indeed, the only hope for a diplomatic solution lay in convincing Saddam that if he didn't withdraw from Kuwait voluntarily, we would use our armed might to evict him.

A few days later, I ran into Dave Obey, a liberal Democrat from Wisconsin, one of the most influential members of the House. He said he disagreed with the position I had taken in the caucus, but he admired my willingness to stand up and speak out for what I believed, even though it wasn't a very popular position. Other members weren't so gracious. Pete Stark of California, a vocal opponent of the use of force, addressed me as "Field Marshal Solarz," and he didn't mean it as a compliment. Clearly a lot of Democrats in Congress were unhappy with and resented my support for military action. Many people in my district disagreed with me as well.

I received a long letter from Roger Hilsman, who had been assistant secretary of state for East Asia during the early stages of the Vietnam War, urging me to resist the administration's apparent determination to use military force, which he said would inevitably lead to another Vietnam. Bill Leuchtenburg, my former professor at Columbia University, with whom I had been close, wrote saying I had betrayed him by supporting the administration. His anger was so deep that to this day he still doesn't speak to me. The *Village Voice*, which had generally supported me over the years, described me as "a loathsome benighted incubus whose reptilian visage has darkened the television screens of America." I had to check the dictionary to find out what "incubus" meant. I discovered that it referred to a demon that had sexual intercourse with a sleeping woman.

My involvement with Iraq dated back to my first visit there in 1982, as part of my effort to develop a better understanding of Arab attitudes

First meeting with Saddam Hussein, 1982.

toward Israel. A key question for me was which Arab states were prepared to make peace with Israel, and which were intent on eliminating it?
I went to Iraq to determine whether Saddam Hussein belonged in the first
camp or the second. Given his subsequent thuggish behavior, this quest
may seem naive. But at the time, and along with many other people, I saw
Saddam as a typical Arab strongman — not any better than the others in
this group, but also not necessarily worse.

The visit started out inauspiciously. The only meetings I had were with
relatively low-level government officials and one mid-ranking Baath Party
functionary. I was accompanied everywhere I went by Iraqi security es-

corts, so the only way I could talk privately with our ambassador, Bill Eagleton, was to take a rowboat ride with him across the Tigris River. On my second day in Baghdad, with no official meetings on my schedule, I was playing tennis under the broiling midday sun at the British ambassador's residence while waiting to find out if I would be able to meet with Saddam Hussein. As often happens in dictatorships, I had not been told in advance when I would see the leader, or if I would see him at all. In the middle of the match, a contingent of Saddam's feared secret police, the Mahabharat, rolled up in their black sedans and informed me that their leader was ready to see me. "Let's go," they said. I protested that I couldn't meet the president dressed in sweaty tennis clothes. "I need to go back to the hotel so I can shower and change," I said. They relented, but to make up for the delay, they took me on a hundred-mile-an-hour race through the narrow streets of Baghdad to get to the palace where he was waiting.

Saddam came into the room dressed immaculately in a military uniform, with a pistol on his hip. "You look very young to be a congressman," he remarked.

"You look very young to be a president," I responded.

Saddam eyed me and said: "Ah, but there's a difference. You came up through the overground. I came up through the underground." Saddam had a somewhat forbidding persona; you certainly wouldn't want to encounter him in a dark alley. I couldn't have imagined then that twenty years later the Mesopotamian megalomaniac's career would end as it began, underground, with American soldiers ordering him to emerge from the rat hole where he was hiding. But I did notice that even though the room was freezing cold, Saddam's aides were all sweating. Only later did I learn about his habit of shooting those who disagreed with him.

We talked for about three hours. The meeting lasted so long beyond its scheduled time that I had to ask him to hold my plane so I could get to Jordan in time for a meeting with King Hussein, which he obligingly agreed to do. During our discussion he seemed to go out of his way to appear moderate. When I asked him whether Iraq would be willing to make peace with Israel, he replied, "Whatever is acceptable to the Palestinians is acceptable to me." Based on our conversation, I came away feeling that Iraq, unlike some other Arab states, was not implacably opposed to peace with Israel.

Subsequent events, including blood-curdling threats to incinerate half of Israel and support for suicide bombers intent on killing as many Israelis as possible, suggested that these expressions of moderation were only tactical, designed to secure American support in Saddam's war against Iran — not a strategic commitment to peace with Israel. He was already embroiled in this charnel-house war, with Iran sending endless waves of youthful religious fanatics armed only with the Koran across his border, so it was in his interest to curry favor with the United States by portraying himself as a moderate with respect to Israel and the Palestinians. Sometime later, he sent Nizar Hamdoon to Washington to project the same image. Hamdoon, a very skillful ambassador who seemed genuinely interested in promoting better relations between Iraq and the United States, subsequently became a shameless flack for Saddam as Iraq's ambassador to the UN during the Gulf War. My initial meeting with Saddam was therefore a useful reminder not to take the words of national leaders, especially dictators, at face value.

I did not issue a public report about my meeting with Saddam when I returned. But about nine months later, the Iraqis released a surprisingly accurate version of it, presumably designed to reap the political benefits of his expressions of moderation, which had been denied him by my decision not to publicize the substance of our discussion. I met Saddam again in 1986, at a time when the United States was protecting Kuwaiti vessels from Iranian interdiction in the Persian Gulf. In this case it was Iran's mullahs whom we saw as the villains, and again Saddam presented himself as a responsible leader interested in better relations with the United States.

I was scheduled to meet Saddam a third time in August 1990, but the week before the date we had set, he invaded Kuwait. I was already in the region but decided that a picture of me with Saddam on the front page of the *New York Times* right after he had annexed Kuwait would not do much to enhance my career. More important, I had no desire to legitimize his aggression. So I cancelled my visit to Iraq while continuing on to other Middle Eastern countries.

To me, Saddam's annexation and brutal occupation of Kuwait was unacceptable — not only in itself but because the invasion was America's first big test as the sole superpower left in the world. Saddam couldn't have made it clearer: in an unprovoked act of aggression he had invaded another country and thumbed his nose at the United Nations, which was determined to secure the withdrawal of Iraqi forces and the reestablishment of an independent Kuwait. At stake was whether, in the post–Cold War world, international relations would or would not be characterized by the rule of law. I thought the answer was obvious. But once I concluded that we had to oppose the annexation, I had to decide how active a role to play in that effort.

Given the aversion of many of my colleagues and constituents to American involvement in a war against Iraq, the prudent course would have been to quietly object to Iraq's action but not play an active or public role in opposing it. Such a stance, however politically convenient, ran counter to my sense of responsibility as a member of Congress. The invasion had taken place in a part of the world where I had spent considerable time trying to understand the local political dynamics. And the Foreign Affairs Committee would clearly be deeply involved in shaping the congressional response. In good conscience, I couldn't take a back seat. If my purpose in being in Congress was to make a difference rather than simply hold my seat as long as possible, I felt morally obligated to work actively to undo Saddam's grab for the wealth and power that the annexation of Kuwait would give him.

This was the most difficult decision I had to make in my eighteen years in Congress. Many of the men and women I had worked with on behalf of peace and human rights were against me on this issue. So were my party's leadership and the majority of my Democratic colleagues in the House. Bucking the party leadership could jeopardize my chances for advancement within the House. And by alienating my constituents, I could lose my seat in Congress. But ultimately I concluded that, if I was going to be faithful to my views and values, I had to go against the wishes of the leadership, the sentiment of my party, the preferences of my colleagues, and the views of my constituents — at least those who cared enough to communicate them to me. And plenty did. A very significant peace constituency in my district opposed the use of force, even against an ogre like Saddam Hussein. During the lead up to the war, I must have gotten 1,000 letters on this issue from people in my district. Most were very personal and heartfelt, and 95 percent were against war. Peace groups held a daily prayer vigil outside my congressional office in Brooklyn. I wasn't sure whether they were praying for my salvation or my defeat. Ultimately I took comfort from the words in the Bible that say, "For what shall it profit a man, if he shall gain the whole world, and lose his own soul?"

The United States had much at stake in the Persian Gulf. An Iraq bent on the conquest of its neighbors represented a serious economic threat to American interests. By annexing Kuwait, Saddam had put himself in control of 20 percent of the world's supply of oil. Had he moved south into Saudi Arabia, he would have controlled up to 40 percent of the oil supplies on which the international community depended. Even if he didn't actually invade Saudi Arabia, an Iraqi army deployed along the Saudi border would have enabled Saddam to intimidate the Saudis into doing his bidding on the production and pricing of oil. Furthermore, a hostile Iraq armed with chemical and biological weapons, which at that time Saddam indisputably had, and eventually nuclear weapons, which he was then trying to develop, represented a "clear and present danger" to American security.

I would have preferred to give sanctions more of a chance to work, if there had been any reasonable possibility that they might. But it soon became clear to me, especially after an assessment of their impact by the Institute for International Economics, a Washington-based think tank, that sanctions could not work. Iraq, after all, was a fertile country able to feed itself. Prohibited but essential items were already being smuggled across the Iranian, Jordanian, Turkish, and Syrian borders. And, unlike President Bush, Saddam was immune to electoral pressure and didn't have to deal with a contentious Congress, a critical press, or daily demonstrations in front of his many presidential palaces. Whatever miseries the sanctions imposed on Iraqis, they were unlikely to induce Saddam to withdraw from Kuwait. Instead, he would have hunkered down and, while we waited in vain for sanctions to work, the inherently fragile, fractious coalition arrayed against him would likely unravel and the sanctions would erode. In the end, Saddam would prevail.

As I thought this through, I also had in mind our failure to stop Hitler in the years before World War II, when that was still possible. Meanwhile, I discovered how stark were the perceptions in other nations of the potential destabilization and dangers created by Saddam's aggression. In the immediate aftermath of the Iraqi invasion, I was still in the Middle East, and I met with Ezer Weizman, a former defense minister and subsequent president of Israel, who was then in private life. To my amazement, Weizman told me that if we opted to use armed force to liberate Kuwait, as he hoped we would, Iraq would be a perfect place to use tactical nuclear weapons. This statement showed just how strongly the Israelis felt about the threat Saddam posed. But I soon saw that the Egyptians and Saudis too perceived an expansionist Iraq as extremely dangerous, although none of them suggested nuclear weapons.

On my return to the United States, I did all I could to generate support for liberating Kuwait by force. I appeared frequently on CNN and other television networks to mobilize public support for military action. After one such appearance, I was told there was a call for me in the control room. The person on the other end said: "Congressman Solarz, this is Saud al-Sabah. I am the Kuwaiti ambassador. I love you." And as Humphrey Bogart said in *Casablanca*, that was the beginning of a beautiful friendship. I got to know Sheik Saud very well and became a great admirer of this man who did so much to secure American support for his beleaguered country.

To counter the widespread opposition to military action, I established an organization known as the Committee for Peace and Security in the Gulf. Its purpose was to secure endorsements from people whose credentials might carry weight with Democrats as well as Republicans. I persuaded Richard Perle, who had been a neoconservative arms control expert in the Reagan administration, and Ann Lewis, Congressman Barney Frank's sister and a prominent liberal activist, to serve as codirectors. I also got Frank Carlucci, who had been secretary of defense under President Reagan, and Tony Coelho, the former Democratic whip in the House of Representatives, to serve as honorary cochairmen. Other members included Democrats Tom Lantos, Stu Eisenstadt, Dave McCurdy, and Bob Torricelli, and Republicans Howard Baker, Richard Lugar, Alan Simpson, and John McCain. All in all, this list of luminaries demonstrated broad bipartisan support for the use of force.

In early January, President Bush invited to the White House the senior members of the Foreign Affairs Committee plus some others, including Les Aspin, a Wisconsin Democrat and Chairman of the Armed Services

Announcing the Gulf War resolution with Bob Michel (second from left).
Back row (from left): Reps. Sonny Montgomery, Elton Gallegy, and Ike Skelton.

Committee, and Bob Michel, the Republican leader in the House, who had supported the president's position on Iraq. I was also asked to attend. We met in the Cabinet Room to help the president decide whether to seek a resolution from Congress supporting military action against Iraq. I argued strongly, as did others, that we should seek such a resolution. We thought we could persuade a majority in the House to support it. We also argued that going to war without Congress's approval would produce tremendous domestic discord and divide the country at a time when unity was essential. In fact, I'm convinced that if President Bush had followed the advice of Secretary of Defense Dick Cheney, who was urging him to ignore Congress and go to war without congressional backing, at least some Democrats would have tried to impeach the president.

After hearing us out, President Bush decided that he would seek congressional support. Because of their stature, I suggested that Dante Fascell, the chairman of the Foreign Affairs Committee, and Les Aspin, his counterpart on Armed Services, should be the lead sponsors of the resolution. But both declined, and it was agreed that, in order to demonstrate bipartisan support, Bob Michel and I would be lead sponsors. The president then asked me to go with John Sununu, his chief of staff; Boyden Gray, his White House counsel; and a few others to the Roosevelt Room to hammer out the text of the resolution, which we did with relative ease. In those days, bipartisanship — particularly on foreign policy — was far more common than it has since become.

Over the next few days, I devoted all my time to mustering Democratic support for the Solarz-Michel resolution. Virtually all the Republicans could be expected to support it, but a significant number of Democratic votes would be needed as well. I invited a number of my Democratic colleagues, who had already announced their support, to my office to establish an informal whip operation to persuade undecided Democrats to join us. By the time the vote took place, one-third of the Democrats, including the chairmen of the Foreign Affairs, Armed Services, Ways and Means, Government Operations, and Veteran Affairs Committees, voted yes.

To maximize support for the resolution, I had hoped to have it reported out favorably by the Foreign Affairs Committee, where we had the votes to pass it. Ordinarily this would have been the correct procedure — bills were rarely brought to the floor without first being passed in committee — and it would have given the resolution an additional measure of political respectability. But Tom Foley, the Speaker of the House, under pressure from the Democratic caucus, met with the Democrats on the Foreign Affairs Committee and insisted that we refrain from reporting it to the full House, precisely because he wanted to minimize the prospects for its passage. The mild-mannered Speaker actually grew red in the face and banged his fist on the table as he demanded that the committee not take it up. Chairman Fascell and the rest of us reluctantly acquiesced.

A few days later, the resolution reached the floor of the House. The debate went on for a full day, since virtually every member felt compelled to participate. On January 12, 1991, at the close of this historic debate, I rose to address the House as the resolution's lead sponsor. During most House debates only a handful of members are on the floor. But at the climax of this debate, with the issue of war or peace hanging in the balance, hundreds were in attendance. The gallery was also filled to capacity. I wasn't aware of it at the time, but millions of Americans were listening on NPR or watching on television.

I began by admitting that I found myself in an anomalous position. Almost twenty-five years earlier, I had begun my political career as the campaign manager for one of the first antiwar candidates for Congress in the country. It would never have occurred to me then that I would one day be speaking on the floor of the House in support of a bipartisan resolution that many members I highly respected believed could lead to another Vietnam. But the difference between these two wars was stark. In Vietnam, vital American interests never were at stake. In the Persian Gulf, they were. In Vietnam, the cost in blood and treasure was out of all proportion to the expected benefits of successfully defending South Vietnam. In the Gulf, the benefits of ejecting Iraq from Kuwait far outstripped the price we would have to pay if force had to be used.

I then noted that there had been much talk during the debate about the need for patience. But, I pointed out, we were patient when Japan attacked Manchuria in 1931. We were patient when Italy attacked Ethiopia in 1936. We were patient when Nazi Germany blitzkrieged Poland in 1939. We were patient when Germany overran France in 1940. We were patient right up to December 7, 1941, when Japan attacked Pearl Harbor — by which time Germany had conquered almost all of Europe and Japan controlled much of Asia. This, I contended, was the great lesson of our time: evil exists and when evil is on the march, it must be confronted. Almost a half-year after the brutal, unprovoked annexation of Kuwait, the time for patience had ended, and the time for firmness had arrived. Saddam had gone to war twice in the last ten years. He had used chemical weapons not only against his enemies but against his own people, and he was well on his way toward acquiring nuclear weapons as well. (Indeed, after the war was over we discovered that Iraq had not one but three separate clandestine programs underway to develop nuclear weapons.)

To those who believed that sanctions should be given longer to work, I argued that they were a formula for failure rather than a strategy for success. I pointed out that Judge William H. Webster, the director of the CIA, didn't believe the sanctions would be sufficient to get Iraq out of Kuwait, nor did the British, the French, the Egyptians, the Saudis, or any of our other coalition allies.

None of us wanted war, I said. But the truth was that not until Saddam Hussein was stripped of any lingering illusions he might have about our willingness to use force would there be any real chance for a peaceful resolution of the crisis. That was why, with only three days left before the expiration of the UN deadline for the evacuation of Kuwait, the Solarz-Michel resolution, by confronting Saddam Hussein with a choice between leaving and living, or staying and dying, represented the last best chance for peace. With the adoption of the resolution, I contended, we would be in a better position to achieve our objectives, by peaceful means if possible, but by force if necessary.

"If we prevail, as surely we will, we will have prevented a brutal dictator from getting his hands on the economic jugular of the world," I concluded. "We will have protected and stabilized the Arab governments courageous enough to have opposed him. We will have eliminated his weapons of mass destruction and greatly reduced his conventional military power. We will have enhanced the prospects for progress in the peace process between Israel and its Arab neighbors. And perhaps most importantly of all, by demonstrating that aggression does not pay, and that the international community will uphold the sanctity of existing borders, we will have established a precedent that could lead to the creation of a new world order governed by the rule of law rather than by the law of the jungle, and in which nations shall not make war against other nations any more."

When I sat down, the Speaker banged his gavel and called for the vote. The resolution passed by a comfortable margin of 250 to 183, with significant bipartisan support; more than a third of the Democrats voted for it. Shortly afterward it was adopted in the Senate by the much closer vote of 52 to 47. I was convinced that this course of action was in the best interests of the country. But that feeling was tempered by the fact that, throughout history, men far more intelligent than I had been equally convinced they were right on issues of war and peace, but turned out to be tragically wrong. Some of the most respected foreign policy specialists in the country, including Zbigniew Brzezinski, James Schlesinger, and Sam Nunn, had vociferously opposed the use of force. Some had even predicted that there would be thousands of American casualties and that our tanks would break down in the desert sands. I couldn't preclude the possibility that they were right and I was wrong. I felt real humility, plus a prayerful hope that my analysis would be validated by events.

I also remember thinking, not only as a member of Congress who had voted for the resolution, but as someone who had beaten the drums loudly for war, that I was morally responsible for the consequences. I had a strong sense of the difficult emotions President Johnson must have experienced during the Vietnam War, especially when he had to sign condolence letters to the families of soldiers who were killed. Now, an unknown number of Americans would die in the Persian Gulf. It was a sobering thought.

About an hour after the vote on the House floor, I received a call from President Bush in my congressional office. He was on Marine One, the presidential helicopter, flying to Camp David, and apparently wanted to thank me for the role I had played. Unfortunately, it was a terrible connection and I couldn't hear him clearly. But I also couldn't bring myself to say to the president of the United States, "Can you call back? Can you repeat that? I can't understand what you're saying!" So I let him go on without hearing what his exact words were, just knowing that basically he wanted to say thanks. It was an example of the customary graciousness he was well known for.

A few days after the war began, President Bush held a reception in the White House living quarters for the members of the Committee for Peace and Security in the Gulf, who had been out in front of the effort to generate public support for the war. Among the other guests were Dick Cheney, Colin Powell, John Sununu, and Brent Scowcroft. Suddenly the president called on me to say a few words. I hadn't had any advance notice, and I don't remember what I mumbled except that I gave him credit for his leadership and expressed confidence that we would prevail.

Meanwhile, I had begun receiving death threats through my Brooklyn and Washington offices. When the House sergeant at arms heard about this, he assigned bodyguards to provide me with around-the-clock protection for the duration of the conflict. They advised me to take my name off the mailbox in front of our house in McLean and to remove it from the telephone directory. They also suggested I wear a bulletproof vest during my public appearances. With some reluctance, I agreed. As much as I appreciated their devotion to duty and willingness to protect me, I was not sorry to see them go when the war ended and the sergeant at arms concluded I was no longer in danger. It was also a relief to go around without the bulky vest.

Six weeks after the war began, the impressive coalition assembled and led by the United States succeeded in driving the Iraqi army out of Kuwait. Despite the fears of those who thought the Gulf War would be another Vietnam, less than 150 Americans lost their lives and, thanks to the global fundraising efforts of Secretary of State James Baker, the entire cost of the war was covered by other countries. On the day the ground war began, General Powell came to Capitol Hill to brief members of Congress about the coalition offensive. A couple of hundred attended. After Powell finished his report on the rout of Iraqi forces then underway, but before he answered any questions, I had to leave for another appointment. As I passed him, I offered my hopes and prayers for the war's successful conclusion. In response, he leaned over and whispered in my ear, "I told you there was nothing to worry about."

A few days after the war ended, I attended a mass meeting convened by antiwar groups in my district in a church in Brooklyn Heights. A few hundred people were there. When I rose to speak, I was greeted with sustained boos and catcalls. If this was the reception I received after we won the war at a minimal cost in blood and treasure, I could only imagine what the response would have been if we had lost.

My four-year-old granddaughter, Leah, had quite a different response when she visited us at home soon after that. "What's the name of the bad man in the Persian Gulf?" I asked her. "Saddam Hussein," she said, without missing a beat.

"And what did Grandpa do to Saddam Hussein?"

"You gave him a spanking," she quickly replied, "but you should have thrown him in the trash can." About a week later, at a meeting in the White House, I repeated Leah's comment to President Bush and suggested he consider putting her on his staff, since she was likely to give him better advice than what he seemed to be getting from his existing team. Understandably enough, the president declined to do so and, while Leah remained in kindergarten, Saddam remained in his palace in Baghdad.

Actually, I supported President Bush's decision not to march on Baghdad when the war ended. Sending American troops all the way to the Iraqi capital in order to overthrow the regime would have violated the UN resolutions authorizing "all necessary means" to liberate Kuwait and would have split the coalition we had assembled. But I did object to our failure to use our air power when Saddam used his remaining armor and artillery to crush the uprisings of the Shiites in the south and the Kurds in the north that President Bush had called for. Particularly upsetting was Saddam's use of the helicopter gunships that General Norman Schwarzkopf had allowed him to fly—ostensibly to facilitate communications between his generals in Baghdad and his commanders in the field—to slaughter those who had the courage to rise up against him. Several years later, I participated in a symposium on the Gulf War at Stanford University. Referring to this incident, another participant, former Secretary of State George Shultz, observed that General Schwarzkopf had acknowledged he had been "snookered" into letting the Iraqis use the helicopters. "Since we won and they lost," Shultz said, "I never understood why he simply didn't unsnooker himself." Neither did I.

THE YEAR OF THE *SHLEMAZEL*

One day, after I had been in Congress for a while, Nina asked how long I expected to remain in the House. I assured her I would only stay as long as Manny Celler did. Emanuel Celler, a distinguished and venerable congressman from Brooklyn, had served for forty-nine years, until he was defeated in a Democratic primary by Liz Holtzman in 1972, so this was my way of saying that I expected to be a member of Congress for many years to come. Given the nature of my district and the enormous advantages enjoyed by incumbents, I had every reason to believe I could stay as long as I wanted. Since the House had what looked like a permanent Democratic majority, it was not unreasonable to expect that I would eventually become chairman of the Foreign Affairs Committee. Moreover, the job was exciting, challenging, and fulfilling. It gave me the opportunity to make a difference on issues I cared deeply about, plus it amounted to a license to do good — help my constituents deal with personal and community problems and lend succor and support to those struggling for democracy and human rights around the world. It was not a job I planned to voluntarily relinquish.

Then came 1992–93, the year I became a *shlemazel*. In Yiddish, this word denotes someone with chronic bad luck, someone for whom nothing turns out right. A classic definition distinguishes between the *shlemazel* and the *shlemiel*, another loser type. The *shlemiel* is the fellow who goes up a ladder with a bucket of paint and drops it. The *shlemazel* is the one whose head it falls on. And so it was for me. Within that one year, my political world collapsed: my district disappeared, I was caught up in the House banking scandal, and I lost the ambassadorship I had been nominated for.

The main threat to my continued tenure in Congress was the congressional reapportionment every ten years. In 1982, when New York lost five seats in the House of Representatives, I narrowly escaped this political version of the hangman's noose. When I went to plead my case with Meade Esposito, the leader of the Democratic Party in Brooklyn who held my political fate in his hands, he heard me out and then said, "Stevie, your ass is

in a tub of warm butter." Never having experienced that particular sensa-
tion, I wasn't sure what he meant. I knew enough not to expose my innocence by asking him to explain it in the King's English, but I immediately
called Nina to report it. She said it sounded encouraging and, as usual, she
was right. Despite some additions and subtractions, my district remained
fundamentally intact. My only possible competitor was Fred Richmond,
part of whose district I picked up. However, a few weeks later he pleaded
guilty to bribery and tax evasion, and my reelection was assured.

Ten years later, New York was slated to lose three more seats in the
House. Once again I hoped to escape cartographic evisceration. But this
time I wasn't so fortunate. With the Assembly controlled by Democrats
and the Senate controlled by Republicans, the state legislature was unable
to agree on a reapportionment plan. Governor Mario Cuomo, who might
have brokered a compromise, chose to remain aloof and did nothing. The
issue wound up before a state supreme court judge in Brooklyn who appointed a special master to draw a new set of district lines.

When the Special Master's plan was released, I discovered that he had
done to my district in Brooklyn what the British and French diplomats
Mr. Sykes and M. Picot did when they carved up the remnants of the
Ottoman Empire after World War I. My district was split into six different pieces, five of which were attached to the districts of neighboring
congressmen. In each of those five, the incumbent had a much larger percentage of the new district than I did. Since they were all popular in what
were essentially, even after these changes, their old districts, my prospects
for defeating any of them were minimal.

My own house in Manhattan Beach, at the southern tip of Brooklyn,
was now in Congressman Ted Weiss's district, which ran from Brooklyn north up the West Side of Manhattan all the way to Riverdale in the
Bronx. In the context of New York City's geography and demography, it
was a bizarre configuration. Nevertheless, because it included more of my
old district than any of the others, I considered running there. But when
we analyzed the district politically, it became clear that my chances were
minimal. Seventy-one percent of the votes in the Democratic primary —
the key to victory in this overwhelmingly Democratic district — came out
of Weiss's old district, and only 29 percent came out of mine. Since Ted
was fairly popular in his district, running against him wasn't politically at-

tractive. In addition, the campaign would unfold in the aftermath of the Gulf War. With the beating heart of American liberalism centered in the West Side of Manhattan, the core of the district, the role I had played in the lead up to the war would have been a very big problem.

A further complication was that Ted was quite ill, although few of his constituents knew this. In a survey we conducted to determine what district I should run in — if at all — it turned out that more people in Weiss's district thought I was unwell than thought he was unwell. Since I was in perfectly good health, it was clear that my only real chance of winning would be to make Ted's health the major issue. But Ted was a good friend, whom I liked and admired, and my conscience would not let me campaign against him on that basis. In any event, Ted was unopposed for renomination, but sadly he died on primary day. In retrospect I realized it probably was a good thing that I didn't run against him. If I had, I would have been blamed for his death. And to make matters worse, I likely would have suffered the ignominy of being defeated by a corpse.

The sixth part of my old district was added to a newly created district in which the overwhelming majority of residents were Hispanic. Only 10 percent of this new district consisted of parts of my old district. But since there was no incumbent to run against, this was the constituency I chose to contest.

The main reason I decided to run again was that I was next in line to become chairman of the Foreign Affairs Committee. If I had any realistic ambition, it was to achieve that chairmanship. Since the current chair, Lee Hamilton, was a likely prospect for a cabinet-level position in the next Democratic administration, I felt I simply couldn't walk away from the opportunity such a promotion would have given me to play a significant role in shaping American foreign policy.

Another factor was that in anticipation of the problems I might have in a reapportionment year, I had raised more than $2 million from over 25,000 contributors from every state and territory in the Union. I had more money in my campaign account than any other member of Congress. Legally, if I had chosen not to run again, I could have kept these funds. But it would have been unethical to use for personal purposes money that had been contributed to my campaign for political purposes. The law concerning the use of campaign funds for personal purposes was

subsequently changed to prohibit this. But legalities and ethical considerations aside, I felt I had an obligation to these thousands of contributors
not to retire without a fight.

The district I was now running in included parts of Manhattan, Brooklyn, and Queens; it looked like an octopus whose tentacles extended to
every predominantly Hispanic neighborhood within reach. With four
Hispanic candidates plus me vying for the nomination, I hoped the others would divide the Hispanic vote, enabling me to squeak through with a
majority of the non-Hispanic votes in the primary. I assumed—perhaps
mistakenly—that after I won this election, I would be reelected in subsequent years through an assiduous commitment to community service and
the many advantages of incumbency.

I still needed to make a reasonable showing among the district's Hispanic majority, which understandably hoped to be represented in Congress by one of their own in what was supposed to be a Hispanic district.
The fact that my ancestors had left Spain five hundred years earlier when
they were expelled from the Iberian Peninsula didn't qualify me as a Hispanic in their eyes, and it was a very difficult campaign. Debates among
the candidates were conducted in Spanish, which I didn't speak except for
a few remembered words of high-school Spanish. I had to wear earphones
so someone could interpret the attacks my opponents leveled against me.

It was also the first time in my political life that I was exposed to
anti-Semitic slurs. Some people campaigning for my opponents clearly resented the fact that I was running in a district designed for Hispanics. The
arguments that I had a proven track record of accomplishment and that
my seniority would enable me to do more for the new district than my opponents counted for little against the ethnic realities that dominated the
campaign. As it turned out, if I almost lost my first campaign for public office because the voters in my predominantly Jewish district thought I was
Hispanic, I actually lost my last campaign for Congress because my putative constituents knew I wasn't Hispanic.

To add insult to injury, the district was later declared unconstitutional
by the US Supreme Court on the ground that the number of Hispanics
included in it was not simply one factor, but the only factor, in shaping it.
Determined to preserve a majority Hispanic district, the legislature made
only a few changes in its shape and composition. This time it passed con-

stitutional muster but, recognizing that there was little desire for my services there, I declined to run again.

While this reappointment drama was unfolding, my name was, unfortunately, prominently mentioned in connection with the House banking "scandal." Well over 300 other members had overdrawn their accounts at this bank, which allowed members to write checks against their deposited salaries. But I was clearly one of the worst offenders. It turned out that over 700 overdrawn checks had been written on my account. I had to assume responsibility for this; it was, after all, my account. But in fact, 98 percent of the checks were written either by Nina or by my secretary because I didn't handle the expenses they paid for. I used to joke that I took care of war and peace, while they took care of paying the bills.

Still, I was occasionally aware that my account was overdrawn. From time to time, I got a call from someone at the House Bank saying I needed to deposit money to cover checks written against nonexistent funds. I would then arrange for enough money to be deposited to cover the shortfall. Everyone to whom checks were made out was paid in full. Nevertheless, even though no one was ever stiffed, I should never have let the overdrafts happen in the first place. When the story first broke, I was flabbergasted to discover how many overdrawn checks there were on my account. The calls from the bank had been infrequent, and I had the impression there were only a few overdrafts. Still, I should have been more sensitive to the appearance of impropriety and taken steps to make sure there were no more such checks. The fact that I didn't is a source of lasting embarrassment and regret.

Politically speaking, I'm convinced that if my district had remained more or less intact, I would have been reelected despite the banking scandal. In the new district, it was more of a handicap. Nevertheless, given the district's ethnic realities, I would probably have lost even if the bank brouhaha hadn't been an anchor to leeward.

The House Bank affair turned out to be more of a problem for me after the election than before it. I strongly supported Bill Clinton in his campaign for president and was the first member of the New York delegation to endorse him. I provided foreign policy advice and campaigned actively for him in the general election. During the Gennifer Flowers affair, I defended him on national television, pointing out that other presidential candidates from Jefferson through Kennedy had been accused, fairly or unfairly, of sexual indiscretions.

During the transition, *New York Times* foreign affairs columnist Tom Friedman called me at home in Mclean to say he had been told on good authority that Clinton was going to appoint me deputy secretary of state. I would have welcomed and been honored by such an offer, but it never came. One reason for this had to do with the House banking scandal, which a special prosecutor had been appointed to investigate. Because it was an election year, the hundreds of members with overdrawn accounts were clamoring for letters from the special prosecutor saying they hadn't done anything illegal. Understandably, in reviewing each member's case, the special prosecutor gave priority to those running for reelection. Since I had lost the primary and was no longer a candidate, my case was put on the back burner, without any clear indication of when it would be resolved. Since President-elect Clinton was not going to nominate me for deputy secretary of state or anything else until this matter was resolved, my prospects for joining the administration in some high-level position were correspondingly diminished.

My letter of exoneration did not arrive until April. By that time, the position of deputy secretary had already been filled. Soon after, I received a call from Tony Lake, Clinton's national security advisor, who said President Clinton wanted to nominate me as ambassador to India. After consulting with Nina, I called Lake back and told him I would be honored to accept. India, after all, was a country I cared deeply about. I had been the unofficial leader of the effort in the House to strengthen Indo-American relations, and I felt that this appointment would give me an opportunity to put the relationship between the most populous and powerful democracies in the world on a stronger and more secure basis. The appointment was announced in India and well received; if most Americans were unaware of my work regarding India, the Indians both knew and appreciated it. So when Pat Moynihan told an audience in Mumbai that I would be the next ambassador, he subsequently told me, those present rose to their feet in a standing ovation. Precisely because of its rich culture, commitment to democracy, linguistic diversity, and unique religious faith, as well as the opportunity to make a difference, I was quite enthusiastic about going to India.

In summer 1993, I enrolled in the Department of State's school for new ambassadors, fully expecting to have my nomination confirmed by the Senate when Congress reconvened in September and then leave for New Delhi. After serving for twenty-four years in legislative bodies in Albany and Washington, I looked forward to becoming part of the executive branch. But then the nomination process seemed to stall. I tried to find out what was holding it up, but nobody would tell me. I began to feel like Joseph K. in Kafka's *The Trial*, being judged without knowing the charges against me. After a few months in ignorance, with my nomination in limbo, I finally discovered what the problem was. Richard Williams, our consul general in Hong Kong, had accused me of being bribed by a Hong Kong businessman in my last week as a member of Congress to help get him a multiyear visa to the United States.

It seems that Williams harbored a grudge against me because he felt I had mistreated him at two congressional hearings. He apparently took these encounters personally, whereas from my perspective, they weren't personal at all. The first involved a hearing before my subcommittee after the brutal suppression of the student demonstrators in Tiananmen Square in 1989. President Bush had dispatched two high-level officials on a secret mission to Beijing to let China's leaders know that, even though his administration had publicly suspended all high-level meetings between American and Chinese officials, it still wanted a good relationship with the People's Republic. To those of us who remained deeply offended by the killing of hundreds of students and others in the Tiananmen massacre, this seemed an exercise in diplomatic hypocrisy.

I convened a hearing to find out why the administration was snuggling up to "the Butchers of Beijing." Nobody higher up in the State Department was eager to testify, so they sent Richard Williams, then deputy assistant secretary for East Asia. We subjected Williams to some tough questioning on the administration's duplicity. It wasn't directed at him personally, since he hadn't made the decision to send the officials to Beijing. But he apparently resented the treatment he received and held me responsible.

On another occasion, during a routine oversight hearing, I asked the administration witness, Desaix Anderson, the number-two man in the Asian Bureau, whether we had appointed an ambassador to Mongolia. Mongolia had been the first Communist country in Asia to reject its Communist system after the collapse of the Soviet Union. It seemed important, therefore, to make sure we had an appropriate and effective diplomatic presence there. Told that we had no ambassador in Mongolia, I asked why. Anderson responded that the State Department hadn't been able to se-cure acceptable accommodations for the ambassador and that there were concerns about his security. I observed tartly that American soldiers were living in foxholes along the frontiers of freedom in Korea and elsewhere, and that the ambassador would probably be safer walking the streets of Ulan Bator at night than he would be in Washington, D.C. I strongly sug-gested that we get our ambassador out there as soon as possible, even if it meant he had to live in a cramped apartment rather than a magnificent residence. Williams, who had been nominated and confirmed as ambas-sador to Mongolia, apparently interpreted this as an attack against him, when it was actually a criticism of the administration.

His allegation against me was absurd on its face. Why would anyone bribe me in my last week as a member of Congress, when there was noth-ing I could do for him as a lame duck that I couldn't do a few days later as a private citizen? Nevertheless, once the allegation was made, it had to be investigated. Since the White House couldn't be sure what the outcome of the investigation would be, and there was no way the Senate would confirm me while it was still pending, my nomination was effectively put on hold.

Now that I knew what the problem was, the Justice Department deigned to listen to my side of the story. It was this: In my last week in Congress, I was invited to Hong Kong to give a lecture. Michael Nuss-baum, a friend of mine and cousin of Bernie Nussbaum, arranged this speaking engagement and accompanied me to Hong Kong. While we were there, Michael told me he knew a Hong Kong businessman who might be interested in using my services in the consultancy I planned to establish after leaving Congress.

So, at Michael's suggestion, I went to see Albert Yeung, president of the Emperor Group, which was described to me as the Hong Kong equiva-lent of a Fortune 500 company. Yeung told me he planned to establish banks in a number of foreign countries and asked if I could help. Based on the many contacts and relationships I had established with foreign leaders during my years in Congress, I told him I thought I could, and would welcome an opportunity to work with him. After we agreed on terms, Yeung suggested we sign a contract. I said I would be more comfortable doing that the following week, when I would no longer be in Congress. Yeung agreed, and the signing ceremony was put off for a few days.

Yeung now told me that he visited the United States at least once a year with his wife, who was an American citizen. To facilitate these trips, he wanted to get a multiyear visa so he wouldn't have to wait on line for several hours at the consulate each year. He asked if I could help. I told him I was meeting with the consul general — Richard Williams — later that day and would ask. I had forgotten that a few months earlier Michael Nussbaum had called me on Yeung's behalf with a similar request. I had asked Michael if Yeung was an honorable man. Michael said he was, so I directed him to contact Eric Schwartz, a member of my staff, who drafted a letter to the consul general that was sent out over my signature asking him to consider issuing the multiyear visa.

But when I raised the issue with Williams that same day, he said the consulate had decided not to give Yeung a multiyear visa because he had violated the law. Jerry Stuchiner, a representative of the Immigration and Naturalization Service, who handled such matters for the consulate, joined us to explain that Yeung had a gambling conviction. Was this the result of a $2 bet on the horses, I asked, or was it something more serious? If it was a minor offense that in itself would not prevent him from receiving the visa, I hoped they would take that into consideration. Williams indicated that they would look into it. Ironically enough, I learned later that Stuchiner was running a visa fraud operation out of the consulate, selling US visas with stolen Honduran passports to Chinese desperate to get into the United States. He was eventually indicted and convicted.

A couple of months later, Michael Nussbaum called me to say that Yeung hadn't heard anything from the consulate about his visa request. He asked me to find out where things stood. I called the consul general, who told me Yeung's application had been denied "because he is in the triads." Since I had never heard that phrase before, I inquired what it meant, and was told that the triads were the Hong Kong equivalent of the mafia.

In Hong Kong a few weeks later, I saw Albert Yeung and told him the consul general would not give him the visa because he "believes you are in the triads." Yeung said he certainly knew people in the triads. "Everybody does in Hong Kong," he claimed. "But am I a member of the triads? Absolutely not."

The next day I met with the consul general and told him Yeung claimed he was not in the triads. Williams responded that he had it on good authority that Yeung was. I asked if he could give me the source of his information. I was thinking that the last thing I wanted was to work for a mobster. On the other hand, I didn't want to walk away from a remunerative relationship with someone who had never asked me to do anything wrong, purely on the basis of hearsay allegations. Williams refused to tell me his source, and I asked, "If you don't want to give Yeung a multiyear visa because he's in the triads, why did you give him a one-year visa?" I never got an answer because at that point he got up and asked me to leave his office.

I then called an old friend who happened to be a prominent attorney in Hong Kong, and asked him to find out if Albert Yeung really was in the triads. A day later he called to say that according to his contacts in the Hong Kong police, Yeung was, indeed, a member. Just to make sure, when I returned to the United States a few days later, I contacted Jules Kroll of the international detective agency Kroll Associates and asked him to investigate. Jules told me that the people in his Hong Kong office also thought Yeung was in the triads.

Now that I had confirmation from two independent, trustworthy sources, I called Albert Yeung and told him that unless he could convince the consul general and the Hong Kong police that he was not in the triads, I would have to terminate my relationship with him. That action cost me $150,000 in fees and retainers that I was about to receive for arranging for him to get a bank license in Sri Lanka. I also called my contact in Sri Lanka to inform him that Yeung was apparently a member of the triads. The Sri Lankan official thanked me and promptly put the proposed bank license for the Emperor Group in the circular file. Since I had left Congress a few months earlier without a cent to my name, $150,000 was nothing to sneeze at, but I didn't want to be associated with someone I had reason to believe was a mobster.

About a month after I explained all this to the Justice Department, I got a letter from an assistant attorney general saying they had concluded there was no basis for any charges against me. I thought my nomination to

India would now proceed without any further hitches. But about a month after that, Tony Lake asked me to come to the White House, where I met with him and Sandy Berger, the deputy national security advisor. They said the president had decided not to go ahead with my nomination because the State Department would not give me a security clearance. But this could not possibly have been true. As a member of the Foreign Affairs and Intelligence committees, I had already received the highest clearances and — as I subsequently discovered through a Freedom of Information Act request — the Bureau of Diplomatic Security had recommended that I receive a security clearance in connection with my ambassadorial appointment. Under these circumstances, it is inconceivable that the State Department would have denied me clearance.

To this day, I have not been able to discover why the White House decided to withdraw my nomination even after I had been exonerated. I was convinced at the time — and remain so today — that Senate confirmation wouldn't have been a problem. Most Democrats would have voted for me and, because of my support of the Bush administration on the Gulf War, presumably many Republicans would as well. Indeed, two nationally syndicated columnists who wrote about the withdrawal of my nomination — William F. Buckley and Ken Adelman, both conservative Republicans — deplored the decision and wrote warmly about my qualifications for the job.

Lake now asked on behalf of the president if I would be willing to chair the Central Asian American Enterprise Fund. This was one of several funds established by Congress in the aftermath of the Cold War to facilitate the creation of market economies in the previously Communist former Soviet republics and Eastern European countries. The CAAEF had $150 million to invest in small and medium-size private sector enterprises in the five Central Asian republics. I suppose the administration saw this unsalaried, part-time position as a consolation prize. But I thought it would be an interesting challenge, and I accepted it. For the next five years, I traveled a couple of times a year to Kazakhstan, Uzbekistan, Turkmenistan, Tajikistan, and Kyrgyzstan. It was a long way from my district in Brooklyn to Bishkek, the capital of the Kyrgyz Republic, but it marked the end of the journey I had begun over two decades earlier with my election to the House.

So that was my year as a *shlemazel*. In twelve miserable months, I was caught up in the House banking scandal, my congressional district was eviscerated, I was defeated in my bid for reelection, I became the subject of a criminal investigation, and the administration withdrew my nomination as ambassador to India. It wasn't the happiest ending to my congressional career. Nevertheless, I consider the years I spent in Congress, and the opportunity to take part in the "passion and action" of my time, the most exciting and rewarding experience of my life. I wouldn't have traded it for anything.

EPILOGUE
Lessons Learned

Those who do not remember the past
are condemned to repeat it.

✦ GEORGE SANTAYANA ✦

Each reader will no doubt take away a different set of lessons from this account of my experiences as a member of Congress. Following are those that have most impressed themselves on me.

In both domestic politics and foreign affairs,
take nothing for granted and expect the unexpected.

When I arrived in Washington in 1975, the Soviet Union seemed indestructible and the Cold War an immutable fact of international life. Yet when I left Congress in 1993, the Soviet Union had ceased to exist, Communism had collapsed throughout Eastern Europe, and the Cold War was a relic of history. In the same way, when I was first elected to Congress the Democrats had what appeared to be a permanent majority in the House of Representatives. I even got Thomas "Doc" Morgan, the Foreign Affairs Committee chairman, to sign a document I drew up as a joke in 1976, promising that in twenty years I would be committee chairman myself. Yet two years after I left Congress in 1992, the Republicans became the majority. If I had remained in the House, I would have had to wait another fourteen years to become chairman.

The fact that a conflict has remained unresolved
for a long time doesn't mean it can never be resolved.

The peace treaty between Israel and Egypt, the Good Friday agreement between Unionists and Republicans in Northern Ireland, the triumph of People Power in the Philippines, the rescinding of martial law in Taiwan, the UN-sponsored settlement in Cambodia, and the abolition of apartheid in South Africa all demonstrate that even the most seemingly intractable conflicts can be made tractable, under the right circumstances and with courageous, effective leadership.

Bad situations can be made worse.

In Uganda, the overthrow of Idi Amin in 1979 by the armed forces of Tanzania looked like an unalloyed benefit for that country's suffering people. But by the time he died in exile, more people had been killed by his successor, Milton Obote, than by the murderous Amin himself. Mobutu Sese Seko plundered Zaire's wealth for his own benefit, driving the standard of living below what it had been when the country was still a Belgian colony, but his overthrow led to foreign interventions and a civil war resulting in the deaths of over three million Zairians. In Zimbabwe, the end of the liberation struggle and the election of Robert Mugabe improved conditions for a while but ultimately led to the ruination of the agricultural sector, the collapse of the economy, and the establishment of a ruthless tyranny that has resulted in the torture, death, and impoverishment of countless Zimbabweans. I don't suggest that because things sometimes go from bad to worse we should refrain from efforts to make them better. But I emphasize that we should make those efforts with our eyes wide open.

War should be a last resort, but
at times it becomes a necessary resort.

One of the great lessons of our time is that evil exists — as in Cambodia in the 1970s and when Iraq invaded Kuwait in 1990 — and must be confronted. If it can be dealt with and its depredations undone by diplomacy and/or sanctions, so much the better. But if it can only be countered by force, the exercise of America's armed might should be seriously considered. To be sure, the United States is not in a position — nor should it aspire — to become the policeman of the world. Such a role would be far beyond our military and political means. But the fact that we're not in a position to intervene everywhere doesn't mean we should intervene nowhere.

If the Holocaust demonstrates the limits of indifference,
Vietnam illustrates the hazards of intervention.

We must always strike a balance between the moral imperative to act and the potential consequences of such action. This balance was struck during World War II when we were allied with the Soviet Union, whose determination to continue resisting Nazi Germany was a necessary condition for the defeat of Hitler. President Roosevelt and Prime Minister Churchill concluded it would not be appropriate to make the provision of desperately needed supplies to the Red Army contingent on an improvement in the human rights situation in the USSR, however badly Stalin was treating his own people. Churchill, who had tried to strangle the Bolshevik baby in its crib after the Russian revolution in 1917, put it best when he said, after the Nazis invaded the Soviet Union, that "if Hitler invaded hell, I would make at least a favorable reference to the devil."

The balance was also struck by George H. W. Bush when he decided to use American military power to liberate Kuwait despite the fact that several of our allies in Desert Storm—including Saudi Arabia, Egypt, and Syria, as well as Kuwait itself—were not exactly enlightened democracies. But the balance was not struck by George W. Bush when he launched the second Gulf War against Iraq. Removing Saddam Hussein and his Baathist regime was undoubtedly desirable. But the price we paid in American blood and treasure—not to mention the tens of thousands of Iraqis killed in the resulting insurrection and sectarian war, and the millions forced to flee the country—was out of all proportion to the benefits we gained from his removal, especially once it became clear that the weapons of mass destruction that were the ostensible justification for the invasion no longer existed.

In assessing the need for and consequences of
military intervention, much depends on the extent
to which vital American interests are involved.

If the United States is attacked, as we were at Pearl Harbor on December 7, 1941, and in New York and Washington on September 11, 2001, striking back is morally justified and strategically necessary. Where vital American interests are not at stake, but the lives of hundreds of thousands or even millions of people in other countries may be at risk, we must weigh whether military intervention will do more good than harm. In two hypothetical cases, Tibet and Chechnya, an American military intervention would involve us in wars against nuclear-armed China and Russia, clearly putting far more people at risk than it could possibly help. By comparison, our decision to go to war against Serbia to prevent the ethnic cleansing of the Kosovars from their ancestral homeland saved far more people than it put at risk. In order to secure and sustain the American people's support for humanitarian interventions where vital American interests are not involved, it is important to have the support of other countries, especially in the region where the intervention occurs, to demonstrate that we are not acting alone.

> *Between doing nothing and going to war, there is a*
> *range of possible responses to injustice and aggression.*

Private diplomatic démarches represent the minimal level of response to threats to our interests or violations of our most cherished values. When quiet diplomacy doesn't work, public protests and denunciations can sometimes shame potential aggressors and human rights abusers into doing the right thing. When quiet diplomacy and public criticism fail, we can try sanctions, although the effectiveness of sanctions often depends on other countries' willingness to apply them too. More often than not, sanctions fail to achieve their objective — yet not invariably. The sanctions against South Africa, for example, clearly played a role in convincing the white leadership that the time had come to abandon apartheid.

> *In determining how to promote democracy in nations*
> *with repressive regimes, consult the leaders of the struggle*
> *for democracy there, who usually know their countries'*
> *political dynamics better than we do.*

In South Africa, the African National Congress, which clearly had the support of the black majority, urged the United States and other countries that abhorred apartheid to put economic pressure on the Afrikaner regime. In South Korea, on the other hand, Kim Dae-jung and Kim Young-sam, the leaders of the opposition to the military dictatorship, urged us to diplomatically pressure the regime to hold genuinely free and fair elections, but not to apply sanctions or withdraw our military forces. As much as they wanted a transition to democracy, they feared another war even more and didn't want us to do anything to diminish Seoul's and Washington's ability to deter another North Korean invasion. In Poland, the leaders of Solidarity, who clearly spoke for a majority of the Polish people, wanted us to impose sanctions after martial law was established in 1981 but then called on us to lift sanctions several years later, when they thought that would enhance the prospects for economic development and political reform. I don't suggest that we turn the formulation of American foreign policy over to citizens of other countries, no matter how courageous and commendable they may be. But they should be carefully consulted and their advice taken seriously. We are more likely to advance our objectives if we follow their advice than if we reject it.

Be careful about supporting groups that use violence,
because the mouth you feed may turn and bite you.

In the 1980s, Pakistan began providing support to Lashkar-e-Taiba, a militant Islamic group that was launching terrorist attacks against India in Kashmir (and was later responsible for attacks in New Delhi and Mumbai as well). But over time Lashkar-e-Taiba turned against the Islamabad government, which it is now trying to overthrow through the use of suicide bombers and targeted assassinations of key Pakistani leaders, in an effort to establish a strict Islamic regime in Pakistan. In a similar way, as recounted in chapter 8, India suffered the assassinations of two prime ministers — Indira Gandhi and her son Rajiv — as blowback from attempts to manipulate the political situation in Punjab and in Sri Lanka.

Also during the 1980s, Israel began providing surreptitious support to Hamas, a fundamentalist group then focusing on delivering social services to needy Palestinians in the West Bank and Gaza. The intention was to undermine support among the Palestinians for the PLO, then considered much more threatening. But over time, the PLO moderated its views toward Israel and embraced a two-state solution, while Hamas evolved into a terrorist movement committed to the elimination of Israel and the use of suicide bombers and rocket attacks that were intended to kill as many Israelis as possible.

Nor was the United States immune to this kind of blowback. Elements

of the mujahedin we supported in the 1980s to counter the Soviet invasion of Afghanistan morphed into the Taliban, which, after taking power
in Afghanistan, provided sanctuary to Osama bin Laden—also the ben-
eficiary of American support—who gave the orders for the 9/11 attacks.

Foreign policy may in practice be the primary
responsibility of the executive branch, but Congress
has an important role to play as well.

The Constitution clearly makes the president *primus inter pares* in the formulation and conduct of foreign policy. But Congress, in exercising its
own constitutional duties, clearly has the capacity to influence our relations with other countries. Through its power of the purse, it can impact
both our foreign aid program and our policy toward countries that receive aid. Through its power over commercial relations with other countries, it can impose or repeal tariffs and sanctions against them. Through
the Senate's ability to consent to treaties and confirm ambassadors and
other executive branch officers, including top State Department officials,
it can directly influence our international relations. Finally, in our democratic society, implementing any foreign policy ultimately depends on the
support of the American people. Thus Congress can also influence foreign
policy through holding hearings that shape US public opinion.

Even congressional actions that are little noted
at home can have a significant impact abroad.

I was often amazed to discover that hearings I held or resolutions we adopted that went mostly unnoticed at home were big news overseas. In chapter 5 I described how Prince Sihanouk told me, when I first met him in
New York in January 1979, how much it meant to him to hear on the Voice
of America about my efforts to focus attention on what was happening in
Cambodia. A few years later, mass protests in Burma brought the Burmese
dictatorship to the brink of collapse. I met with Aung San Suu Kyi, the opposition leader, in Rangoon, and the following day secured House approval
for a resolution calling on the Burmese government to resign and permit
a genuinely democratic election. The day after that, our embassy in Ran-
goon tried to distribute news releases about this resolution to the media.
In front of one newspaper office, a mob surrounded the vehicle carrying

With Aung San Suu Kyi and US Ambassador to Burma Burt Levin, at his residence, 1988.

copies of the release and demanded to know where it was going and what it was doing. When the embassy officer inside told them he was distributing a press release about an action Congress had taken the day before, someone from the crowd shouted out: "That must be the Solarz resolution. Let him through." They had obviously heard about it over the VOA.

In 1990 the leaders of the Nepali Congress Party launched a campaign to restore democracy in this Hindu kingdom, and the government arrested many of those involved. I sent a letter to King Gyanendra calling on him to release them and faxed a copy to the Congress Party leaders, who promptly had thousands of copies pasted up all over Katmandu. In the Philippines, South Korea, Taiwan, South Africa, and many other countries, people struggling for democracy and human rights were well aware of efforts in Congress to support their cause and drew encouragement from them.

Just as Congress as a whole can influence
foreign policy, so can individual members.

This book has tried to demonstrate the truth of this assertion in my own case. But I was far from the only member of the House or Senate who could reasonably claim credit for affecting American foreign policy. Senator Henry Cabot Lodge of Massachusetts, for example, was largely responsible for the Senate's rejection of the Treaty of Versailles and America's refusal to participate in the League of Nations. Without Arizona Senator Dennis DeConcini's crucial vote, the Senate would not have ratified the Panama Canal Treaty of 1977. Senator Richard Lugar of Indiana played a key role in the adoption of sanctions against South Africa and the congressional override of President Reagan's veto of that historic legislation. Congressman Charlie Wilson of Texas was single-handedly responsible for securing hundreds of millions of dollars in military assistance to the mujahedin in Afghanistan. Speaker of the House Jim Wright was instrumental in cutting off our covert aid program to the Contras in Nicaragua. Throughout Congress's long history, many others have left their mark on US foreign policy and international relations.

Key to the ability of a member of Congress to influence
foreign policy is a deep understanding of the issues.

It helps, of course, to be Speaker of the House, majority leader of the Senate, or chairman of a relevant committee or subcommittee. But for those who do not hold such an influential position, the best way to have an impact is to thoroughly master the issue under consideration. Serving on the committee with jurisdiction over the issue is important (though not essential) because it is easier to shape legislation in committee than after it reaches the floor. But in either case, other members are more likely to follow your lead if they realize that you know what you're talking about. And there is no better way to grasp the essentials of an issue than to go to the country and region where it is playing out and talk to the people on the ground who are most involved.

Individuals can have an impact on history.

Historians have long debated whether history is shaped by large impersonal forces or by the actions of individuals. Certainly geography, culture, demographics, economics, history, and religion all play a role in a nation's destiny. But it is clear to me that individual leaders do as well. Without Nelson Mandela, it is doubtful that there would have been a peaceful transition from apartheid to majority rule in South Africa. Without Lech

Walesa, Solidarity would probably not have prevailed in Poland. Without Anwar Sadat, there would have been no peace treaty between Egypt and Israel. Without Fidel Castro, the Cuban revolution would probably not have lasted its current fifty years. Without Lee Kuan Yew, Singapore would not have been transformed from a backward port into one of the world's most advanced economies. Without Cory Aquino, it is hard to imagine the transition to democracy in the Philippines occurring without a violent eruption. Without Mikhail Gorbachev and Boris Yeltsin, Communism might have lasted much longer in the Soviet Union than it did.

Looking back on my eighteen years in the House of Representatives, I like to think I made a difference as well, though on a much smaller scale than the political titans above. I can sum up my approach to politics and policy by saying that, like John F. Kennedy, I was "an idealist without illusions." That phrase still describes my view of America and its role in the world. To succeed, our foreign policy must be rooted not only in our most basic national values but in a realistic assessment of what is possible in our complex and challenging world.

But I have to confess that there's another way of looking at my congressional career. In the mid-1980s I held a fundraiser in the Boston suburbs at which Barney Frank, an old friend and colleague, introduced me. "Steve was first elected to Congress," said Barney, "by running against an incumbent who was under indictment for bribery, conspiracy, conflict of interest, and perjury. He was elected, and his opponent was convicted and went to jail. He then served as a back-bench member of the Foreign Affairs Committee until the chairman of the Subcommittee on Africa was convicted of payroll padding. When he went to jail, Steve became chairman. Then in 1982, when New York lost five House seats, Steve's district was merged into the district of a neighboring congressman. Two weeks later, that House member pleaded guilty and was convicted of tax evasion and payroll padding. What Steve's career demonstrates," Barney concluded, "is the importance of convictions as a way of getting ahead in American politics." I could hardly disagree.

ACKNOWLEDGMENTS

Hillary Clinton reminded us that it takes a village to raise a child. I don't pretend to be an expert on child rearing, but I can say that it took a village to make this memoir possible.

There was, first of all, Bob Greenberger, a former diplomatic correspondent for the *Wall Street Journal*, who helped me organize and write an initial draft, which ultimately went through several revisions. Without his help and the discipline it imposed, I doubt the project would ever have gotten to first base.

Second, there were Stephanie Golden, who worked her editorial magic on the manuscript, eliminating redundancies, tightening up the language, and in the process making it a much better read, and Jeanne Ferris, whose fastidious attention to detail enabled me to avoid a host of embarrassing errors. It was a collaboration I found most enjoyable, and I am very grateful to them.

Third, a number of friends and former staffers read and commented either on the entire manuscript or on chapters dealing with issues they were involved in. They include Mort Abramowitz, Ken Adelman, Richard Bush, David Frank, Bob Hathaway, Mike Lewan, Irv Matus, Richard Pious, Stanley Roth, David Steinberg, Charlie Twining, and Steve Weissman. Their stylistic and substantive suggestions enabled me to correct errors and fill in blank spots I had overlooked. I am grateful to them all for helping me make this a better book.

Fourth, my Brooklyn staff did an outstanding job handling constituent complaints and representing me at community meetings. Without their superb work helping me consolidate my political position in the district, I never would have been able to devote the time I did to foreign affairs. Peter Abbate, Adam Barnett, Mary Boyle, Shlomo Braun, Mary Jane Burt, Helene Coburne, Sandy Cooper, Steve Denker, Rena Diamond, Pat Ferris, Ruth Gilden, Dennis Holt, Josh Howard, Peter Kelley, Ben Lederman, Annette Lidawer, Ken Lowenstein, Laurie Mason, Rick Miller, Rosie Nebenhaus, Andrea Nordell, Al Padow, Jules Polonetsky, Eric Roth,

Jack Russak, Renee Sherman, Ruth Tannenbaum, Glen Thrush, Stephanie Twin, and Sylvia Wurf were more to me than just staffers. They became part of my extended family, and I consider myself privileged to have worked with them on behalf of my Brooklyn constituents.

Fifth, there was my administrative and policy staff in Washington. I don't think it an exaggeration to say that I was blessed with one of the most outstanding staffs on Capitol Hill. Little that I accomplished would have been possible without their assistance: Lynn Arnold, Bill Barnds, Mary Boyle, Stu Brahs, Richard Bush, Dawn Calabia, Johnnie Carson, Tor Cowan, Carol Ditta, David Dreier, Dan Ertel, Marvin Feur, David Frank, Ed Friedman, Audrey Gallagher, Vicki Halloran, Bob Hathaway, Mia Higgins, John Isaacs, David Lachmann, Bert Levin, Mike Lewan, Susan Lewis, Valerie Mims, Jeremy Rabinovitz, Pat Rivalgi, Phil Robertson, Stanley Roth, Eric Schwartz, Steve Silbiger, and Gene Sofer. They too became part of my extended family.

Sixth, a number of my closest friends accompanied me on trips abroad (at their own expense). Their companionship made my journeys more pleasant, and I benefited greatly from their insights. They include Dr. Ross Brechner, Jay and Diana Goldin, Gary Grossman, Jules Kroll, Franz Leichter, Bernie Nussbaum, Sig Rolat, and Steve Shalom.

Seventh, without the support and votes of my constituents in New York's Thirteenth Congressional District, I would never have been elected to Congress and then reelected for eight subsequent terms. I deeply appreciate the confidence they reposed in me and consider myself privileged to have represented them in Congress.

Last, but by no means least, without my wife, Nina, I never would have been elected to Congress in the first place, and without her love and support I couldn't possibly have achieved whatever I did accomplish. Her shrewd insights into the people and leaders I encountered and her invariably sagacious advice were an enormous help in making sense of the varied situations I encountered at home and abroad.

These encomiums notwithstanding, I alone am responsible both for this memoir and for the actions it describes. No one mentioned above is in any way accountable for what I've written or what I did while I was in Congress.

INDEX

159, 161; nuclear weapons program,
155–57, 161; Solarz's travel to, 154, 157,
159–60; and Soviet Union, 154–55;
U.S. support for, 150
Pakistan Peoples Party, 157
Palestinians, 52–53
Park Chung-hee, 34, 130
Passover Seder, 55, 65
Pastora, Edén (Comandante Zero), 171
Patman, Wright, 24
Paton, Alan, 75–76
Patriotic Front (Zimbabwe), 87–90
peace agreements, 41, 51–57, 166, 194,
219–20. See also country entries;
Middle East peace process
"peace for peace," 53
Pell, Claiborne, 143
Percy, Charles, 80
Peres, Shimon, 41
Perle, Richard, 199
Perlmutter, Bennet, 2
Persian Gulf. See First Gulf War;
Second Gulf War
personal relationships, importance of,
32
persona non grata (U.S. designation),
Waldheim as, 69
Peru, Solarz's travel to, 167
Philippines: democratic transition, 98,
112–29; Solarz's travel to, 113–16,
124–25, 128–29
Phnom Penh, 99
Pickering, Thomas, 42
Pike, Otis, 25
Pious, Dick, 12–13
piracy, 107
Plaskow, Johnny, 2, 4
PLO (Palestine Liberation Organiza-
tion), 41, 223; commitment to

elimination of Israel, 52; as represen-
tative of Palestinian people, 52; and
signing of Oslo agreement, 53
Poage, W. R., 24
Podell, Bertram, 18–20
Pogrund, Benjamin, 82
Poland, 72, 223; Communism in, 177;
democratic transition, 186–91;
Solarz's travel to, 126, 186–90
Polish American Congress, 190
Polish Americans, 190–91
Politis, Victor, 117–18
Pol Pot, 100–101, 103, 108, 110. See also
Khmer Rouge
Ponchaud, François, 100
Popieluszko, Father Jerzy, 188
Portugal, 95
Powell, Colin, 55, 204–5
Prabhakaran, Velupillai, 34, 149
Prasong, Squadron Leader, 107
Premadasa, Ranasinghe, 34
Prendes, Ray, 164
presidential certifications, of human
rights progress in El Salvador, 165–66
presidential election (1972), 18
Presidential Medal of Freedom, awarded
to Jan Nowak, 190
Price, Melvin, 24
Princeton University, 106
Pritchard, Joel, 31–32
PRK (People's Republic of Kampuchea),
99, 108–11
Procaccino, Mario, 15
Project WIANCHOR, 92
Project WIZARD, 92
Psinakis, Steve, 129
public criticism, 222
Puritz, Elliot, 2
Pyongyang, North Korea, 138

Library of Congress Cataloging-in-Publication Data

Solarz, Stephen J.

Journeys to war and peace: a congressional memoir /

Stephen J. Solarz; with a foreword by Norman Ornstein.

p. cm.

Includes bibliographical references and index.

ISBN 978-1-58465-997-6 (cloth: alk. paper) —

ISBN 978-1-58465-998-3 (e-book)

1. Solarz, Stephen J. 2. United States. Congress. House —
Biography. 3. Legislators — United States — Biography.
4. United States — Foreign relations — 1945–1989. 5. United
States — Foreign relations — 1989–1993. 6. United States —
Politics and government — 1945–1989. 7. United States —
Politics and government — 1989–1993. I. Title.

E840.8.S577A3   2011

328.73'092 — dc22

[B]   2011002259

Library of Congress Cataloging-in-Publication Data
Solarz, Stephen J.
Journeys to war and peace: a congressional memoir /
Stephen J. Solarz; with a foreword by Norman Ornstein.
p. cm.
Includes bibliographical references and index.
ISBN 978-1-58465-997-6 (cloth: alk. paper) —
ISBN 978-1-58465-998-3 (e-book)
1. Solarz, Stephen J. 2. United States. Congress. House —
Biography. 3. Legislators — United States — Biography.
4. United States — Foreign relations — 1945–1989. 5. United
States — Foreign relations — 1989–1993. 6. United States —
Politics and government — 1945–1989. 7. United States —
Politics and government — 1989–1993. I. Title.
E840.8.S577A3   2011
328.73'092 — dc22
[B]   2011002259